Studies in modern capitalism · Etudes sur le capitalisme moderne

Economic life in Ottoman Europe

Studies in modern capitalism · Etudes sur le capitalisme moderne

This series is devoted to an attempt to comprehend capitalism as a world system. It will include monographs, collections of essays and colloquia around specific themes, written by historians and social scientists united by a common concern for the study of large-scale long-term social structure and social change.

The series is a joint enterprise of the Maison des Sciences de l'Homme in Paris and the Fernand Braudel Center for the Study of Economies, Historical Systems, and Civilizations at the State University of New York at Binghamton.

This book is published as part of the joint publishing agreement established in 1977 between the Fondation de la Maison des Sciences de l'Homme and the Press Syndicate of the University of Cambridge. Titles published under this arrangement may appear in any European language or, in the case of volumes of collected essays, in several languages.

New books will appear either as individual titles or in one of the series which the Maison des Sciences de l'Homme and the Cambridge University Press have jointly agreed to publish. All books published jointly by the Maison des Sciences de l'Homme and the Cambridge University Press will be distributed by the Press throughout the world.

Economic life
in Ottoman Europe

Taxation, trade and the struggle for land, 1600–1800

BRUCE McGOWAN
Director, American Center in Ljubljana, Yugoslavia

Cambridge University Press

Cambridge
London   New York   New Rochelle   Melbourne   Sydney

& Editions de la Maison des Sciences de l'Homme

Paris

CAMBRIDGE UNIVERSITY PRESS
Cambridge, New York, Melbourne, Madrid, Cape Town, Singapore,
São Paulo, Delhi, Dubai, Tokyo

Cambridge University Press
The Edinburgh Building, Cambridge CB2 8RU, UK

With Editions de la Maison des Sciences de l'Homme
54 Boulevard Raspail, 75270 Paris Cedex 06, France

Published in the United States of America by Cambridge University Press, New York

www.cambridge.org
Information on this title: www.cambridge.org/9780521135368

First published 1981
This digitally printed version 2010

A catalogue record for this publication is available from the British Library

Library of Congress Catalogue Card Number: 81-3899

ISBN 978-0-521-24208-0 Hardback
ISBN 978-0-521-13536-8 Paperback

Contents

Illustrations

Preface

This effort to present new information about rural life in south-eastern Europe is partly a response to the challenge implicit in Fernand Braudel's famous study of the Mediterranean basin wherein he understandably neglects the eastern in favor of the western shores, but at the same time provocatively suggests connections between developments in the Ottoman territories and developments upon the continent as a whole. Especially intriguing is the implied relationship between export oriented agriculture in Ottoman territories (i.e. *chiftlik* agriculture) and export oriented or market oriented agriculture elsewhere.

I did not know at the outset of this research that the subject of export oriented agriculture and its social effects was to receive new prominence with the publication of Immanuel Wallerstein's first volume on the emergence of a world scale economy in the early modern period. The 'seigneurial reaction' discussed along the way by Braudel moved to the center in Wallerstein's work, where modes of coerced labor are seen as characteristic in the emerging peripheral world with which Western Europe traded. However, like Braudel, Wallerstein also gave the Ottoman territories brief and diffident treatment within his ambitious conception.

Obviously scholars like Braudel and Wallerstein are in need of more facts on the Ottoman territories. The few at work in this relatively undeveloped field are duty-bound to provide more basic statistical information, both for themselves and for other scholars. It is partly for this reason that statistical tables have been appended to these case studies; but partly, of course, these tables are included to support conclusions which would seem unwarranted if offered without statistical evidence.

In response to Braudel's implied challenges, an effort has been made

ix

to relate both the Ottoman export trade and the social effects of that trade in south-eastern Europe to developments elsewhere on the European continent. (Such comparison could conceivably be further extended to place the Ottoman territories within the entire center–periphery scheme conceived by Wallerstein, though this was not attempted here.) At first glance, there is a temptation to relate the quasi-serfdom (the *reaya* institution) established by the Ottomans directly to the 'second' or 'later' serfdom which developed more or less contemporaneously throughout Eastern Europe. Yet it is difficult to show persuasively any causal connection between the Ottoman quasi-serfdom and the serfdom variants to the north despite their coincidence in time and their proximity. Indeed, the Ottoman institution cannot with certainty be linked to earlier Byzantine or Slavic models, despite the survival in the Ottoman system of certain vestigial forms inherited from earlier states. In the moderate spirit of the Ottoman *reaya* institution we tend rather to see a reaction against earlier, more oppressive modes of serfdom, a reform program which contributed greatly to the Ottoman state-building potential. And, as in Eastern Europe, there is a striking disjuncture in time between the rise of this serfdom variant and the rise of a domestic export trade: the *reaya* institution was fully established long before the sixteenth-century 'wheat boom' which marked the rise of a significant trade in indigenous Ottoman products, in contrast to an earlier entrepôt trade in silk and other luxury items originating further east.

A related hypothesis entertained by the author at the outset of these investigations was that south-eastern Europe of the sixteenth, seventeenth and eighteenth centuries would probably be shown to divide into two more or less distinct economic zones – an outer seaward zone greatly affected by waterborne trade and an inner zone which remained within the command economy preserve of the capital city with its staple policies. This expectation has been only partly substantiated by the evidence developed so far.

The subjects of the five essays in this collection are logically related. Their publication together is intended to intensify their complementary character. Like the exploratory trenches of the archaeologist, they are aimed at revealing the outlines of the reality remaining to be uncovered. Briefly, these subjects are: the development of an international trade in indigenous Ottoman products on a scale sufficient to affect land use in south-eastern Europe (chapter 1); an analytic model with which to rationalize the deployment of land and labor during the disintegration of the classic Ottoman land regime, and an application of that model to south-eastern Europe (chapter 2); an attempt to establish demographic trends and their spatial distribution by using the head tax data pertaining to south-eastern Europe (chapter 3); a parallel attempt to measure demographic trends and/or economic strength by studying changes in the distribution of a second body of tax data, the so-called 'tax houses' of the inner provinces (chapter 4); and an attempt to follow fiscal and interrelated agricultural developments at one Balkan location through the use of local judicial records (chapter 5).

The spatial and temporal framework for these essays was significantly affected by the limits of the documents consulted. Originally the plan was to take the entire period of the Black Sea closure (i.e. 1475–1783) as a time frame and to measure the effects of this occlusion – this arrested circulation – upon the whole of south-eastern Europe, at first conceived as including the Romanian and Hungarian territories. Unfortunately, the tax house and head tax series (chapters 3 and 4) exclude territories north of the Danube and are relatively weaker for Bosnia and Serbia than for the remaining south-eastern European territories. The judicial records used for the Manastir study (chapter 5) are similarly limited in time although they begin somewhat earlier and end somewhat later than the other series used. Limitations in time were also a feature of trade estimates by non-Ottoman sources (chapter 1). Since Ottoman customs records are little concerned with content of trade and because they ignore contraband, it was imperative that non-Ottoman estimates of trade be brought into play. But the best of these pertain to the seventeenth and eighteenth centuries rather than the earlier period. For these reasons, the original scope of study was reduced in order to concentrate on the last two centuries of the Black Sea closure.

I feel a keen gratitude towards certain individuals who encouraged this lonely project at critical moments. Above all I wish to thank Charles Issawi for his role in clearing the way for its publication. Halil Inalcik has been constant in his encouragement and has allowed an early look at his most recent writings which were of special interest as they deal with this same period. Immanuel Wallerstein has also been generous and helpful. Bernard Lewis, Alan Fisher, John Smith and William Schorger each for different reasons deserve my thanks. The writer is also indebted to Michael Cook for a thorough critique, and to Traian Stoianovich for helpful comments.

These studies would not have been possible without institutional funding. Credit for backing this line of research is owed to the International Research Exchange, to the Social Science Research Council, to the Fulbright faculty research program, to the Rackham grant program at the University of Michigan, and to the Council for Research on Economic History.

My wife and son cheerfully tolerated an absence of a year and a half while I worked in archives at Skopje, Sarajevo, Istanbul and Vienna. Their understanding eased that separation and gave me peace of mind while I was far from home.

Bruce McGowan
Ann Arbor, Michigan

1 ❧ Ottoman exports to pre-industrial Europe

The Levant trade,[1] though partly a trade in luxuries, functioned primarily to supply European traders with unprocessed commodities from the Ottoman territories. These commodities originated in regions where land was relatively abundant, and labor correspondingly cheap as well, and were destined for regions further west where land was less abundant and labor consequently somewhat more costly in absolute terms. Thus in Europe's pre-industrial centuries – the sixteenth, seventeenth and eighteenth – a pattern of trade developed which expressed an emerging regional specialization in production and trade which went beyond the limits of Europe itself and which permitted the European trading partners to share cheaper Ottoman factor supplies as embodied in the traded commodities.

Geographers who have studied the progress of trade during the pre-industrial and early industrial periods have pointed to the overarching influence upon land use everywhere of an emergent distribution of population densities, with centers of density in north-western Europe and, on a lesser scale, in northern Italy.[2] An interpretation of the Levant trade which takes into account these differences in population density gives us a view of this half-conscious, backdoor relationship between Europe and the Ottomans which places available information on the trade on a more rational plane. Seen in this way, the Levant trade exercised a continuous influence upon the history of European land use in the modern era, a role which Ottoman authorities had no way of understanding and to which they probably would not have consented if they had.

WP

1

The field effect of population concentration in Western Europe

The brave new world of exploration and trade which opened up in the sixteenth century was a world with swiftly changing demographic proportions. In Western Europe the traumatic plague-related losses of the fourteenth century had long since been effaced, and population densities in most areas were edging upwards to unprecedented levels. An older tendency towards a concentration of population in the north-west reasserted itself; population density in the Low Countries became two to three times that of less populous parts of Europe. To the east, the Ottoman territories – like most of Eastern Europe – remained relatively far less populous in terms of density, even though evidence of flourishing Ottoman towns persuades us that the populations under Ottoman rule – in line with populations on the western rim of the Mediterranean and in Europe generally – were also growing dramatically throughout the sixteenth century.[3]

The emergent east–west density gradient persisted and became a long term influence in shaping modern European history. Whereas in the seventeenth century population levels on the shores of the Mediterranean faltered or foundered, human populations in the north-west continued to edge upwards.

One effect of this gradient was its influence upon long run patterns of trade both on the European maritime periphery and later, as the maritime world expanded, world wide. By altering the ratio between men and the land the population concentration in the west created new demand conditions, operating (to borrow Warntz's phrase) like a 'field quantity, analogous to gravitational potential – (with) similar characteristics such as mathematically derivable intensities, gradients, forces and energies.'[4]

Yet the field created by the economic needs of the population clusters in north-western Europe was not a simple and unobstructed field. It had two main parts, on conducive to trade, the other resistant to trade. Whereas the waterways surrounding Europe were exploited to carry trade as rapidly as maritime technology was developed for their mastery, land routes burdened with mud, dust and customs men resisted mastery until their gradual displacement by canals and railroads. Fox speaks of two Frances, one accessible to water, the other not. Peet speaks of rivers such as the Oder and Vistula as 'low cost intrusions' upon the northern plain of Europe.[5] In a similar vein, Karl Polanyi has emphasized the relative poverty of intraregional trade in the same centuries relative to interregional trade. It was by ships and by water that the demands born from the changing demographic constitution of Europe were transmitted. Therefore, concentrated population alone was not a precondition for an enlivened trade in primary goods, but it was rather population concentration at or near waterside – together with the income potential and buying power which such concentration implies. It was the waterside capitals of Europe – above all Amsterdam and London – which were the arbiters of the emerging trade empires.

Ignoring for our purposes the far flung colonies of the trading powers, let us consider the flow of primary goods upon the seas bounding Europe north and south. These seas became in the sixteenth century, and remained, avenues for a continuous, predominantly east-to-west flow of primary goods. A traffic in staples was, of course, not a new thing – one need only think of the wheat of Sicily or the Crimea, or the wool of Spain or England, among other frequently traded commodities of the late medieval world. But increasingly from the sixteenth century onwards Western Europe became the destination for unprocessed commodities which answered its needs, usually food and fibers, sending back textiles, other processed commodities, or coin.[6] The needs of the east–west trading partners became asymmetrical. Thus from the Baltic shores a flow of grain (predominantly rye), which had appeared intermittently in earlier centuries, became a major feature of the sixteenth-century world and, although diminishing as a portion of a steadily expanding total world trade, remained important in the seventeenth and eighteenth centuries, with its all-time peak occurring in the first half of the seventeenth century.

As for the relatively more important Levant trade (see Fig. 1), it was far more heterogeneous. Founded on wheat and silk in the sixteenth century, it grew to include cattle, wool, mohair, hides and finally cotton and tobacco in copious quantities. The erstwhile entrepôt trade in luxury goods, in which the Italians and Egyptians had been the major actors, survived as but a tiny part of the Levant trade of the later Ottoman centuries. Though subject to fluctuation in volume and content, the Levantine exports reached new levels in the seventeenth and eighteenth centuries, steadily feeding Western markets with commodities which, generally speaking, required extensive use of the land, thereby freeing land in the vicinity of the ports of destination for more capital-intensive and labour-intensive uses. Thus as fallow became increasingly scarce in waterside Europe, and as land was turned over to raising fodder and other industrial and more intensive uses, the relatively more abundant land of the eastern Mediterranean – in a development paralleled to that in the eastern Baltic – was drawn into the emergent Europe-centered international system of trade and production. Ottoman fallow products were drawn into the service of Europe.

The West European pattern of land use supported by the Baltic and Levant trades during the centuries following the sixteenth was already in formation during the demographic trough of the fourteenth and early fifteenth centuries. Vacancies created by plague and famine had slackened pressure upon the land and had released some land for purposes other than to raise grain for the everlasting porridge pots of medieval times. Renewed space for pasture, orchards, vines, and such industrial crops as flax, hemp, hops and woad had made possible shifts in consumption habits which were to survive the new general upward trend in population of the sixteenth century and *the renewed pressure upon the land* which accompanied that surge in population. As a matter of course, rents rose near population centers and near the waterways which communicated with them. Although a modern market for land, with market consensus on grades of value, would only emerge gradually, the enhanced value of land in waterside Europe in the sixteenth century would be reflected in the now more frequent short-term tenure arrangements, as well as more frequent sales of land and other land transfers. Rural wages, on the other hand, were held down as the man/land ratio tilted so as to increase the relative value of the land.

Since a more populous, increasingly urbanized north-western Europe, taken as a whole, could afford to sustain more varied (and thus more 'modern') consumption habits, land use closer to home reflected these various relatively recent changes in consumption patterns. Yet obviously as population levels again crept upwards in the sixteenth century (and in the Low Countries continued to move upwards in the seventeenth century) the higher levels of demand for such traditional staples as wheat and wool had also to be accommodated. Gradually part of the increased demand was met by improved agricultural technique (or as at least one authority emphasizes *re*discovered technique) – crop rotation, marling, manuring, and increasing reclamation through swamp drainage and polder making.[7] But even before these rediscovered agricultural techniques had shown themselves in north-western Europe, a much simpler adjustment to the increased demand was made by reaching farther afield for waterborne commodities – to the Baltic tributaries for rye, and less obviously,[8] to the Ottoman territories for cattle, wheat, wool and hides.

With the exceptions of cotton and tobacco, which became important Ottoman exports in the eighteenth century (and in the north the forest by-products which came to supplement rye) the staple goods sent to Europe from the Mediterranean and Baltic shores were goods which could also have been produced near the ports of destination – indeed they could have been raised more efficiently closer to home than in the distant zones which actually supplied them had land been freed from other uses. But under the new conditions fostered by the growth of population in the sixteenth century, there was not enough land to sustain the more modern consumption patterns with the agricultural techniques then prevailing. Thus some commodities were produced closer to home while other products were imported from the distant periphery. Naturally as north European agricultural technique was improved in the direction of intensivity, the need for certain imports slackened, so that England, for instance, could become intermittently a grain exporter in the eighteenth century. Spain, on the other hand, did not make comparable improvements in technique, and thus at the beginning of the seventeenth century was obliged to drop its hitherto exorbitant policy of supplying its overseas colonists with oil, wine and biscuit.[9]

It was not chance which determined which commodities the European markets would bring from abroad and which from their immediate hinterland. Those crops (or combinations of land uses, since crop rotation was evolving) which could afford to pay the highest rents (after the subtraction of capital inputs and transportation costs) were the crops raised closest to the waterside population concentrations where rents were highest.[10] Thus an emerging hierarchy of rents (which systematic data gathering would surely show to have described an isobaric configuration centered upon north-western Europe) had as its concomitant a hierarchy of land uses (or combinations of land uses) whereby those crops least able to pay high rents were pushed outward, away from the center of the demographic field. Conversely, crops which could pay higher location rent would dominate in regions closer to the center; examples would be the olive and wine specialties so well developed in Spain and Portugal that grain, a partly displaced commodity, was continuously imported; this paradoxical effect was noticed by Braudel, who found it puzzling.[11]

The fact that the greater part of Europe was still a landlocked enclave in relation to the waterside population concentrations has obscured this pattern; otherwise it would have long since been as

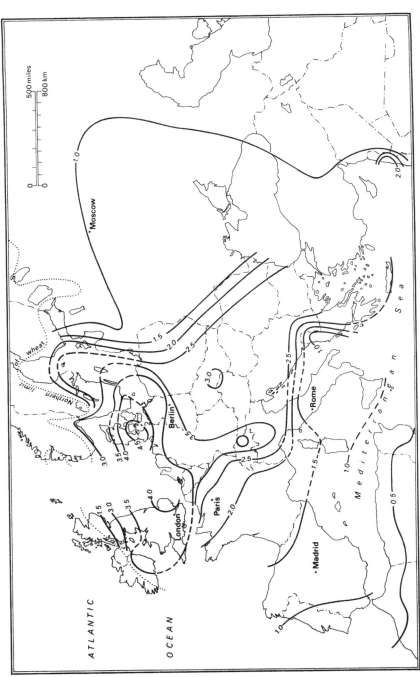

Map 1 European yields of wheat in metric tons per hectare based on twentieth-century data (demonstrating the field effect of demographic concentration)

Source: after J. Kolars and J. Nystuen, *Geography: The Study of Location, Culture and Environment* (New York, 1974)

6

apparent to historians as increasingly it has become to geographers. A pattern which would eventually be meaningful for the European whole in all its parts was at first manifest largely on the watery periphery: thus whereas Amsterdam drew regularly on the Baltic for its rye staple, Paris was supplied from the Ile de France. Only by standing back to gain the geographers' perspective upon Europe as a whole can we begin to appreciate the effects of the emergent European demographic field upon both near and distant land use.

A striking demonstration of the demographic field effect can be obtained from maps encompassing the whole of Europe which show concentric zones of agricultural intensity (i.e. intensity of inputs) based on early twentieth-century data.[12] By the twentieth century, the penetration of Europe by railroads was sufficiently complete to obliterate the earlier dependence upon water transport, so that the hierarchy of agricultural intensity in this latter period no longer features a great landlocked enclave of the sort just referred to in connection with the sixteenth century land-use hierarchy. Nor is the latter-day example based on intensity of inputs simply illustrative, for it demonstrates a fundamental corollary effect of the megascale hierarchy of location rent which had begun to develop with the population surge of the sixteenth century. Thus not only were certain crops and products designated by an economic logic as Baltic or Ottoman export specialties, but even the intensity of cultivation which could be justified in these outlying regions was also influenced by the demographic field effect. Since commodities produced far from the market had to pay relatively higher transport costs, more intensive inputs of labor or capital could not be justified economically if they were to be competitively priced in the faraway markets.

Ottoman agriculture, in other words, was destined to be more 'extensive' (i.e. less labor and capital intensive) than agriculture in the West to the extent that it supplied European markets with its products at prices which could bear the transport costs involved: this is a corollary effect of the evolving European demographic field.[13]

To say that the Ottoman territories were located on the periphery of the European demographic field is not to say that their exports were 'marginal,' 'peripheral' or inessential. Ottoman exports, though they amounted only to a small fraction of total world trade in the seventeenth and eighteenth centuries, made an important contribution to European economic evolution and to the evolution of land-use patterns in Europe. The nature of these exports was determined not only by the

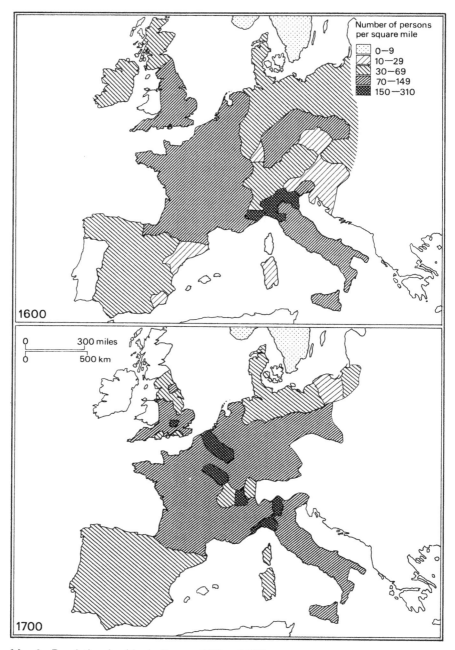

Number of persons
per square mile

0—9
10—29
30—69
70—149
150—310

1600

0   300 miles
0   500 km

1700

Map 2   Population densities in Europe, 1600 and 1700

Source: after A. P. Usher, 'The history of population and settlement in Eurasia,' *Geographical Review*, 20 (1930), 120

demand for them in Europe but by economic characteristics inherent in them.

The cattle of the Hungarian, Wallachian and Moldavian plains embodied extremely low factor costs – both land and labor – and had the additional advantage of transporting themselves to market, driven in herds via Vienna as far west as Frankfort. The wool, hides, and mohair exported by the Balkan and Anatolian zones respectively also embodied low factor costs and were compact enough so as to bear the cost of transport over combined land and water routes which reached deep into the hinterland behind the ports of embarcation.

Silk and cotton were somewhat different cases. Both of these fibers, whether raw or in semi-processed form, are labor intensive. But since they embodied the relatively low cost of Ottoman labor, and were compact, they could easily bear the additional cost of overland transport. Cotton, as time would prove, could also be grown economically at other southerly locations where land was good and abundant and labor cheap. Both silk and cotton were vulnerable to displacement as Ottoman specialties when other zones came into play which offered labor which was as cheap or cheaper: varying grades of finished silk made from native raw silk were established as Italian and Far Eastern specialties (being very easy to transport), while cotton was displaced to Egypt and to the American South in the nineteenth century.

Wheat, which also embodied low factor costs, but which could not bear the cost of transport so well as fibers, was traditionally a waterside export, especially from Thessaly and, by smuggling, via the Archipelago. In this case also a displacement took place in the nineteenth century as even cheaper land became accessible in the Ukraine and in North America, and as transport costs fell relatively as the result of the introduction of steam powered ships and railroads. By the late 1920s Turkey, which had formerly supplied wheat to other countries, itself became the occasional buyer of wheat from Australia, where the land was incomparably cheap. In this way the scope of the demographic field centered upon north-western Europe (and in the nineteenth century also upon the eastern seaboard of the United States) widened with successive improvements in transport and agricultural technique to permit the rise of a true world system in which the Ottoman territories lay nearer the center than to the periphery.

There is a difference of opinion among students of the developing world system of trade and production regarding the dating of its origins. Certainly the concentricity of the system and its far reaching field effect, are most clear and dramatic in the later nineteenth and early twentieth centuries when the buying power of the North Atlantic community was unrivalled in international commodity markets, as compared to the weaker concentration of earlier centuries or the greater dispersion of power in today's world. Certainly it can be argued that the demographic field effect which is already perceptible in the sixteenth century is nonetheless quite incomplete, limited as it was to waterside and largely dependent upon water transport. The intervening centuries – the seventeenth and the eighteenth – witnessed the institutionalization of international commodity markets, centered first in Amsterdam, then in London. As these markets stabilized their influence penetrated the European continent as well as the seas beyond, so that the prices of various commodities in various distant localities converged under the influence of internationally determined prices. (For a map series which illustrates the concentrating influence of the great commodity markets upon grain prices at various European localities, the reader is referred to the fourth volume of the new edition of the *Cambridge Economic History of Europe*.) Seen in retrospect, long after the 'perfection' of the world commodity markets via the price mechanism, the sixteenth-century developments may seem blind, embryonic and relatively unimportant. But because the Levant trade in primary commodities and the counterpart Baltic trade to the north were among the first responses to a new European demographic constitution, we permit ourselves a special interest in the genesis period of the world system of trade and production.

The Ottoman staple reserve

The fact that the main exports from Ottoman territories were raw, mostly unprocessed commodities – similar in that respect to the trans-Atlantic commodities – will probably always tempt some to call the Levant trade a 'colonial' trade. But at least until the nineteenth century the political subordination implied by that term was almost wholly missing. To the contrary, on the Ottoman side the Levant trade was first institutionalized (i.e. included in treaties) in the period of greatest Ottoman power, before the close of the sixteenth century. Thus clauses on trade agreed to by the Ottoman authorities expressed at first Ottoman convenience, then later a *quid pro quo* bargaining for mutual advantage and only finally, in the nineteenth and twentieth centuries, a tutelary relationship with a succession of Great Powers.

The fact is that the Ottoman role in the emergent world trade system was neither deliberately chosen, nor understood, nor effectively controlled by the Ottoman authorities. To the extent that they were consciously concerned with economic as opposed to fiscal priorities, their first priority from the late sixteenth through the early nineteenth centuries (military exigencies aside) was the provisioning of the capital city complex from its staple reserve zone.

A 'policy of provision,' which reserved for towns and cities the staple commodities produced in their vicinities, was characteristic in medieval Europe.[14] Byzantine Constantinople had a well developed staple policy which was only one among an array of state controls. Following the Byzantine example (but with what degree of consciousness we do not know) the Ottoman authorities reconstituted a staple policy of their own to serve the needs of their capital city of Istanbul, the Der-i-Saadet, or 'Door to Happiness.' Again, as in the Byzantine case, the Ottoman staple policy is only one element (though a very important one) in a command economy which included other interlacing elements – a system of price controls, controls over craft guilds and merchants, a system of service villages and service groups, a commodity purchase system, and prohibitions on foreign purchases of foodstuffs inside the straits and on the exports of anything which could be regarded as war material, as well as specie. The prevailing economic philosophy of the Ottomans, insofar as they had one, has yet to be precisely defined. Loosely speaking, they preserved a medieval pre-mercantilist outlook on economic life until at least the period of Selim III at the end of the eighteenth century, although to characterize them in this fashion is to use Western, non-Ottoman categories. Their command economy will surely one day receive systematic study as an integrated system. For the limited purposes of characterizing the Ottoman export trade, we interest ourselves only in the extent to which the imperial staple policy in the service of the capital city impinged upon their total export situation.

It is tempting to look at the Ottoman staple policy as the simple continuation of Byzantine policy. The depopulation of Constantinople/Istanbul in the late Byzantine and the first Ottoman century was so marked that a staple policy requiring that a special effort be made to provide the capital with basic foodstuffs scarcely seems necessary. Nonetheless Polish–Ottoman treaties of the late fifteenth and sixteenth centuries already reserve for the Ottomans a right to pre-emptive commodity purchases on the Black Sea coast, the Danube and in

Bulgaria.[15] The flourishing of the multi-ethnic Ottoman capital in the sixteenth century would in any case require the reconstruction of such a policy, a policy which once fully adopted would not be finally relaxed until the Romanian principalities escaped from effective Ottoman control in 1830.

The so-called wheat 'boom,' identified by Aymard, found its reflection in at least one Ottoman source, which points in the direction of a policy of provision, the construction of a staple reserve for the capital city. In 1548 a law written for the province of Damascus stipulates that it is forbidden to sell grain anywhere except at market.[16] The intent of the law was surely to protect the provincial grain supply from the demands of buyers from the western Mediterranean.

Unfortunately few of the records of the Ottoman veziral council (known today as the *Mühimme* registers) survive from the years before the end of Süleyman's reign. Thus the best evidence for the earliest stage in the development of the Ottoman staple policy is unrecoverable. Nonetheless a considerable number of items dealing with the operation of the system of provision survive from the 1580s and 1590s. From these we can see clearly certain essential features of the system which survived more or less until its dissolution:[17]

(1) The customary sources for Istanbul's grain (especially wheat) were the Bulgarian shore, the Dobrudja and the cluster of ports at the mouth of the Danube, as well as the western shore of the Marmara, and Egypt; secondary areas drawn on in times of special dearth were the eastern shore of the Marmara, the Black Sea coast of Anatolia, the Aegean shore as far as Euboea, and least frequently the Mediterranean and Aegean shores of Anatolia. (Reliance on the Asian shores increases, however, in the late eighteenth and early nineteenth centuries.)

(2) The customary sources for Istanbul's sheep (usually divided into military and non-military, i.e. *yeniçeri* and *esnaf*, sheep) were Wallachia, Bulgaria and Thrace.

(3) A contraband trade was already chronic outside the Straits; the Ottoman sanctions on this trade included the death penalty.

(4) Contraband and unauthorized transfers of grain and sheep between Ottoman provinces seem to have been just as great a source of worry for the authorities as the smuggling done for foreign buyers.

(5) Foreign flag traffic within the Straits was already under strict control and only under special circumstances permitted north of the Bosphorus.

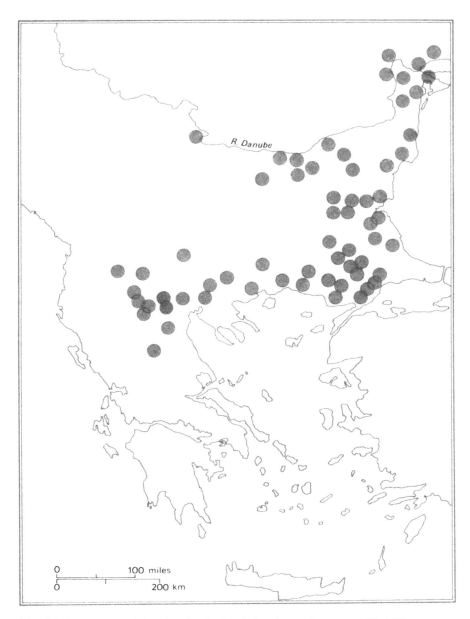

Map 3   European assembly points for the Istanbul grain supply system, 1668–1836

Sources: BVA*Maliyeden Müdevver (MM) 15381 (1080н); MM 6865 (1079–80н); MM 554 (1084н); and BVA Kâmil Kepeci (KK) 5529 (1087н); KK 2749 (1104н); KK 2806 (1113н); KK 2706 (1096н); KK 2719 (1097–8н). There are many other registers in both collections bearing on state wheat purchases both from the European and Asian sides. For lists of European assembly points for Istanbul's supply of sheep, see Ahmed Refik, *16 asırda Istanbul hayatı* (Istanbul, 1935), items 10 and 39. (*BVA = Istanbul Prime Minister's Archive.)

Because of the special geography of the empire, the Ottoman reserve policy also implied from its very inception a reserve zone. Control of the entire Black Sea periphery, and of its tributary the Danube, had always been thrust into the hands of whatever power controlled the Straits, as an accident of geography and a geopolitical circumstance of prime importance since the days of Troy. The Ottomans made the most of this situation. After driving the Italians from the Black Sea in the late fifteenth century, down to 1783, when they were forced by the Russians to accept foreign flag commerce through the Straits, the Ottoman authorities permitted regular entry to the Black Sea only to the Ragusans, who were their tributary (and even in this case permitted them to proceed only as far as the Bulgarian ports). Occasional permits to enter, which were granted to the English in the seventeenth and to the French in the eighteenth centuries, were marks of momentary favor, exceptions to the rule. The attempt by the Linchou family of France to break through this barrier and create a regular business inside the Black Sea reserve in the mid-eighteenth century ended tragically for the family.[18]

Although the Ottoman provision policy also brought to the capital city such varied products as dried fruits, dried fish, honey, pressed beef, butter, cheese, timber, hides, wax, tallow, metals and horses, the perennial preoccupation was with grain (wheat, barley, and sometimes rye, millet or flour) and with sheep. The quantities involved were substantial: Mantran cites a document showing Istanbul's consumption of sheep to be about 6 million in the year 1674. Thornton speaks of half a million sheep annually from the Romanian principalities (late eighteenth century); Güçer has computed the total grain deliveries to Istanbul under the state-run system to have totalled in the single year 1758 6,510,000 Istanbul *kiles*, or 237,000 metric tons.[19]

Always vitally important to Istanbul and the army, the staple provision system took on added importance after supplies from Egypt dwindled owing to political problems there in the mid-eighteenth century, and again more after the territorial losses which followed the wars with Russia in the 1770s and 1790s. Thus in 1748 the control system, which had always involved written certificates of authorization for buyers and shippers, was stiffened with the introduction of a system of purchase quotas for each of the contributing districts.[20] After 1755 Wallachia was required to contribute grain annually, rather than sporadically as before. Here is one Ottoman institution of the sixteenth century which became more powerfully organized with the passage of time.[21] Naturally whether the buyers were *kapanlıs* buying for the needs of the palace and the military, or whether they were merchants buying under franchise for the Istanbul public, the state-run grain purchase (*mubayaa, ishtira*) and sheep purchase (*jelb*) systems were so open to abuse as to be intermittently demoralizing in their effects upon the contributing districts.[22]

The Danube was not, in the centuries before the opening of the Straits, the commercial artery which it later became. Only exceptionally did grain traffic reach west of the Iron Gates, when the garrison at Belgrade could not find sufficient supplies locally.[23] Generally speaking, landholders along its banks had no markets which could be reached via the river where their grain or other commodities could be sold profitably. The Polish and Russian borders were separated from the Black Sea shore by the Cossack–Tatar barrier. Thus the *boyars* of the Romanian principalities could resist the Ottoman purchase system only by sending their surpluses overland for sale into Transylvania and beyond. Usually these were animals – pigs and cattle – or wine and spirits; even as late as the 1830s grain formed only a small portion – less than 20 per cent – of Wallachian exports.[24]

The overland contraband trade in the north and north-west had as its southern counterpart the chronic seaborne contraband trade from the Aegean shores and via the Archipelago. Thus along the frontier and outside the Straits, Ottoman borders were not fully under government control. Yet the vital Istanbul reserve system inside the Straits for the most part functioned effectively in the service of the capital until the suppression of the Ottoman purchase privileges in the Treaty of Balta Liman (1838),[25] and by the same token made it impossible, before the opening of the Straits, for foreign demand to make itself felt at all on the Black Sea shores and along the lower Danube, or for a normal commercial life to arise which could respond to international trends.

The trading partners

A review of Ottoman exports from the mid-sixteenth to late eighteenth centuries discloses three noteworthy trends. The first of these is the marked rise to and fall from prominence of a series of trading partners: the Adriatic traders Venice and Ragusa (Dubrovnik) joined by France in the sixteenth, then English and Dutch supremacy for the better part of the seventeenth, then French domination for approximately a century, followed towards the close of the eighteenth century by the rise of neighboring powers to the north, Russia and the Habsburg empire.

Just as land use in exporting regions is affected by land use in importing regions, so also levels of demand are affected by changes in taste and industrial technology, and in shipping technology and the organization of trade on the part of the trading nations. The mutual interaction of these factors has been stressed by R. Davis in his studies dealing with England's Levant trade. 'Trade,' as Ohlin points out, 'is usually fairly reciprocal, both as to value and transport requirements.'[26] Shipowners and merchants could not for long afford to sustain the losses of a one way trade. A nation which wished to sell in the Levant had also perforce to buy in the Levant, and if changing tastes or changing technology endangered the capacity of a nation to maintain the *reciprocity* of its trade in the Levant then that balance either had to be restored by dealing in new items or the level of both imports and exports would fall.[27]

Wars and alliances, both those in which the Ottomans were directly involved and those in which they were not,[28] naturally also often played

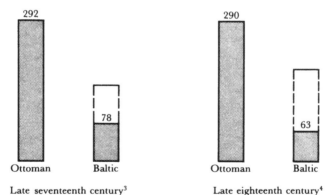

Figure 1   Estimated Ottoman exports[1] to pre-industrial Europe (in millions of grams silver),[2] compared with Baltic grain trade
(dotted line represents hypothetical totals of Baltic exports *including* products other than grain)

Notes:
[1] The peak of the Baltic grain trade came in the first half of the seventeenth century, with a half-century annual average from 1600 to 1649 which was 23 per cent higher than the annual average of the period 1650–99. Before the mid-seventeenth century the grain of the Baltic represented one-half to two-thirds of the total value of the westbound Baltic trade, but by the eighteenth century its proportion of the westbound trade had fallen to one-third, or less. The late seventeenth-century figure of 78 mgs is derived from the half-century average offered by J. A. Faber, 'The decline of the Baltic grain trade in the second half of the 17th century,' *Acta Historiae Neerlandica*, 1 (1966), 108–31, at 118; his figures in general agree with the indices proposed by

a decisive role in handing a trading advantage first to one nation's traders, then another's. It was between the two wars of the Holy League against the Ottomans, i.e. between 1538 and 1571, that Ragusa shared with Venice the benefits of the short-lived Ottoman 'wheat boom' identified by Aymard.[29] Ragusa, which because of its special status as an Ottoman tributary was able to enter the Black Sea to find

---

P. Jeannin, 'Les comptes du sund comme source pour la construction d'indices generaux de l'activité économique en Europe (xvie–xviiie siècle),' *Revue Historique*, 231 (1964), 55–102, 307–40, from which the late eighteenth-century figure (actually 1750–80) is extrapolated. The rye price used to monetize the earlier average is 140 fl. per last; for the latter average, 130 fl. per last. These articles largely supercede an earlier work: A. Christensen, *Dutch Trade to the Baltic about 1600* (Copenhagen, 1941). It should be added that Baltic trade figures, like the Mediterranean figures, fluctuate dramatically. We are fortunate to have these hard-won secular averages.

[2] Sources for the silver content of various coins in which the component estimates of trade were expressed were for the *livre tournois*: Natalis de Wailly, 'Mémoire sur les variations de la livre tournois,' *Mémoires de L'institut impérial de France*, 21 (Paris, 1857), 177–427, at 404–6; for the *'real* of eight' (the Castillian 'piastre' favored by the French in their seventeenth-century Levant dealings): A. P. Usher, *The Early History of Deposit Banking in Mediterranean Europe* (New York, 1967), p. 512; for the Dutch *gulden* (also known as *florin*): N. W. Posthumus, *Nederlandscher Priesgeshiednis* (Leyden, 1943), Table cxii (this work also contains a treasury of commodity prices over a three-century period, including rye); for the Austrian *gulden/florin*: W. A. Shaw, *The History of Currency, 1252 to 1896* (New York, 1967), p. 375; cf. also J. McClusker, *Money and Exchange in Europe and America, 1600–1775* (Chapel Hill, 1978).

[3] Source for the late seventeenth-century annual average of Ottoman exports by sea (base period actually 1670–83): P. Masson, *Histoire du commerce français dans le Levant au XVIIe siècle* (Paris, 1897), p. 236. Masson's estimate (equalling 289 mgs/ann) may be compared with Dovière's report, an elaborate, unpublished memoir detailing the French Levantine trade, today preserved in the Paris archives (photocopy in the writer's possession), based on a *single* war year (1686) in which seaborne exports equalled about 171 mgs. An additional 2–3 mgs, at the very least, must be added to represent the approximate 20,000 cattle which annually were herded westward from Hungary in the late seventeenth century: K. Glamann, 'European Trade, 1500–1750,' in *The Fontana Economic History of Europe*, vol. 2, ed. Carlo Cipolla (London, 1971), p. 50. Note that a mid-seventeenth-century estimate of Ottoman exports by G. Tongas, *Les Relations de la France avec l'Empire durant la première moitié du XVIIe siècle* . . . (Toulouse, 1942), pp. 208–10, yields an annual average of 180 mgs by sea. All western trading partners are included in these estimates.

[4] Sources for the late eighteenth-century composite annual average for Ottoman exports are C. F. Volney's estimate of seaborne trade as of 1784, 'État du commerce du Levant a 1784, d'après les registres de la chambre de commerce de Marseilles,' reprinted in C. Issawi (ed.), *The Economic History of the Middle East, 1800–1914* (London, 1966), pp. 30–7 (approximately 230 mgs). The northward export trade by land offered for the year 1780 by J. Winkler and appearing in I. Sakazov, *Bulgarische Wirtschaftsgeschichte* (Berlin and Leipzig, 1929), p. 253 (approx 74 mgs) was compared with a figure equalling 41 mgs offered for the decade average 1771–80 by S. Gavrilović (drawing on work by Marianne von Gerzfeld and Adolf Beer) in *Prilog Istoriji Trgovine i Migracije Balkan Podunavlje XVIII i XIX Stoljeća* (Beograd, 1969), p. 12. To a compromise figure of 50 mgs annually for the northward landborne trade we have added another 10 mgs representing seaborne exports to Venice via Zadar and Split: N. Čolak, 'Bradovlasnici Zadarske Komune izmeďu Karlovačkog i Požarevačkog Mira,' *Pomorski Zbornik*, 3 (Zadar, 1965), 775–808, and, in the same issue, Traljić 'Izvoz Bosanske robe preko Splitske luke u XVIII stoljeću,' pp. 809–27, especially pp. 823, 825.

Naturally such a composite falls short of the desired degree of certainty, nor is it entirely appropriate to compare fifty-year and thirty-year Baltic averages with Ottoman estimates for far shorter periods (especially single year estimates like Volney's or Dovière's). Alas we must make do with what we have at hand!

cargo on the Bulgarian coast, continued thereafter to make its living as a trading city state, but not to any marked degree as a grain trader. Both of these Adriatic traders were affected adversely by Venetian–Ottoman hostilities connected with the Ottoman conquest of Cyprus in 1570. French ships were already bringing to Marseilles in the 1560s a part of the trade formerly concentrated in Venetian hands.[30] The war over Cyprus was a stimulus not only to the French but to English

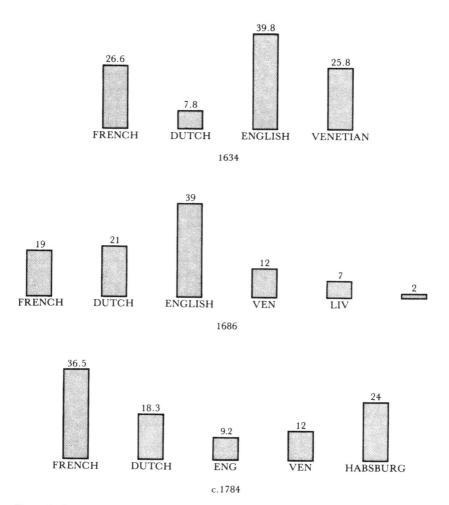

Figure 2   Levant traders' percentage shares of Ottoman exports, 1634, 1686 and c. 1784

Sources: 1634 Stoianovich; 1686 Dovières; c. 1784 Volney, Winkler, Čolak (see Fig. 1 for detailed references)

traders, who picked up again the desultory attempts at trade in the Levant which their predecessors had made earlier in the century. In France chaotic political conditions dampened the growth of trade generally. But the English, after the sack of Antwerp (1576), which closed the overland route from the Adriatic, came in increasing numbers to fetch their own raisins, wine and spices.[31] Every piece of business which these Western traders, soon joined by the Dutch, were able to complete in Ottoman waters constituted a subtraction from Venice's erstwhile entrepôt trade.

At least four other factors helped unseat the Venetians from their former preeminence as Levantine traders towards the end of the sixteenth century. The thrill of fear which had seized San Marco's square when word arrived in 1501 that the Portuguese Cabral expedition had returned from India with spices, was ultimately justified in 1595 when the Dutchman Cornelius Houtman rounded the Cape, thereby opening the long but profitable Dutch sea route to the East Indies and dealing a body blow to the already diminished Venetian spice trade.[32] A second fact of life in the late sixteenth century was the dawning recognition of the technical superiority of the Atlantic ships, with the result that Venice's merchants allowed more and more trade to be carried in foreign hulls and even themselves purchased or commissioned ships from the Atlantic traders.[33] Thirdly, there was the failure of the Venetian woollens industry to compete successfully with the new, lighter, brighter woollen cloths being produced for the Levant trade by the Dutch and English.[34] Perhaps it was in response to these unpalatable developments that there arose at Venice during the latter quarter of the sixteenth century a tendency to reinvest commercial capital in agricultural estates in the Venetian hinterland, not in itself a negative development since it led quickly to near self-sufficiency in food supplies for the merchant republic.[35]

Hence by the beginning of the seventeenth century Venice had already assumed a subordinate role as a Levantine trader, following a successful career lasting four centuries. In the seventeenth century, even this second role was further eroded by the effects of the Thirty Years' War, which largely destroyed Venice's trade across the Alps, and by the twenty-five year Candian War (1644–69) in which Venice exhausted its resources in a vain attempt to deny Crete to the Ottomans.[36] Both the Genoese and the Ragusans profited from Venice's predicament in the Candian War, and, to a lesser degree, during the long war from 1683 to 1699, in which Venice was a principal.

Venetian commerce with the Ottmans survived at a diminished level until its final resurgence in the late eighteenth century. Although Venetians lost their footing in the east Mediterranean and in the Black Sea, they intensified their hold on the Adriatic after the Ottomans successfully reclaimed Morea in 1718. During the eighteenth century the Dalmatian and Albanian shores were treated as part of the Venetian staple reserve, in a small scale (and less complete) version of Istanbul's own provision policy. The pattern of trade in the Adriatic of the seventeenth and eighteenth centuries was also affected by the prosperity of two lesser ports sponsored by Venice – Split and Zadar on the Dalmatian coast. Through these non-Ottoman ports the merchants and drovers of Bosnia were able to move, both to Venice and to Ancona, considerable numbers of livestock and considerable quantities of other Ottoman fallow products – wool, hides and wax. Although neither Bosnia nor the denuded and rocky Dalmatian coast offered vegetable exports in significant quantities, south of Kotor the Albanian coastal plain was capable of such surpluses. Thus in the eighteenth century coastal Albania for the first time found a significant export role as landholding families, such as the Bushatlis, provided cotton, oil, tobacco and rice for the local trade with Italy which already in the seventeenth century had included occasional shipments of other grains, as well as wool, leather and wax.[37]

The Ottoman tributary port of Ragusa, pressed on the north by the newer Dalmatian ports offering a vent to Bosnian products, drastically revised its trading system in order to compete in the seventeenth century, but failed to adjust successfully to a new set of conditions after the peace of Karlowitz (1699). Dropping an older trade through Bosnia, in which metals and slaves had been important, Ragusa/Dubrovnik constructed a vast network in the seventeenth century which drew upon a great portion of the Balkan peninsula, as well as Hungary, the Dobrudja and Bessarabia, for wool, cattle hides and other types of skins which were funneled into the home port and transshipped, largely to Italy. This admirably successful reorientation did not survive into the eighteenth century. The most reasonable explanations which can be offered for Ragusa's demise as a trader in the eighteenth century (war years excepted) are that, like Venice, Ragusa suffered from competition with western *caravanaires* at sea and perhaps even more on land from competition with the new network of indigenous Balkan traders and trade fairs which rose in the interior during the eighteenth century.[38]

The French trade in the Levant, which had originally profited from

France's unique strategic alliance with the Ottomans, was superceded, even dwarfed, in the early seventeenth century by the trade carried on by Dutch and English ships. Both of these Atlantic sea powers had participated, since 1590, in the rise of the free port of Livorno, there joined by Hanseatics in bringing Baltic grain into the Mediterranean, where it became a frequently supplied staple. From 200 ships in 1592–3, arrivals at Livorno rose to the level of almost 2500 in 1609 and 1610.[39] Silks from the eastern Mediterranean were resold at Livorno on so plentiful a scale that the port became in the seventeenth century the chief silk market in Europe.[40] Venice itself gave an impetus to the Livorno trade with a 'navigation act' in 1602 which had the effect of forcing the Atlantic skippers to do business elsewhere than at Venice.[41] Often these northern skippers whiled away the months between voyages home (which were timed to take advantage of seasonal markets in the Levant) by carrying on a trade between Mediterranean ports, a trade for which, because of the economic superiority of their ships, and particularly the Dutch ships, they were well suited.[42]

After 1600, both Dutch and English merchants were pleased to find a ready market in the Levant for their woollen fabrics in preference to the heavier woollens of the Venetians.[43] The superiority of their quickening Levant trade over that of France is shown in the mid-seventeenth-century figures supplied by Tongas:

> France, about 6–7 million livres annually
> England, about 15 million livres annually
> the Dutch, about 12 million livres annually.[44]

The Dutch evidently lost some of their interest in the Levant trade after 1617, being distracted by burgeoning opportunities in the Far East.[45] Except for the disturbance of England's trade during the English civil wars, from which the Dutch drew some profit, the English were the undisputed leaders in the Levant trade between 1620 and 1683. The temporary decline of Dutch trade in the eastern Mediterranean after 1660 is thought to have been the result of the interplay of silk prices in which Levantine silk was displaced by Bengal and Chinese silk in the Dutch market.[46] Dutch interest in the Levant trade recovered in the eighteenth century in rhythm with the rise of the port of Izmir, which they preferred to all other Levantine ports.

English interest waned later and took longer to revive. English woollen fabrics, though still in the lead in 1700, steadily lost ground to French cloth after that date. Furthermore, English interest in the silk of the Levant, which comprised the bulk of their imports from the area in the early eighteenth century, dropped sharply after 1730, after which English trade with the Ottomans was of minor significance for almost a century.[47]

The doldrums in which the French traders languished throughout the better part of the seventeenth century was only partly the result of competition. The French 'nations' of the Levant were plagued by the arbitrary levies (*avanies*) of Ottoman provincial governors because they never learned the art of propitiatory voluntary bribery practiced by other 'nations.' Lack of direction, and a confusion of authority over the Levant trade within France, hurt badly. Moreover, the French were very vulnerable targets for pirates of every kind not only because their ships tended to be small but because they did not employ a convoy system.[48] The French–Ottoman trade, which had recovered after the close of the religious wars in France, amounted to 30 million livres in 1600.[49] Between 1620 and 1635 that trade fluctuated between 12 and 14 million livres, declining thereafter until in 1661 France was importing only 3 million livres of Levantine commodities at a time when combined Dutch and English imports from the zone were approaching 25 million livres annually.[50] However, a concerted effort to improve France's position, directed by Colbert, resulted in a recovery after 1670. The advantages produced by the favored treatment which the Dutch and English had received at the Ottoman court during the better part of the seventeenth century were finally matched by a renewal of the Ottoman–French alliance after the catastrophic Ottoman defeat at Vienna (1683).[51] As a reward for French friendship, the Ottomans reduced the customs rate paid by French traders in Egypt from 30 per cent to 3 per cent (1685). The French were also granted the privilege of participating in an intra-Ottoman *caravanaire* trade between Egypt and other Ottoman ports, among them Istanbul.[52]

Colbert's policy involved the conversion of Marseilles into a 'free port' with greatly reduced taxes, encouragement for the French woollens industry, and the organization (1670) and reorganization (1678, 1685) of a national company for trading in the Levant.[53] Owing at least partly to these shifts in policy, and to France's recovery of prestige at the Ottoman capital, marked by the Nointel capitulations of 1673, French trade figures once again rose, this time for a long period. France also had other advantages which began to count. Less interested than the English or Dutch had been in the silk offered in the East, France was nonetheless far better able to absorb other raw materials obtainable there: cotton, grain, wool and hides.[54] The reciprocity rule began to work in France's favor, and French woollens firms helped the turnabout by gradually developing ever cheaper, lighter and brighter fabrics to cater to Muslim tastes. According to the report of a Venetian ambassador, French trade had already edged out English trade by 1713.[55] The growing importance of France's Levant trade can be judged numerically by the preponderance of Levantine exports within total French imports: by 1717–20 the Levant trade accounted for 13,500,000 livres out of a total of 18,000,000; by 1786–9 it represented 30,200,000 livres out of 36,450,000 livres.[56] In 1784, towards the end of the period of French predominance, Volney estimated the relative shares in the total Levant trade as follows: France 4/8; the Dutch 2/8; England 1/8; Venice 1/8.[57]

This estimate obscures two vital developments. The disruption of French trade in the eastern Mediterranean during the Seven Years' War (1756–63) resulted in the displacement of the French *caravanaire* fleet by a new group of sea-going merchants – Greek and Albanian subjects of the Porte who used this opportunity to their advantage.[58] It was this group which flew the Russian flag after 1783 (making up the bulk of the first foreign flag commercial flotilla on the Black Sea since the departure of the Italians in the fifteenth century), taking up the slack after the collapse of French trade after 1789. About the same time Habsburg trade through Trieste and Fiume (Rijeka) was undergoing a marked development. Although Charles VI of Austria had opened these as free ports in 1719, with an eye to reducing further Venetian trade, the real development of this Habsburg sea route took place only late in the eighteenth century. The tardiness of the prosperity of the Habsburg sea route was the result of natural obstacles which had to be removed, and of sluggish coordination between domestic and external Austrian policy.

The Treaty of Passarowitz of 1718, besides handing spectacular territorial gains to the northern power, also gave (through an appended trade agreement) continuity to conditions encouraging trade between the two powers, a liberality which had been a Habsburg treaty objective since their first trade agreement with the Ottomans in 1617. Thus the 3 per cent *ad valorem* customs rate which had found a place in the Treaty of Karlowitz was repeated at Passarowitz. However, current Austrian policy simultaneously imposed upon domestic merchants imposts on imported goods amounting to 30–40 per cent. Therefore it was the merchants from the Ottoman territories who were able to profit immediately and directly from the low customs rate. The result was that for the better part of the eighteenth century the trade initiative was unintentionally handed over to Ottoman subjects, Stoianovich's 'conquering Balkan Orthodox merchants.'[59] The Romanian-speaking *Kutzovlah*, Macedonian Slav and Serbian merchants who constituted the great majority of the Ottoman trading group made good use of their opportunities in the decades after 1718. Avoiding routes which would lead directly into Austrian territory, they built a vast trade network which followed Hungarian, Romanian and Transylvanian routes, and easily suppressed the remnants of the Ragusan trade empire. Favored by the Hungarian nobility, which both taxed them and invested with them, merchants from the Ottoman territories monopolized the overland Ottoman export trade, making full use of river routes to deliver Ottoman primary commodities – above all raw cotton – to Vienna and other northern destinations, and in the reverse direction sold northern manufactures through the circuit of seasonal fairs which became a regular feature of Balkan life in that century.

Only after 1771, when the Habsburgs signed an agreement with the Porte differentiating between manufactured items and raw materials, did Habsburg merchants begin to participate in this trade on something like an equal footing. In contrast to the little regulated Ottoman style of trade, the Habsburg trade offensive required elaborate preparation: (1) the improvement of the port of Trieste, (2) the successive improvements of the Carolina Road connecting the port of Fiume/ Rijeka with the Danube River system, and (3) the organization of official trading companies intended to facilitate the movement of primary commodities from the Hungarian plain to the Adriatic ports: the Trieste–Rijeka Company (1750) and the Temisvar Company (1759). Following these gradual improvements, which had bilateral effects, Ottoman exports into Habsburg territory, though averaging only about 3 million florins in the period 1741–71, had by 1778 reached the level of 9 million florins.[60] The former predominance of the Morava– Belgrade–Tisa route was now gradually eclipsed by the sea route from Salonica to Trieste, a transition marked by the establishment of Graf Staremberg's firm at Salonica in 1776 and the subsequent placement of that firm's agents at Seres (Siroz) and Larissa (Yenishehir).[61]

The long interruption of the north–south trade between 1683 and 1718 is worth noting. The seventeenth-century and eighteenth-century trades were very different in character. Whereas in the later seventeenth century the Ottoman–Vienna trade was carried on by 'Raizen'

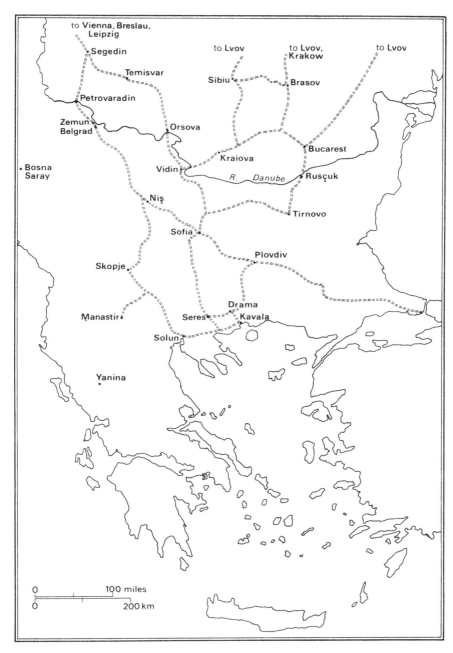

Map 4 Primary South-east European overland trade routes, eighteenth century

(presumably Ragusans as well as Serbs) and Armenians, the eighteenth-century trade was largely in the hands of 'Greeks' (i.e. predominantly traders from the Macedonian zone, with colonies at Vienna and at key points on the northward route). The seventeenth-century exports to Vienna had been quite heterogeneous – cattle, leather, hides, linen, tobacco, spices, sturgeon, vitriol, rugs, sponges, etc. – whereas the eighteenth-century export trade was almost wholly a trade in a limited number of primary commodities – especially Macedonian cotton, but also tobacco, wool and hides. The cattle trade from the Hungarian plain westward had peaked in the first half of the seventeenth century; a plausible explanation for this is that the empty spaces (*Wüstungen*) created by the Thirty Years' War had made room for cattle raising closer to western markets. However, a flow of cattle from the Romanian principalities, not only westward but northward toward Lvov and Krakow, also remained a feature of the Ottoman export trade in the eighteenth century.[62]

The Danube below the Iron Gate was but a minor trade route during most of the eighteenth century, although its strategic and military importance was appreciated by both powers. Ottoman supplies for the capital were mustered near the river mouth, particularly at Isakchi (Isaccea). Westward from the Gate little traffic moved toward Belgrade, which in the eighteenth century received its regular grain supply from Srem and Slavonia, provinces now under Habsburg control, in return for which Hungary accepted Serbian pigs and oxen. Some traffic *crossed* the lower Danube, however, especially goods of Bulgarian and Macedonian provenance which crossed northward at Ruse and Vidin. The Romanian and Transylvanian towns, especially Bucharest and Brasov, were the destinations for some of this traffic, being among the most populous places in south-eastern Europe. But some of the Ottoman goods went on as far as Leipzig, where an increasing number of Ottoman (i.e. largely Macedonian) merchants made regular appearances.[63]

During the reign of Joseph II Austria made a successful effort to break free into the Black Sea, as well as into the Adriatic. Until the time of the Danube voyages organized by Graf Festetics in the 1780s, any downstream Austrian traffic was still obliged, under a longstanding rule, to be transferred into Ottoman bottoms before issuing into the Black Sea. But this condition became intolerable to Austria after the Treaty of Kuchuk Kaynardja of 1774, when Ottoman weakness was again clearly revealed. Thus when the Russians finally received ratification of their own right to navigate the Black Sea in 1783 the Austrians were fast on their heels. By the late 1780s Austrian flag commerce was first among the non-Ottoman flags on the Black Sea and remained so until the mid-nineteenth century. Polish commerce, which had been limited to the Principalities, was also stimulated by these changes, so that Polish grain was a factor on the Black Sea immediately after 1783. Not until 1802, however, were Russian ships flying their own flag (in contrast to Greek ships flying that flag) actually permitted *south* of Istanbul, a relaxation which came about in connection with concessions to the English (1799) and the French (1802) with respect to navigation on the Black Sea.[64]

At the eastern end of the Black Sea, a circumvention of the Ottoman reserve zone had been instituted long before the northern powers made their breakthrough. There the French, imitating an earlier initiative by the English and Dutch in that area, established a network of *barataires* (agents protected by letters of patent, i.e. *berats*) connecting the Black Sea and Persia with the Gulf and the Levant.[65]

The ports of the Levant

A second noteworthy trend during the period under scrutiny was the northward shift of the export trade through Ottoman ports away from Egypt and Syria in favor of ports further north. While the decline of the trade from the Arab provinces to the south is explainable partly in terms of the chaotic political conditions of the eighteenth century, the rise of Smyrna (Izmir) and Salonica (Thessaloniki), the natural debouchments respectively of the western Anatolian plateau and the Macedonian plain, are explicable as agricultural responses to overseas demand.

Egypt

Issawi's assessment of Egyptian trade, that except for the period 1530–1600 Egyptian trade declined from the mid-fourteenth to the nineteenth century, should be modified somewhat.[66] Although the trade through the Egyptian ports was trifling so far as the English were concerned until the nineteenth century,[67] the French case was different. There was still a quite considerable trade with France from Alexandria in 1658,[68] and the 1686 agreement, permitting the French to participate in a coastal trade between Egypt and other Ottoman ports, meant a real boost in the activity of the French, though not in trade figures recorded at Marseilles.[69] French trade with Egypt did decline in the eighteenth century, however, as increasingly erratic and arbitrary behavior by local Egyptian authorities added to the already high level of harassment which the French had endured there in the seventeenth century.[70] According to a 'well informed' source, the Ottoman empire was in 1776 consuming about five times more Egyptian goods in value than the Europeans.[71]

Syria

Although Aleppo was the leading Ottoman export entrepôt at the beginning of the seventeenth century, by 1671 it had slipped to fourth place among the French *échelles* (i.e. merchant colonies), surpassed by Smyrna, Alexandria and Sidon.[72] This relative decline has been attributed by Europeans to three causes: the rapacious *avanies* and other impositions of the successive pashas of Aleppo, interruptions in the silk caravan route from Isfahan owing to the long Ottoman–Safavid wars

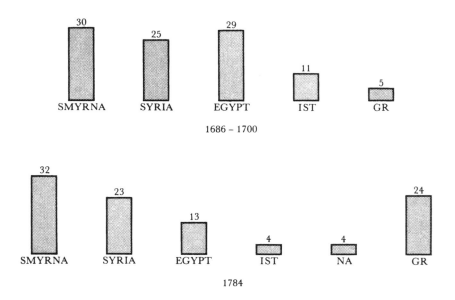

Figure 3   Ports of the Levant, percentage share of exports to Marseilles, 1686–1700 and 1784
Key: IST = Istanbul, GR = Greece, NA = North Africa
Sources: 1686–1700 Paris; 1784 Volney (see Fig. 1 for detailed references)

which dominated the first four decades of the century (to 1639), and the draining off of Persian silk by Dutch and English traders who, with Safavid support, had established themselves as successors to the Portuguese at Hormuz (1623) and had, at least until the 1640s, succeeded in carrying away considerable quantities of Persian silk through the Gulf.[73] But whereas French trade at Aleppo slipped during the seventeenth century, the English entrenched themelves there; a memoir of 1671 shows them solidly established,[74] and using the old French warehouses as though t y were their own. Therefore total exports through Aleppo (in contrast to French exports through Aleppo) sank only as the English interest in Levantine silk declined in the early eighteenth century. When exports through Aleppo's port of Alexandretta (Iskenderun) revived in the last quarter of the eighteenth century, the bulk of this trade was no longer raw silk, as formerly, but cotton thread, cotton cloth and raw cotton.[75]

The French hold on the Damascus trade through the port of Sayda (later through Acre) was never loosened by foreign rivals. Consequently total French exports from the Syrian coast as a whole did not fall as dramatically in the seventeenth century as did the French trade at Aleppo. Masson's figures on total French exports through the ports of the Levant during the period 1685–1714 (a period when the French were resuming their supremacy in the Levant trade, it should be noted) show an almost equal trade from Anatolia, Egypt and Syria, taken together, with a still decidedly minor trade from Istanbul and Rumelia (Ottoman Europe):

Smyrna (Izmir): 88 million livres, climbing steeply towards the end of the period
Alexandria: 84 million livres, also rising in 1714
The Syrian ports (Iskenderun and Sayda) combined: 82 million livres
Istanbul: 31 million livres
Rumelia, Crete and the Archipelago combined: 16 million livres[76]

The Levantine export flow shifted dramatically northward in the eighteenth century. Although Masson's figures are a patchwork based on averages for different periods in the second half of the eighteenth century, and although they pertain to the French export trade (which predominated strongly at Salonica, in Syria and in Egypt) rather than the total export trade, they nonetheless give us good reason to believe that Rumelia and Egypt changed places in the rank order of the exporting zones. Approximate annual averages gleaned from Masson's work on later eighteenth-century trade are as follows:[77]

Smyrna (Izmir): 14,500,000 livres (base period 1787–9)

Rumelia: (Salonica during the base period 1768–87 plus Morea and the Archipelago during the base period 1787–9) 3,318,000 plus 1,800,000 respectively, for a total annual average of 5,118,000 livres

The Syrian ports: (Iskenderun in the base period 1787–9 and Sayda/Acre in the base period 1787–9) 2,372,000 livres plus 800,000 livres respectively, for a total annual average of 3,172,000 livres

Alexandria: 2,600,000 livres (base period 1787–9)

Istanbul: 1,800,000 livres (base period 1763–7)

Volney's totals, which purport to show French imports from the Levant in 1784, and which also are based on the Marseilles registers, naturally differ from Masson's averages yet preserve the same rank order among exporting zones:[78]

Smyrna: 6,025,845
Rumelia (Ottoman Europe except Istanbul): 4,574,563
Syrian ports combined: 4,419,411
Alexandria: 2,465,630
Istanbul: 682,043

Paris offers imperfect but suggestive figures on the relative importance of the Levantine *échelles* from the point of view of exports to Marseilles over the entire period 1686–1789, as follows (all figures percentages):[79]

	Constantinople	Salonica	Smyrna	Morea	Candia	Aleppo	mid-Syria	Cairo
1686–1700	11.00	—	30.00	—	—	9.00	16.00	29.00
1711–15	8.00	1.75	15.50	1.00	6.25	6.75	16.00	25.50
1736–40	6.00	2.75	13.60	7.00	6.25	11.50	23.25	14.30
1750–4	4.00	6.25	22.70	8.00	2.00	9.35	16.65	11.25
1765–9	3.00	13.00	37.00	6.75	0.75	10.00	12.00	11.00
1773–7	5.75	14.50	33.00	5.75	2.75	8.25	7.00	11.75
1785–9	6.75	7.50	38.00	4.75	6.00	9.00	5.00	7.50

If the records of the chief Levantine traders of the eighteenth century can be taken as a guide, Smyrna (Izmir), already the leading exporting harbor in the late seventeenth century, by the mid-eighteenth century was far ahead of Salonica and the other Greek ports combined, while Egypt had fallen behind.

Smyrna

The steady rise of Smyrna, especially after the town was rebuilt following the earthquake of 1688, is due at least in part to the relatively steadier and more moderate government of this port by local Ottoman authorities, placed as they were much closer to the capital city than the ports to the south and east. Smyrna apparently received a great boost in trading skills with the transfer there of many Jews from Salonica in connection with the Candian War, involving Venice and the Ottomans in the twenty-four-year struggle from 1645 to 1669.[80] Was it for this reason or for some other that Smyrna became in the 1640s, and remained, the preferred port of the Dutch in the Levant?[81] Both the Dutch and the English seem to have been only moderately, though steadily, interested in the heterogeneous trade through Smyrna, and as their interest in silk declined (first that of the Dutch, later the English) their trade totals also declined, though they were to revive late in the eighteenth century on the basis of cotton and dried fruit.[82] The French, however, after their great trading drive in the last quarter of the seventeenth century, were able to carry on in Smyrna a trade well balanced between imports and exports, and since French *caravanaires* did a great coastal trade there, total trade at the port maintained a relatively high level during the eighteenth century.[83]

Salonica, Cyprus, Morea and the Albanian ports

Exports from Cyprus gradually dwindled to almost nothing during the seventeenth century (following its occupation by the Ottomans) but revived on the basis of cotton after 1715.[84] Morea[85] suffered greatly as a consequence of the final war with Venice and the Venetian occupation (ending in 1715), which reduced its capacity to offer surpluses for a long time. Salonica, although designated as a French *échelle* in 1685, failed to become an important port until the mid-eighteenth century from which time it rose, it would seem, in tandem with Trieste.[86] Masson believed, however, that though Salonica may have been the official port of call, most French ships went on to other places in Greece and the Archipelago to load additional, usually clandestine, cargoes,[87] and his conviction is borne out by many other sources.

The rise of export oriented agriculture in coastal Albania during the eighteenth century lengthened the list of Ottoman ports. Visited by Italian ships, these ports were also served by the nascent Greco-Albanian navy, which became increasingly important in the wake of the Seven Years' War. Thus although none of these ports was large, the cumulative importance of the newer Adriatic ports was considerable; besides Durazzo/Durrës (already important in the seventeenth century) we must place the names of Messolonghi, Galaxidi, Arta, Prevesa, Valona and Dulcigno/Ulcinj.[88]

The reappearance of a trade in staples

A third trend in Ottoman trade, intimately correlated with the north-ward shift of ports and the shifts in trading partners, was the gradual dwindling of the long distance trade in luxuries passing westward through the Egyptian entrepôt, then the dwindling of the long distance trade in silk and their replacement by an interregional trade in staples grown in Ottoman provinces – grain, animal hides and animal fibers in the sixteenth and seventeenth centuries, cotton and tobacco in the eighteenth century. The phasing out of the so-called 'spice trade' through Egypt during the course of the sixteenth century has been discussed in a number of places and requires no demonstration here.[89] On the other hand, the Ottoman trade in staples from the mid-fifteenth to the late eighteenth century, although it can be inferred by collating monographs on aspects of the trade written from the point of view of one or another of the Western trading nations or their Levantine companies, has not until now been discussed with all the trading partners in mind. A brief but comprehensive summary is attempted in the following paragraphs, deliberately simplified to include only the major primary commodities exported from the Ottoman territories, particularly those which directly influenced land use.

Wheat

Although relatively minor quantities of other foodstuffs were exported, such as rice (from Egypt and in the eighteenth century Albania), dried fruit and olive oil (from the Archipelago), the only food which was exported from Ottoman territories in sufficient quantities and over a sufficient length of time to have affected land use in an important way was wheat. Barley was occasionally mixed with the wheat to make what the Ottomans called *mahlut*, a 'mixture.' American corn (i.e. maize) made its appearance in south-eastern Europe and upon the Black Sea shores in the seventeenth century, but although maize eventually became locally important as an animal feed (and in the nineteenth century as human food too) there is no evidence that it was exported from Ottoman territories. On the other hand, the traffic in wheat, at least until the mid-eighteenth century, went beyond sporadic

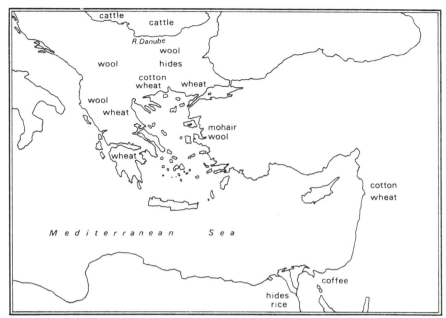

Map 5   Indigenous exports of the eastern Mediterranean, later seventeenth century

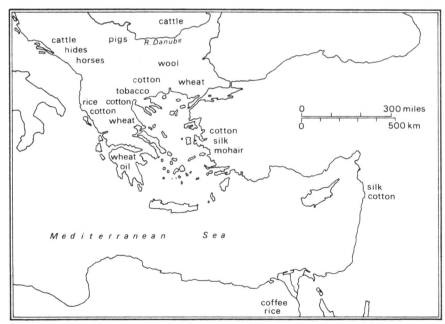

Map 6   Indigenous exports of the eastern Mediterranean, later eighteenth century

adjustments to momentary shortages which Braudel assures us took place occasionally on all the Mediterranean shores.

A regular trade in grain was not at all a new feature of Mediterranean life. The Roman past aside, in the period immediately preceding the Ottoman centuries Salonica, Crete, Cyprus, Anatolia and Egypt were all areas outside the Black Sea where traders could usually or very often find grain surpluses.[90]

The upward surge in population, which is now thought to have involved most shores of the Mediterranean in the sixteenth century, was accompanied by a quickened trade in wheat. This was partly an erratic trade, as Braudel has shown us, since harvest patterns were never twice the same. But since local inequalities were an annual reality, wheat was ever on the move. (Parry estimates an annual shift of grain throughout the Mediterranean amounting to 50,000 tons annually.[91] Despite the fact that Ottoman population was also rising in the sixteenth century, the Ottomans seem to have been always the suppliers, never the recipients of foreign grain.[92] Long before the general Malthusian peak towards the end of the sixteenth century, the Ottoman government became concerned about its supplier's role, anxious about supplying bread for its own populous capital, and wishing therefore to remain in control of a trade in this essential commodity, which was also thought to be a strategic military supply which ought to be denied to the enemy. Outside the Straits, as we already know, the Ottoman fleet – even at its peak of effectiveness in the mid-sixteenth century – was unable to do more than dampen a clandestine trade in wheat.[93]

The 'Ottoman wheat boom' identified by Aymard for the period 1548–64 is, of course, the obverse of the *crise de blé* which had become a serious problem for Italian cities when Sicilian export duties on wheat were raised in 1546. Although wheat surpluses were at that time sold from Ottoman ports without much control, 1551 is suggested as the last year in which permission was given by the Ottoman authorities to load wheat at Varna, inside the Bosporus enclosure.[94] A law drafted in 1539 for the districts of Bosnia, Herzegovina and Zvornik prohibited exports from Ottoman soil of military cloaks, armor, weapons, horses, iron and 'all else that could be useful to the enemy,' but does not mention grain, or even foodstuffs as such. However, a provincial law for the Damascus province already indicates a prohibition on the sale of grain away from the market at Damascus in 1548 (although this may have more to do with local price control than with the export trade).[95] In succeeding years, partly owing to the burgeoning population of Istanbul (put tentatively by Barkan at 400,000, but no survey exists), partly owing to the deflection westward of Egyptian and other surpluses outside the Straits, the Ottoman capital itself saw shortages. Aymard identifies 1564–8, 1572–81 and 1585–90 as periods of particular stress, naming the following years when actual bread shortages were noted by foreign observers in the Ottoman capital: 1555, 1565, 1574–5, 1576, 1578, 1580, 1587 and 1588.[96]

The external drain on Ottoman grain supplies tapered off rapidly around 1590. Stimulated by attractive prices, Italian merchants had turned to investing in agriculture on a large scale. Venice had expanded its production of rice and was practically self-sufficient in food after 1586.[97] A dramatic improvement in the Italian supply situation as a whole came with the arrival at Livorno and other ports, starting in 1590, of grain carried all the way from Danzig, the Baltic entrepôt. This Baltic grain was henceforth a factor in meeting the needs of the western half of the Mediterranean.[98] This new supply was, of course, available only at a price. The poor still suffered in the trade depressions of the next century, and plagues swept back and forth across the basin without respect for political boundaries. Malnutrition and plague being good bedfellows, periodic grain shortages are blamed along with poor sanitation and other factors for the regression of population on the seventeenth-century Mediterranean scene, a trend in which the Ottoman shores are certain to have participated.[99] (See pp. 83–7 below.)

In 1555, after a famine in Egypt and three days without bread at Istanbul, the first Ottoman ban on the export of grain is recorded.[100] A second followed in 1560. Starting as an exception, the ban on the export of foodstuffs quickly became the rule for which exceptions were occasionally made (referring here, of course, only to the supplies which the government was actually able to control). By 1574 there had come into being a permit system under which all grain movement, even from province to province within the empire, was subject to official surveillance and certification.[101] Numerous decrees aimed at stopping the contraband trade have been found for the period 1570 to 1610.[102] Stringent warnings on the subject by the sultan personally are recorded in 1614 and 1633.[103]

The subject of controlling traffic in grain began to be incorporated, after a certain delay, into the so-called 'capitulations'[104] granted to foreign powers. The first such capitulation granted to France, in 1569, contains no mention of the grain trade. The second such promulgation granted to France, in 1597, permits the export of grain.[105] The third, granted in 1604, contains several clauses extending certain immunities to French merchants, mariners and ships apprehended with *victuailles* or *provisions de bouche*. This capitulation (or *lettre patente* as it was called in French) extends to French merchants (and by extension to merchants of several less favored nations sailing under the protection of the French flag) permission to purchase and ship certain specific items yet withholds permission to trade in other prohibited commodities which, oddly enough, are not specified (Permettons aux marchands françois – d'enlever des cuirs, corduoans, cires, cotons, cotons files, sauf que ce soient des marchandises prohibées et défendus d'enlever[106]). The 1604 French capitulation seems to have served as a model for all subsequent capitulations, insofar as contraband trade was touched upon, down to the nineteenth century. Later capitulations, both for France and for other powers, also extended immunities to merchants, mariners and ships apprehended while loaded with wheat or with foodstuffs under conditions variously defined. Later capitulations also specifically permit traffic in certain specified items (much the same list as that offered above) which fall far short, however, of the list of items actually traded. These later capitulations also make reference, *de rigueur*, to the 'prohibited items' which from other contexts we know to have included horses and all war material, as well as foodstuffs.[107] The capitulations, therefore, should not be taken more seriously by the historian than they were by the Ottomans themselves. Even a slight acquaintance with the accounts of European travellers in the Levant will suffice to show how far actual diplomatic and commercial practice at the *échelles* differed from the texts deposited at Istanbul. Yet despite the vagueness of the capitulatory articles touching upon the subject, it is clear that there was an official interdiction on the sale of Ottoman grain to foreign traders extending from 1604 down into the nineteenth century. A memoir by Vergennes mentions this interdiction in 1767,[108] and it was still in force in 1810 when a decree reinforcing it was circulated among provincial governors outside the Straits.[109] Perhaps the provincial governors themselves wanted it that way; Masson believed that bribes received by them on contraband formed an increment to their incomes which they were loath to lose. Efforts by a series of eighteenth-century French ambassadors to regularize this trade therefore came to naught.[110]

Generalizations about the level of the trade in wheat outside the

Dardanelles during the two centuries following the first interdiction are extremely hard to make, partly because the trade was only fragmentarily recorded, partly because by its very nature this trade was irregular. We know that Dutch and English ships were used by Genoese, Livornese and Greek merchants to remove wheat from Greece and the Archipelago, and rice from Egypt throughout the seventeenth century. These cargoes helped the northern captains to occupy their slack season, and for the Dutch, at least, loading grain in the Archipelago was the most common of their duties. These Archipelago exchanges often involved wheat from mainland Greece and perhaps sometimes from the Anatolian shore as well. From Egypt little except the intra-Ottoman *caravanaire* trade was expected, a trade which the French were officially enfranchised to carry on after 1686, but which all Western traders had already been involved in on an ad hoc basis. From Syria virtually nothing could be expected by way of grain. Tunisia supplied grain sporadically during the eighteenth century, then after a spurt during the Napoleonic years, lost this role.[111]

Wars, like harvest failures, might intensify the competition for grain. Or, as in the case of the long struggles between the Ottomans and Venice, first over Crete, later over the Morea, wars might destroy a former capacity to produce surpluses for many years. Cyprus, which had been a grain surplus zone before its conquest by the Ottomans, no longer offered such surpluses after the early seventeenth century.[112]

Although various sets of figures exist pertaining to the wheat trade in the eighteenth century, they are all so erratic that it is hard to build generalizations upon them. However, there seems to be a consensus between Masson, Romano and Paris, that seen from Marseilles, the Levant (i.e. in effect, the Greek provinces and islands) is no longer an important supplier of wheat after the Seven Years' War; although Provence, as a region of monocultures, continues to need foreign wheat, it is supplied increasingly thereafter by the Compagnie Royale d'Afrique.[113] Yet seen through the sporadic consular records of Salonica,[114] published by Svoronos, it seems somewhat more likely that the Greek-speaking littoral did remain an important supplier of wheat in the latter half of the eighteenth century, although no longer so orientated to Marseilles as formerly. Leon's study of the newly born Greek merchant marine leads him to conclude that wheat was still the leading commodity carried in Greek ships, which by 1800 carried (according to his estimate) three-quarters of the Levant traffic, including the *caravanaire* business. Most of that wheat was bound for western Mediterranean ports.[115] On the other hand, inside the Straits in the Romanian principalities veritable grain sowing campaigns had been organized by Russia and Austria in connection with the wars of 1768–74 and 1788–92, a foretaste of the role of grain suppliers which the principalities would assume in the nineteenth century after the final relaxation of the Ottoman provision policy.[116]

Animal fibers

Studies of the Jelali crisis of 1596–1610 have noted that lands emptied of villagers as a result of depredations and seizures were most commonly turned over to herds of sheep, or sheep and goats, supervised by the new occupiers.[117] In economic parlance wool is a 'passive' product: easy to transport, requiring little labor and capable of being produced on a small or large scale even in regions which are relatively barren and inaccessible.[118] Although wool cannot yield an output per unit area comparable to a sown crop, the required labor input is so low that wool may nonetheless pay a competitive economic rent when demand is strong and steady. England and Spain, located on the periphery of a concentration of population centered upon Flanders, hovered for centuries between grain and wool production, moving first towards one then the other depending upon the interplay of grain and wool prices over long periods. These shifts in production may also be seen as responses to demographic trends.[119]

The pan-European population expansion of the sixteenth century led to an expansion of the arable in Spain at the expense of pasture during the period 1560–1609. The same period, as noted above, saw an expansion of herds in Anatolia. To the extent that they were responses to export conditions, these shifts are easily explained in von Thünen's terms as a widening concentricity. As Spain in the middle ring (in terms of economic distance from the population vortex) moves away from the momentarily less profitable production of wool, Anatolia, in the outer ring increases production of the commodity being displaced in Spain. Because of changing demand conditions, the relative economic rents which wheat and wool can pay has changed, with the commodity paying the lesser economic rent being pushed outward towards the periphery.

It would not do to overstress this picture. Spain continued to produce a vast quantity of wool throughout the seventeenth century, the bulk of this high quality wool being purchased at Flanders or by the English.[120] This left northern Italy drawing some of its wool supply from the (lower quality) surpluses of Africa or the Levant. Nothing has been done to follow wool prices from Ottoman sources, but it is defensible to assume that the bulk of Ottoman wool was consumed at home and that the quantities exported were of secondary importance. Yet there are signs that demand conditions in Europe did directly affect the Ottoman markets and therefore did contribute to changing modes of using the land, particularly in Anatolia and Rumelia (Ottoman Europe) in the seventeenth century.

A cloak called the 'Leiden Turk,' made of mixed wool and camel hair, was popular in France and the Low Countries from about 1630, its use tapering off towards the end of the seventeenth century. In England mohair (goats' hair) imported from Anatolia was used for buttons until its replacement in the eighteenth century by metal.[121] The English and Dutch were the paramount traders in the Levant throughout the better part of the seventeenth century, and their needs account for most of the Ottoman export of animal hair except from the Adriatic coast, which supplied Venice and other Italian ports. Although figures on the level of Ottoman exports of wool, goat and camel hair have not been developed for the seventeenth century, some generalizations can be made about the trade. One is that animal hair was distinctly less interesting to the Atlantic traders than the silk trade, which was their primary mission in the Levant. Although goat hair and camel hair had its special uses, ordinary Levantine sheep's wool seems to have interested them very little. And since both of the former commodities were available at the same ports which offered silk, they were bought at Aleppo before 1640, and thereafter, with the shift of the Persian silk caravans to Smyrna, it was at the latter port that goat and camel hair were purchased. When the French trade initiative of the last quarter of the seventeenth century began to take hold, the French demand for goat and camel hair was added to that of the Atlantic traders at Smyrna. Thus in the eighteenth century we find that eight of the French commercial houses at Smyrna maintain agents at Ankara to purchase goats' hair, while the Dutch and British maintain two each.[122] More interested in sheep's wool than the Dutch or English, the French also tended to do more purchasing at Istanbul, though sales there were carefully regulated. And since the French were the dominant Western traders of the eighteenth century down to 1789, the annual averages offered by Paris on the animal fiber trade on the basis of the Marseilles registers give a reasonably good idea of the pattern of supply in that century, as follows (in thousands of livres):[123]

Sheep's wool	1701–2	1750–4	1786–9
Constantinople	347	156	1242
Smyrna	172	364	643
Salonica	90	368	237
Archipelago	36	12	—
Aleppo	34	5	21
Middle Syria	34	—	—
Cyprus	14	6	—
Total all ports	737	911	2257
Camel hair			
Aleppo, Smyrna, Constantinople	173	849	1021
Goat's hair (Mohair)			
Smyrna, Constantinople	639	1835	1437

Clearly French interest in all three types of fiber (which were destined for Languedoc and Dauphine) was on the rise in the eighteenth century; especially marked is the the rise in sheep's wool exports. These figures also show the increasing importance of Istanbul as an entrepôt for sheep's wool. This pattern is new in the eighteenth century, the result of a shift in the export outlet for wool from the western to the eastern side of the Balkan peninsula.

Interestingly enough, Salonica, despite its position relative to the Macedonian plain at one end of the Vardar–Morava route, does not seem to have provided much wool for foreign buyers in either century, at least not legally. Perhaps this should be explained in terms of Salonica's own activity as a cloth weaving center responsible for supplying the army.[124]

Despite the swift demise of Venice as a cloth exporter to the Levant after 1600, throughout the century that followed large quantities of sheep's wool were gathered in Rumelia by the Ragusan houses and shipped to the head of the Adriatic, part of it doubtless bound for the passes to Germany, part used by the rural north Italian cloth industry.[125] An average annual shipment of 600 metric tons of wool is suggested for Ragusa in the period 1620–40, making wool-handling the mainstay of the Ragusan economy in this period.[126] Albania was also heavily involved in this trade: a Venetian import invoice offered by Sella, dated 1680, shows twice as much wool from Albania as from

Morea or Constantinople.[127] In 1705–6 wool exports from Durazzo outweigh raw cotton by a factor of fifteen.[128] Much of this wool was gathered for purchase from what are now the Kosmet and Moravlija zones of Yugoslavia, with maximum production from 1620 to 1667.

Whereas Old Serbia raised wool for export, in the same period Bulgaria provided mostly hides. (Perhaps this pattern reflects Istanbul's demand for Bulgarian sheep to feed its populace.) The hides were gathered in by Ragusan merchants. In 1628, 50,000 buffalo and cattle hides were collected at Novi Pazar when a dispute with Ottoman customs officials took place. In 1629 Ragusa shipped 43,000 animal skins of various types from Sofia alone.[129] Meanwhile, before the mid-seventeenth century some Balkan wool was being carried to Vienna by Serbian merchants (i.e. 'Raizen') along with a variety of other commodities.

This pattern did not persist in the eighteenth century. New territorial arrangements following the Peace at Passarowitz (1718) brought new trading patterns. By mid-century Ragusan trade within the peninsula was almost nil.[130] To replace it, the routes across the Danube towards Central Europe were put to greater use.[131] Wool raising shifted eastward. Bulgaria shipped increasing quantities of its best wool via Nicopolis and Ruščuk (Ruse) across the Danube while much of the rest now was sold at Istanbul, as Paris's figures show. Wool gave way to cotton at Salonica, but by 1763–7 accounted for half of Istanbul's export sales.[132]

Cultivated fibers

Raw silk was primary in terms of value among the seventeenth-century Levant exports. The great bulk of this silk came to Syria and to Smyrna by way of caravan from Persia. Ottoman zones suitable for mulberry raising, especially around Bursa, had been pressed into use in the sixteenth century when rivalry between the Ottomans and the Safavid dynasty closed the traditional silk roads. Inalcık's research has shown that the domestically grown silk was already very important at Bursa in the time of Selim II. But Ottoman silk, the so-called 'white silk,' found little favor with the European traders until the second decade of the eighteenth century. Deprived of Persian *sherbasse* during the Persian time of troubles, the Europeans finally accepted the gradually improving Ottoman product, which throughout the eighteenth century was able to compete with Persian silk.[133] Antakya also became a silk-producing zone, so that 'white silk' was sold through the Syrian ports as well as through Smyrna.

Nevertheless, the interest of the English in silk of the Levantine sort was declining in the eighteenth century. And since silk is very compact and easy to transport, Ottoman and Persian silk were both thrust into international competition with silk thread and silk fabrics coming from Bengal and China, inundating the Dutch, then the British and finally the French markets.[134]

In the case of cotton, Ottoman landholders in the most suitable zones (above all in the Seres zone north-east of Salonica and the Smyrna hinterland) experienced a transitory advantage – a very common phenomenon with respect to lucrative monocultures. The advantageous conditions they enjoyed were eventually nullified by even more advantageous conditions existing in other parts of the world (e.g. Egypt and the American South) as hitherto unexploited resources in climate, cheap land and/or labor were brought to bear.[135]

The record on cotton exports does not suggest any sudden change based on foreign demand until well into the eighteenth century. Cotton, like sugar, is one of the traditional Near Eastern products, and the name itself derives from Arabic. All those places which were later associated with the *chiftlik* style of cotton-raising were already raising some cotton long before. In Syria and Turkey enough cotton to meet domestic needs was being grown in the fifteenth century.[136] Cotton had been in use in Europe to make fustians for centuries; therefore there had long been some demand for it abroad.[137] The earliest English cargoes from the Mediterranean, loaded at Patras, Zante and Syrian Tripoli, were predominantly cotton wool and cotton yarn.[138] Ottoman customs records from Damascus verify a certain outflow of cotton thread in the sixteenth century despite conditions unfavorable to commerce.[139] Cotton-raising was already known in the sixteenth century in Thrace, near Plovdiv (Phillipopolis) and around Seres in Macedonia (later the center of the Macedonian cotton culture).[140]

The moderate cotton exports of the seventeenth century seem to have been evenly distributed among Syrian and Anatolian ports. Cotton was then of little importance to the Dutch,[141] but the English, whose spinning industry in Lancashire was built upon Levantine cotton, collected their cotton wool mostly from Smyrna, and from Cyprus, where they dealt in futures purchased by loans.[142] In Syria, the French bought cotton at Sayda (the port of Damascus), where it was the major export, and at Aleppo.[143] Nonetheless, by the end of the century England was beginning to receive cotton from the Caribbean, and French demand was still rather slight, so that at Aleppo cotton wool ranked third among the French items of trade.

The eighteenth century witnessed the intensification of cotton cultivation in all the areas where it had formerly been grown, especially in Anatolia and Macedonia. The falling interest in silk was more than made up for by the interest in cotton and cotton fabrics in France. Whereas England was drawing increasingly on non-Levantine sources for its cotton, Levantine exports to France of raw cotton and cotton cloth multiplied tenfold between 1700 and 1788. The pattern of the French demand can be seen in the following annual averages (in thousands of livres), taken from Paris:[144]

Raw cotton	*1701–2*	*1750–4*	*1786–9*
Middle Syria (Sayda, Tripoli, Acre)	95	1134	69
Aleppo (through Iskenderun)	10	15	71
Cyprus	41	15	412
Smyrna	22	1621	6923
Constantinople	12	800	235
Salonica	30	908	2136
Total all ports	225	3760	9853
Cotton thread, all ports	1303	1924	2939

From these figures it would be justifiable to speak of a cotton 'boom' already underway by mid-century at Smyrna and, following the Seven Years' War, at Salonica.[145] Also noticeable is the drop in raw cotton exports from middle Syria after mid-century. This may be due to increased local demand for raw cotton, as mentioned by Smilyanskaya,[146] or to the depredations of the Palestinian pasha Ahmed Jezzar.

On the Rumelian side, cotton thread or yarn joined the wool which began to take the Belgrade–Vienna–Leipzig or Niš–Braşov routes after the Peace of Passarowitz.[147] Most of this cotton came from the Seres zone,[148] hence was deducted from what might have otherwise passed out through Salonica. The retirement of the Ragusans from their earlier role did not affect the cotton trade between Albania and Venice, which remained lively.[149] The trade through Trieste, on the other hand, maintained a medieval character until about mid-century, then began to draw increasingly upon Salonica.[150] By 1765, 27 per cent of the value of goods imported at Trieste comprised raw cotton; Levantine products accounted for one-third of total imports at the same port. Later in the century, cotton accounted for an even greater share of Austrian imports from the Ottoman territories whether these entered by land through Zemun or, as was increasingly the case, by sea through Trieste.[151]

2 ✤ Men and land: south-eastern Europe during the seventeenth and eighteenth centuries

When in his famous treatise on the Mediterranean world Fernand Braudel spoke of the second serfdom ('second servage') being evident in Turkey,[1] he was using an expression which goes beyond the usual frame of reference in Ottoman historiography. Following the lead of Busch-Zantner and other German geographers, Braudel was making an implied comparison between Ottoman *chiftlik* agriculture on consolidated estates and seemingly similar plantation-like estates east of the Elbe and in Poland. In both parts of the world peasants lived under degraded conditions. In both worlds foreign demand for the commodities produced by such estates seemed to be part of the causal formula. Were they parallel and independent developments, or parallel and linked? How in the ordered society which the Ottomans had attempted to create had these sad conditions come about? In this chapter answers to these questions are suggested, first by considering briefly the most important features of the whole coordinated Ottoman land regime in the period of its florescence, then by presenting an analytic model for an understanding of its transformation and an exploratory application of that model to south-eastern Europe.

The classic Ottoman land regime

The Ottoman land regime is best known to us in its classic period, the sixteenth century, in which we see the system replete and functional. It was indispensable, the foundation of the Ottoman state. The greater and lesser parts of the total system show every evidence of having been deliberately, pragmatically and effectively coordinated. At present we can infer (but have a hard time proving) what the antecendents of the system were and how it arose. The patient engineering behind the early

45

Ottoman state system is obvious largely from the end product, from the legal and fiscal documents of the middle period, i.e. roughly speaking, from the time of the Fatih codes of the mid-fifteenth century to the revised but conservative codification by Ayni Ali in the early seventeenth century. There is no evidence at all to suggest that the system was inspired by contemporary examples in Eastern Europe beyond the Danube, despite the fact that the shaping of the Ottoman land regime is simultaneous with the vast enserfments of Eastern Europe.

If the origins of the Ottoman system are unhappily obscured by simple lack of evidence, the dénouement too has been poorly understood. Yet there is much evidence with which to work out the disintegration of the system. Neglect alone has prevented an understanding of the processes of the later Ottoman world, especially the seventeenth and eighteenth centuries.

Certain generalizations can already be made about the later transformed Ottoman land situation on the basis of research so far. One is central: although the construction of the Ottoman system was the outcome of a concentration of political power in able hands with almost no reference to the contemporary world beyond, the disintegration of the Ottoman system was by contrast greatly influenced by contemporary international economic trends. One cannot say of the seventeenth and eighteenth centuries that Ottoman agriculture was as a whole dominated by foreign demand. That became far more true in the nineteenth century. Yet Ottoman *chiftlik* agriculture, in the sense that we usually mean it – market orientated, consolidated agriculture – was clearly not an isolated development in the preceding two centuries. Consolidated monoculture was in those centuries almost always a response to foreign demand pressing on the Ottoman shores. Thus in the long relationship between the Ottoman empire and its neighbors, Ottoman *chiftlik* agriculture of the seventeenth and eighteenth centuries introduces visible evidence of the slide from isolation to communication, from independence to interdependence. Not all so-called *chiftliks* were consolidated estates, and not all of them were related to foreign economic demand (as will be seen below from the evidence on location), but to the extent that they were, they represent the participation of the Ottoman territories in an emergent world wide system of regional specializations, the international division of labor.

Prebendalism in the Ottoman state

Much of the power of the early Ottoman system lay in the creation and control of a formidably large *sipahi* cavalry, supported by and among the common people of the provinces of the heartland, and available for campaigning throughout several months of each year. This was an army which collected its own income in cash and in kind under a closely regulated understanding with the central government. And because this cavalry army lived dispersed throughout the provinces, it constituted a pervasive police force which contributed greatly to the security of the realm.

It was Max Weber who first identified the Ottoman system as 'prebendal', thus emphasizing features which made it distinct from West European 'vassalic' feudalism: (1) appointment from the center with a minimum of local control, (2) retrievability of the prebend (the *timar*) in case of default of duty, and (3) adjustment of the responsibility of each prebendary (*timarlı*) in proportion to the income expected from his living.[2] At the time that Weber wrote, he could not have known the extreme to which the *timar* system went in matching incomes with responsibilities. Here is a list promulgated in the second half of the fifteenth century, of *timar* holders' responsibilities for supplying the army on campaign. Each level of income brought with it sharply defined requirements for service and supply:

timar of 1000 *akches*[3]	one cuirassier (*jebelu*)
timar of 2000 *akches*	one cuirassier, one valet (*gulam*)
timar of 3000 *akches*	headgear denoting rank, one valet
timar of 4000; 4500; 5000 *akches*	headgear, one cuirassier, one valet, one small tent
timar of 5500; 6000 *akches*	headgear, one cuirassier, two small tents
timar of 7500; 8000 *akches*	headgear, two cuirassiers, one valet, one small tent
timar of 9000 *akches*	headgear, three cuirassiers, one medium tent
timar of 10,000; 10,500; 11,000 *akches*	headgear, three cuirassiers, one valet, one medium tent
timar of 12,000 *akches*	headgear, four cuirassiers, one medium tent
timar of 15,000 *akches*	headgear, five cuirassiers, one medium tent
each additional 3000 *akches*	one cuirassier
each additional 1500–2000 *akches*	one valet[4]

Naturally a system which demanded graded responsibilities in proportion to graded income could not operate solely on the basis of promulgated ideals. Not only was it essential to keep a careful record of all prebendal assignments and anticipated incomes, it was also necessary to punish defaulters if the system was to work as intended. Therefore the Ottoman treasury authorized special agents, known as *mevkufchus* to retrieve the *timars* of defaulting individuals or of individuals deceased without heirs. The following excerpts from laws promulgated by Fatih Mehmet (the Conqueror) show what kinds of considerations affected the *mevkufchu* in punishing the culpable and thereby helping to maintain the efficiency of the system:

And whoever goes from the army into service on his own with the permission of a provincial commander, a general or a lesser officer, his *timar* is to be suspended. Demand its income, let my agent take it over.

And the *timars* of those who are using them without my patent or the patent of a general are to be suspended. Demand their income, let my agent take them and let them not hide suspended *timars*, villages, cultivated sites away from the village, or homesteads. Whoever does hide them or prevents their being known shall merit my wrath. The aforesaid provincial commanders and judges and stationed troops will give the necessary assistance and will not show neglect. Let them know this![5]

Those *timar* holders who do not go on campaign when the army does and do not complete service, (their) *timar* income is suspended. Until that *timar* is given to someone else and a patent written and a date established, it goes to the *mevkufchu* on duty.[6]

However:

If a *timar* holder goes on campaign and if there is a battle and he is in it but is wounded and this becomes the cause of his incapacity . . . and if his wounds prevent him from going on campaign in person and in his place he sends a cuirassier and a capable man and if they complete service so that the provincial commander witnesses it or so that it can be proven with witnesses, those are acceptable and should not be interfered with.[7]

The process by which the Ottomans adopted and adapted the *timar* system remains rather obscure. But that the Ottoman variant developed early in the career of the dynasty is scarcely to be doubted. One of the best informed of the earlier chroniclers, Ashıkpashazade, writing in the third quarter of the fifteenth century, includes in his chronicle the record of a pronouncement by Osman, founder of the dynasty, in which basic principles relating to the descent and retention of cavalry livings were promulgated. Another passage from the same chronicle makes Osman's father-in-law Ede Balı the recipient of a *timar* income.[8] Even if Ashıkpashazade was projecting fifteenth-century concepts backwards in his account of the fourteenth-century past, there is other evidence to corroborate the view that the *timar* system was part of the bedrock of the state. A report to Orhan Gazi by his Süleyman (dated 1358) and a letter attributed to Murat I (dated 1386) both include *timar* terminology.[9] Certainly the Albanian survey of 1431, edited by Inalcık, gives the impression of a system of livings already much evolved.[10] Unfortunately the law code regulating *timar* affairs, which is believed to have been promulgated in 1375[11], has not survived, so that our intimations about the early system must be inferred from such scraps as these.

Although impressive parallels have been drawn between the *timar* on the one hand and the late Roman *emphyteusis*[12] and the Byzantine *pronoia*[13] on the other, there is a consensus of scholars using Muslim sources that the Ottoman *timars* are the functional descendants of similar grants found in the Türkmen *beyliks* which the Ottomans displaced, and that these in turn were the descendants of the Seljuk small *ikta* grants.[14] Opinions differ, however, whether the Türkmen grants were up to the Seljuk standard or whether, for instance, the Türkmen grants included pure alienations of property (*mülk*), thus making them different in their intent and outcome.[15] Inalcık, for one, is not willing to tie the *timar* to the *ikta* and prefers to regard the *timar* as a special form of *havale*, roughly speaking a transfer of revenues.[16] Not until the character of the Türkmen grants, which were the link between the Seljuk and Ottoman forms, is better established can we even guess the extent to which the Ottomans reinvented a prebendal system in their own style, or borrowed from the Byzantines and their Muslim contemporaries. But however that issue is resolved, it is obvious that the Ottoman system could not have been possible without a prior deeply rooted agreement about ultimate authority over the soil.

Eminent domain in the Ottoman state

Marxist historians in particular have laid great emphasis upon the development among the Ottomans of a concept of eminent domain, the widespread principle which reserves to the ruler or to the state a penultimate claim upon all the land of the realm. They link it to Marx's idea of the trusteeship of the ruler on behalf of a community, an idea which lay at the center of Marx's conception of an 'Asian mode of production.'[17]

According to the estimate of the Turkish historian cited above,[18] fully 87 per cent of Ottoman soil was in 1528 legally regarded as within the eminent domain of the state (i.e. as *mirî*). The establishment and continuous reassertion of the *mirî* was the indispensable counterpart of prebendalism, the bedrock upon which the original Ottoman land regime was constructed.

Definitive statements on the Ottoman land system and the principles underlying it were published in Ottoman society only after those principles had long since been put into practice. These clarifications of principle are the work of Ebusuud, the Ottoman legist, who wrote theoretical (and quite untypical) introductions for the provincial law codes affixed to the c. 1574 survey registers of Üsküb (Skopje) and Selanik (Salonica), and also for the code drafted for the province of Budin (Buda) in the wake of the annexation of the Hungarian capital by the Ottomans (c. 1541).[19] In these laws, the legist dwells upon peasant (*reaya*) rights and obligations, the relationship of the peasant to his land and the three fiscal categories (excluding religious endowments, or *vakıf*) into which Ottoman territories were theoretically divided. Two of the categories (*öshri* and *haraji*) were practically empty boxes from the Ottoman point of view, being ancient categories created soon after the original Arab conquests and applying merely to a small percentage of the contemporary Ottoman holdings. The great bulk of Ottoman land was *arz-i memleket*, or *arz-i mirî*, i.e. land subject to the eminent domain principle. Residual authority (*rakabe*) over all land in this great category was entrusted eternally to the state and could not be sold by the holder or otherwise alienated. Even conversion into a pious estate (*vakıf*) was proscribed as invalid. As for the transfer of the 'deed' (the *tapu*) in order to endow usufruct (i.e. the right to use but not to own) upon payment to someone other than the one whom the law prescribed as a normal 'heir', this transfer did not, said Ebusuud, constitute sale of property rights. Rather, it was analogous, in his view, to a transfer of the right of renting between the (successive) occupants of shops which happened to constitute a pious foundation (a *vakıf*).[20] As we know from the way these principles operated in the provinces, their effect was not to prohibit transfer of rights, such as the tenant's right of tenure (*hakk-i karar*), but to make all such transfers subject to the surveillance of the *timar* holder, who was assumed to be serving the state's interests as well as his own when allowing or disallowing such transfers.[21] (The authority of the Byzantine *pronoia* holder over transfers of the *bashtina* is comparable.[22])

Inalcık has likened Ebusuud's *arz-i mirî* or *arz-i memleket* to the original *fay* (spoils) of the Muslim law books.[23] For some reason the legist himself did not do so in the laws cited above. Had he done so he would have admitted legal problems which resembled those of the original Arab Muslims as an outcome of the conquests they had made in the first Islamic centuries. Among the later Muslim states only the Seljuks, the Moguls and the Ottomans had made large scale conquests in formerly non-Islamic territory and were therefore confronted with legal and practical issues not typical among Islamic states generally. The decision by the Ottomans to hold the majority of the land in trust for the community was the same one made by the earliest Muslim rulers and legalists after the original wave of Muslim conquests. This approach was elaborated by Ö. L. Barkan in one of his early essays, where he emphasized the continued involvement of early Ottoman governments in schemes to resettle and colonize, and otherwise adjudicate interests in newly conquerered and depopulated regions. His reasoning was that these resettlement operations necessarily required that questions of ultimate ownership, usufruct and transfer of land be thoroughly worked out and institutionalized.[24]

Parallel to the controversy over the origins of the *timar* system, there exists also a controversy over whether the Ottoman *mirî* concept in fact passed in unbroken descent from the *fay* principle of earlier Muslim states. The Türkmen invaders of Anatolia had had their own concept of state, sharing the notion (widespread historically among nations organized on kinship lines) that the state and all its revenues belonged to the ruler personally or to him and his family.[25] Perhaps Seljuk acceptance of eminent domain was less clearcut than that of the Ottomans since they used a multiplicity of terms in reference to it.[26] One view holds that a merging of the Muslim and steppe concepts of state took place in the course of the Seljuk era so that while the nomad concept of complete ownership by the dynasty was still uppermost in the time of Kılıç Arslan, late in the Seljuk era when Nasir ad-Din Tusi wrote his treatise on finance (c. 1260–74), a clear distinction was recognized between the Sultan's private fisc and the public treasury.[27] The consensus would seem to be that a complementary and simultaneous development of the eminent domain principle alongside the prebendal system established by the Seljuks was a natural outcome of the logic of their situation, just as in the case of the Ottomans.

The Ottoman colonate

Without exception the accounts of late Byzantine times leave the impression of a sparsely populated countryside and of fierce competition for labor between landholders. Everywhere in their vicinity the Ottomans inherited provinces short of labor.

This alone would have been sufficient motive, given the concentration of authority which was characteristic of their young state, for them to have invented and imposed some form of serfdom or to have simply prolonged the servile usages associated with the late Byzantine *paroikoi*,[28] or dependent cultivators. M.I. Finley, a student of the ancient world, reminds us that there was a universal tendency in this direction:

> When any society we can trace attained a stage of sufficient accumulation of resources and power in some hands (whether king, temple, ruling tribe or aristocracy) so that a labour force was demanded greater than could be provided by the household or kinship group, for agriculture, or mining, or arms manufacture, that labour force was obtained not by hiring it but by compelling it, by force of arms or by force of law and custom. This involuntary labour force, furthermore, was normally not composed of slaves but of one or another half-way type, such as the debt-bondsman, the helot, the early Roman client, the late Roman *colonus*.[29]

The youthful Ottoman state would probably have devised a colonate even had there been no shortage of labor. Binding was an administrative convenience. Ottoman administrators of the classic period were interested in maintaining a standard prebend with an income which could be more or less precisely controlled. Inalcık acknowledges this need, describing the Ottoman *timar* as 'an indivisible and unalterable unit.'[30] Only by stabilizing the labor available on each *timar* could its registered character (i.e. the income certified for it in the register) be maintained. This also helps to explain the interest of the Ottoman lawmakers in maintaining a standard and indivisible peasant holding. Therefore it could not be an error to characterize the colonate created by the Ottomans as *counterpart and consequence of their prebendalism*, and to regard both institutions as elements in an integrated system of controls designed to maximize the resources at the disposal of the sultans and their *vezirs*.

Like the *colonus* of post-Diocletian Rome, the person of *reaya* status was legally free though saddled with a stigma of inferiority which was expressed in concrete ways, above all by the obligation to remain in the village where he was registered, or if he moved in order to gain some advantage, to pay for the privilege of doing so. Other disabilities characteristic of *reaya* status have received full attention elsewhere – the peasant's inability to change his class status, his liability to taxes characteristic of his class and his being subject to corvée service for the state. Here, however, because our immediate concern is to establish the relationship of man and land, excerpts from a number of laws bearing on this aspect of *reaya* life are quoted verbatim so that the reader may form an accurate judgment on the degree of binding and tenure which were characteristic under the classic regime. These excerpts are grouped according to four topics: (1) the *reaya*'s ability to leave the land; (2) his ability to alienate his rights to land; (3) his right to remain on the land; (4) his right to pass on his tenure to his heirs. (Since there is no fully accepted singular form for a person of *reaya* status, *reaya* will be used to mean the individual as well as the class.)

Leaving the land From the law for the provinces of Bosnia, Herzegovina and Zvornik (1539):

If a *reaya* cultivates in another village and leaves his own place of agriculture destitute, let him be warned. And if in spite of the warning he sows, two tithes will be required: one to the land holder and one he gives at the place where he is registered.[31]

From the law for the reoccupied province of Mora (Morea) (1716):

If a *reaya*, having been registered as a *reaya* in a particular village at the time of survey, later goes to another village with the explanation that he has no land to cultivate in that village, the long standing law has been to resettle him in the village of registration.[32]

From the law for the province of Požega (1545):

And many *reaya* after being registered as the *reaya* of a *sipahi* and bound to production, become woodsmen, or potters, or fishermen, or millers, or stoneworkers, and some do day labor or busy themselves in some other way for a living. And having abandoned agriculture no tithes or taxes from them go to the *sipahi*. Because of their untrustworthiness 80 *akches* in cash have been customarily taken from the poorer of these under the name of *chift bozan* ('farm-breaking') and 120 *akches* from the better off; and for this reason this has been entered into the new imperial survey in that fashion.[33]

From the law for the province of Kütahya (1528):

It is a law of long-standing to collect *reaya* who have separated from their *timars*. But it is forbidden to uproot someone who has lived in a place more than fifteen years. Someone living in a city more than twenty years is registered in that city.[34]

Especially interesting are those regulations bearing on the adjudication of cases where two different *sipahis* have some kind of claim on the same person, usually because the latter has relocated from one *timar* to another. For instance, in the clause relating to the bridal tax in the law for the province of Erzerum (1540):

Wherever a virgin moves to, her bridal tax is paid to whomever her father is the *reaya* of. And it is established law to give the bridal tax of a woman who is no longer a virgin to the master of whatever land she happens to be on.[35]

From the law for the province of Bosna (Bosnia) (1565):

If a *sipahi*'s *reaya* does not live on the land where he is registered but in another district and is not registered in that (other) village, if he has no place to cultivate, he shall give to the *sipahi* of that other place six *akches* as a chimney tax. If he *does* have a place to cultivate he will give a tithe to the master of the land (*sahib-i arz*); the rest of the *reaya* taxes he will give to his own *sipahi* . . . However when he has lived there for over ten years and has settled down there, the master of the land will take all the prescribed taxes and dues and he will give no taxes to his old *sipahi* – even if he is registered on holdings at both places.[36]

From the same law:

If a *reaya* is registered in two villages, he will be definitely confirmed at the time of the survey in that village where he is registered and has lived ten years. He will not give taxes to his old *sipahi*. Place of residence will be the ruling factor, not priority in time. If he has taken land outside a village and has been registered in that way, he will give *sher'i* dues [those regarded as being sanctioned by Muslim religious law books] and customary taxes to the master of the land but *reaya* taxes to his own *sipahi*.[37]

From the law of Semendire (Murat III period):

If the *reaya*'s (*sipahi*) does not have sufficient land for sowing, the *reaya* may sow where he pleases. But then the *reaya* gives his [*sipahi*] only his *salariye* – or if the *reaya* works land on the *timar* of his *sipahi* and also on the *timar* of another *sipahi* he gives his tithe and *salariye* to the holder of the land.[38] [The *salariye* was a typical non-*sher'i* tax incumbent upon the *reaya*.]

Alienation of land Although in his introduction to the Skopje/Salonica law already cited Ebusuud brands as invalid any sale or purchase of land on which the state claimed eminent domain, or its conversion into a pious estate, he nonetheless found it permissible for someone leaving his holding to accept a certain sum from a person wanting to take over the holding, with the (tripartite?) understanding that the *sipahi* will then turn over the holding to the new person. Obviously the *sipahi*'s knowledge is implied; such transfers would be in the *sipahi*'s immediate pecuniary interest since they would allow him to pocket a transfer fee. Such transfers were not sales in Ebusuud's eyes.[39] Yet the omission of clauses regarding such transfers in other laws suggests that the practice was not widespread. Perhaps the legist's interest in accommodating such transfers was to avoid disrupting the situation which confronted him in the zones cited.

Clearly the *sipahi*'s knowledge and permission was the key issue in this kind of alienation. The Bosnian law of 1565 forbade sale or gift of land by *reayas* without the *sipahi*'s knowledge. If such transfers did take place the *sipahi* was entitled to annul them and return the land to its original holder (*sahib*).[40]

Security of tenure The succinct statement found in the Morean law of 1716 reproduces exactly the spirit of Ebusuud's original statements upon security of peasant tenure within the principles of eminent domain in all conquered (in this case reconquered) territories:

This prosperous land is *mirî* land like that of Rumelia, so that the land which was in the hands of the *reaya* at the time of the conquest was settled upon them once more with the ownership held in trust(*beyt ul-mal*) for the Muslim community.[41]

The solidity and permanence of the individual cultivator's claim upon his own holding is suggested by the following clause taken from the law for the provinces of Bosnia, Herzegovina and Zvornik (1539):

And if a *reaya* leaves his place and another person is registered in his place and afterwards that first *reaya* comes back and wants to return to his place, the judges should simply take the place of the aforesaid; if he got it by paying the *tapu* (transfer fee), then the judges should just take back his expenditure, in agreement with the Holy Law, and again give the holding (*bashtina*) back to its owner. Let no one prevent it.[42]

Heritability of tenure Ebusuud's general statements regarding land on which the state claimed eminent domain specify that *reaya* sons should inherit their father's holdings. No distinction was made in this respect between Muslim and non-Muslim subjects.[43] Natural descent of holdings through sons did not require the payment of a transfer fee.

According to the Silistre law of 1569, when a *reaya* died without sons, the *sipahi* must give the *tapu* to the most eligible individual among his relatives. If there were no relatives the *sipahi* might then give the *tapu* to whomever wanted it. The law also countenances the cultivation of a holding on behalf of a minor son until he is competent, the reiteration of a clause found in the Fatih partial code on *reaya* affairs.[44]

The Fatih code had also secured the rights of women to have a holding cultivated for them provided that they paid all taxes on it.[45] The Bosnian law of 1565 cites a decree permitting a daughter to inherit a holding from her father providing that it was he who had originally brought it under cultivation. A similar clause appears in the Morean law of 1716.[46]

Complementary controls on timar holders

To make the regime effective, it was not only the peasant and his place of cultivation but also the *sipahi* and his *timar*–prebend who were held under strict state control. The income, extent and conditions of tenure of each of thousands of *timars* were entered systematically in standardized registers.[47] A complex of other interlocking norms were designed to keep the *timar* holder in his place. He was forbidden to form a private holding from any land in which the *reaya* had any interest, either present or past, including village common pasture.[48] Although earlier permitted a small demesne as part of his *timar*, the holder lost his right to such demesne in the later sixteenth century.[49] Sharp limits were placed upon the *timar* holder's right to pass on his 'living' or his status to his heirs, and upon his right to exercise police power over, or to make arbitrary demands upon, the *reaya* inhabitants of the *timar* registered in his name.[50]

It would be a mistake, of course, to judge this system solely on the basis of its published norms. Abuses were numerous and on the increase in the latter sixteenth century. Yet the total impression given by the laws, and by the minutes of the veziral council still preserved at Istanbul, is of an admirable degree of order, coordination and even justice. The use of the terms 'system,' 'classic system' and 'regime' in speaking of Ottoman prebendal and agrarian arrangements in their home territories of Anatolia and Rumelia seems fully justified.

In a system so hedged about with conditions and controls, personal fealty was held to a minimum. In theory the sultan dispensed all benefits. Yet the sultan remained remote, impersonal and unilateral in his acts. The *timar* holder was related through his grant not only to the sultan but to the system itself – a cool, rational relationship.

The transformation of the old regime

The Hamilton thesis, dealing with the silver inflation of the late sixteenth and early seventeenth centuries, points to the institutional rigidity of wages and rents during the inflation episode.[51] The Ottoman case very aptly demonstrates that part of his thesis. A flurry of bribery and sale of office accompanied the silver inflation which afflicted the Ottoman empire in the 1580s and for a generation thereafter. Salaries and rents – including prebendal incomes – did rise, but too slowly to satisfy the customary wants of the governing class. Therefore the balance between means and ends which had prevailed for so long was broken. Soon after the death of Grand Vezir Mehmet Sokollu in 1578, a pivotal figure and champion of the old order, the rational graded meritocracy constructed by the Ottomans was shaken from top to bottom. The pursuit of personal interest, vital to survival during the inflation episode, became endemic in Ottoman life thereafter.

Because of its meritocratic system, the Ottoman state, among the many states affected by the flow of silver, was peculiarly vulnerable to the irrational and destabilizing effect of sudden changes in price structure. A second and particular vulnerability of the Ottoman state in that era lay in one institution which had hitherto been a source of great strength – the territorially based *sipahi* cavalry. The *sipahis* were more threatened by the inflation than were salaried servants of the regime since their incomes in kind were registered in inflexible cash terms. But inflation was accompanied by a second revolutionizing wind – the shift in international military technology toward infantry and toward firearms. This shift threatened the Ottoman stability in two ways – not only by making cavalry obsolescent but by bringing into question the entire prebend system on which the cavalry was based, a system which had heretofore absorbed a very large portion of the revenues available for use by the state, and which had been the object of an elaborate record-keeping system developed during the fifteenth and sixteenth centuries.

Looking back, it is easy to see that these special challenges to the peculiarly constituted Ottoman state could best have been answered with radical reforms. Could the territorially based standing cavalry have been converted into a territorially based standing infantry? If this solution was ever contemplated, the Ottoman leaders found reasons to reject it. The brilliant leadership which radical reform would have demanded was not found. Instead the groping leaders of the inflation era dealt in makeshift solutions and improvisations, engendering a multitude of evils. One of the worst of these evils was the temporary mobilizations of large numbers of infantry who when released from duty invariably created tremendous disorder in the provinces from which they had come. A second unfortunate outcome of the inflationary era, even worse in its long run effect upon the peasant class, was the piecemeal dismantling of the prebend system and its replacement by tax farming.[52]

The suddenness and the scale of the challenge which confronted the Ottomans was unique among contemporary states: how were they to rechannel the enormous resources which had been tied up in their prebend system? Giving up that system meant losing the vast advantage of having the majority of the beneficiaries of state revenues in a position to make their own collections, without intermediaries in most cases, and without dysfunctional loss of revenues. Surrendering the prebend system almost inevitably involved them in tax farming, since this solution, so widely employed in Europe and so prominent in the long record of Near Eastern states, did not require the development of a large cadre of honest and capable collectors,[53] and yet could provide the state with secure revenues in the short run. In the long run, of course, the social costs of this solution were predictably high. Like an aging body, the Ottoman polity was forced to function with more useless tissue and with less circulation of resources than had once been the case.[54]

In the seventeenth century a large part of the revenue resources formerly assigned as prebendal incomes were reassigned to the treasury itself. A second part of the reclaimed resources found its way into the 'basket', i.e. into the hands of Ottoman dignitaries of all kinds. A remaining part was only gradually withdrawn from the hands of the diminished *sipahi* corps. Both the treasury departments responsible for the reabsorbed revenues and the dignitaries who held such revenue sources on their own needed a network of primary, secondary and tertiary contractors to travel to distant territories and do the real work of collection. Many well placed figures took on responsibilities as primary contractors, then subcontracted the real risks and the real work to others. From the class of fiscal entrepreneurs which grew with the system there would rise influential landholders, bankers, merchants and officials.

The haphazard growth of the tax-farming system had a number of undesirable side effects. Governors who, like *timarlıs*, had lost part of their prebendal incomes, were placed in the hypocritical position of finding their own quasi-legal sources of revenue, including the tax-farming option, and of maintaining the large retinues increasingly necessary to their own survival.[55] The scribal class, as noted by Ayni Ali at the beginning of the seventeenth century and by Sarı Mehmet Pasha at the end, was implicated in the deliberate obfuscation of fiscal records, this being the simplest and most effective means by which the powerful could arrange to have their temporary holdings illegally converted either into something resembling absolute property or into permanent pious estates with themselves as beneficiaries.[56] The most serious lien upon the future, however, was the effect of the tax-farming system upon the great peasant class, whose complaints were often heard but not often acted upon by the governments of the seventeenth and eighteenth centuries. Under the canopy provided by this poorly controlled system a campaign was conducted to deprive the state of control over the land.

Three related processes in the transformation of the land regime

Arrayed against the interests of the state were the private interests of all those individuals who were seeking a way to subvert the old system and to find for themselves and their heirs the kind of material security which had been antithetical to that system. Although many Muslims, including military men, found commercial opportunities or practiced usury,[57] the major assault mobilized against the old system from the late sixteenth century onward, in an economy in which the primary products of the soil were still the predominant source of wealth, was the campaign aimed at the conversion of the land regime for private purposes. This campaign is usually called the *chiftlik*-building process, since the ultimate outcome as seen in nineteenth-century sources was the appearance in many places of sizeable plantation-like estates which, from an all-European comparative viewpoint, were causally and temporally parallel to the reconstructed 'demesne' of which Bloch was speaking in describing the 'refeudalization' of Europe in early modern times.[58]

The most detailed description that we have of the *chiftlik*-building process is the important work done on the north-west corner of what is now Bulgaria by the Bulgarian historian Hristo Gandev.[59] If Gandev's account was typical of the *chiftlik*-building process, then all the changes involved in privatizing and reorganizing the use of the land could be said to be simultaneous, or almost so. The Vidin zone he describes, drawing heavily on judges' records from that area, was for a long time reserved for imperial and veziral *has* revenues and thus escaped privatization. Then, towards the end of the eighteenth century, with the development of a Danube traffic in agrarian primary products marketed commercially,[60] the newly enhanced value of the land of this zone was realized and the agents in charge of the revenues of this reserve found it profitable (personally or for the fisc, or both – it is not clear from Gandev's account) to grant parcels of this well situated land using the traditional deed-like transfer certificate (*tapu*). These parcels were then heritable without restriction, alienable through sale and hence a property-like investment whose value was quickly realized by townsmen, who formed what seem to be shipping cooperatives to take their surpluses up the Danube in barges. The parcels themselves, as they developed, tended to resemble the classic *chiftlik* village operation which Cvijić described in late Ottoman Macedonia – separate habitations for workers with several pair of oxen available for plowing. Wages consisted of lodging and monthly allowances in cash or kind – perhaps clothing and grain. However, in the Vidin zone *chiftlik* owners tended to reside in town, leaving the work of supervision to bailiffs (*subashıs*). About 120 such estates were counted in the Vidin zone. Among the lands thus deliberately alienated by agents of the imperial treasury were former village commons.[61] This encroachment upon the commons tended to force the younger sons of villagers to work on the new *chiftliks*. In a second stage of this development the treasury alienated still more commons to Turks of the province on a similar basis so that the villagers were then contained by their now alienated land. Like the first wave of *chiftlik* owners, the Turks were enabled to dictate arbitrarily the labor conditions of those who worked for them. Gandev implies that the style with which the second wave of land buyers, the Turks (who boxed in what then came to be known as *ağa* villages), exploited land and labor in a different manner from the *chiftlik* owners; unfortunately on this matter as well as on certain others he has not completed the picture.

The situation described by Gandev at Vidin contains many interesting elements: (1) a sudden and compelling commercial motive, (2) wholesale collaboration by agents of the state, (3) the participation of townsmen of means in the process (a parallel with France), and (4) the concentration of this transformation in time and space. One has the impression from this account that the usurpation (or permanent alienation) of land from the treasury, the dispossession of the peasantry who had formerly worked the land, and the reorganization of consolidated estates for commercial production were all simultaneous, coordinated processes exhibiting all the elements usually subsumed in the expression '*chiftlik* formation.' Yet these last named processes, though they may occur together, as at Vidin, are analytically distinct and cannot be expected to coincide in every zone which comes under the scrutiny of the researcher.

Usurpation To wrest control of the land from the treasury and keep it was the first and in general the most difficult of the three processes. Once land was under his permanent control, the usurping individual *might* wish to dispossess the peasants who were on it. He might also wish to reorganize production on a commercial basis. But depending upon a number of factors, he might do neither.[62] Or he might dispossess without converting to commercial agriculture, though this was presumably rare.

The process of usurpation from state control, earlier in some places and later in others, was not fully accomplished before 1858, the date of the fundamental land law legally endowing various classes of landholders with ownership in the modern capitalist sense. The first great wave of usurpation was associated with the 'Great Flight' in Anatolia, the massive abandonment by a badly harassed peasantry of the holdings on which they stood as the accompaniment of the first *jelali* rebellion late in the sixteenth century.[63] Sućeska believes that in Macedonia the most intense period of usurpation came in the second half of the seventeenth century.[64] In Serbia the process is most visible at the end of the period covered by this study, on the eve of the Serbian rebellion of 1804. In each case, the meaning of the process is different. In none of the cases just mentioned was there the exceptional economic incentive which a steady and convenient commodity market would represent. Just as no exceptional economic incentive is required to stimulate the establishment of serfdom institution, likewise no exceptional economic incentive is needed to stimulate the struggle to transfer land to private hands. The prevailing level of rents was quite enough to justify the struggle.

A variety of methods was used. Many, perhaps most of them, were abuses of the tax-farming system in one way or another. An example unearthed by Bistra Cvetkova will serve to suggest one way in which a tax farmer might go about arranging a takeover, in this case with the apparent connivance of someone at the center. According to a document dated 1604, one Mahmudoğlu Ahmet of Florina obtained as a tax farm (*iltizam*) five revenue districts (*mukataas*) in Macedonia totalling 1,700,000 *akches*. This was 564,000 *akches* more than these *mukataas* had formerly been leased for. In return for his generous bid he was demanding that he also be appointed inspector (*Müfettish*) of the tax farm he had just obtained. He did not want anyone looking over his shoulder to criticize whatever methods he had in mind. Whether he obtained the inspectorate he asked for and how he used it are not recorded.[65]

Without question the social origins of individuals who were able to capitalize on tax-farming situations differed depending upon the period and the place. At the end of the sixteenth century, the historian Selanikî portrayed the non-military usurpers (perhaps pejoratively) as vagabonds, brigands, Gypsies, Jews, Lazes, Russians and even 'city people.'[66] In the source of that period they appear as 'strangers' or 'foreigners' (*ejnebi*).[67] The most active role in the usurpation process was however usually played by military men.

Usurpation could be of two types: conversion or displacement. Conversion here means all maneuvers to take land out of the decaying prebendal/tax-farming system and to represent it, usually falsely, if we are to believe the Ottoman treasury official Sarı Mehmet Pasha, as a 'property' (*temlik*) or as a pious estate (*vakıf*).[68] In the long run, the campaign to convert formerly prebendal land into a secure form of tenure was overwhelmingly successful.[69] The government itself eventually deliberately eased the process by the assignment of life-leases and of other property-like grants, as at Vidin. Naturally any successful conversion affected the position of the cultivators. After conversion they became tenants exposed to whatever arbitrary conditions the landlord (or *vakıf* administrator) preferred to impose.

Displacement offers schematically more complex possibilities. First, there was the attack launched upon the position of the prebendary, a position which might or might not be occupied by a genuine *sipahi*. Usually this meant obtaining and, if possible, keeping the tax-farming contract for particular holdings. But it could also mean the use of force by more powerful men to oust weaker *sipahis* from their places.[70] Secondly, there was the possibility of displacing the peasant from titular control over the peasant's traditional holding (the *bashtina* or *reaya chiftlik*). This kind of usurpation has seldom been difficult to arrange in any country or at any time where a decaying feudal situation prevailed. The pretexts and means were numerous: default of heirs, increased entry fines (*resm-i tapu*), encroachment upon the commons,[71] falsification of records, debt coercion and coercion by force. (For the effect upon the dispossessed *reaya*, see the following section.) Individuals who displaced the peasant from his old position then became non-cultivators with legal control of a cultivator's holding, or to use the Ottoman euphemism, an 'interested party' (pl. *ashab-i alaka*) who was theoretically liable to pay all state taxes incumbent upon the parcel but who naturally passed these obligations on to the actual cultivator(s). Finally, and this must have been frequent,[72] there was the scheme by which an individual obtained the tax-farming contract, then used it to obtain first the former prebendary's revenues and then also the peasant's right to his land. Under the second and third alternatives the peasant might be legally displaced without actually being dispossessed, though, as will be clearer in the following section, the peasant might already have dispossessed himself.

Dispossession of the cultivator The development of the judicial habit of honoring transfers of tax-farming leases and other limited rights between individual subjects of the sultan represented a legal shift which for the Ottoman environment was tantamount, because of its profound effects, to the development of contract law in Western Europe in support of the changeover to leasing at the close of the Middle Ages. The Ottoman development has so far received little attention. We do not know yet, for example, what instructions the government may have given the judiciary on this matter, if any. However, concern both over the transfer away from state control of the basic prebend (*kılıch yeri*) and over the usurpation by *sipahis* of the 'deeds' (*tapus*) of peasant holdings which formed the basis of prebendal incomes, can be heard in laws promulgated in the early seventeenth century. Clearly, without

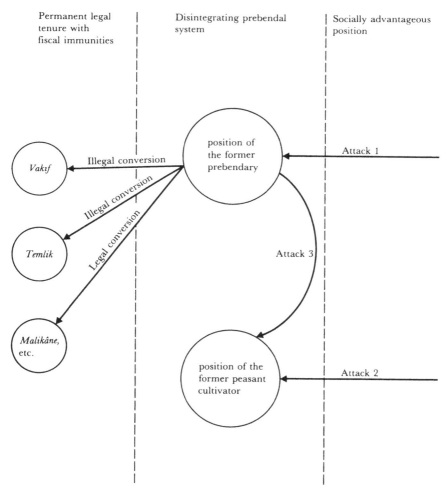

Figure 4   A simplified scheme showing three modes of attack upon the classic Ottoman land regime

the collaboration of the judiciary neither the usurpation of the state's land nor the legal dispossession of the peasantry could have taken place, or would have been much more difficult. The position of the provincial judges after 1600, in fact, was much more vulnerable than before. Their superiors speeded up their alternation in office in order to obtain increased revenues from sale of office, and in zones where central control was weak, and local figures correspondingly active, the judge was no longer his own man, despite his expanding role.

To the extent that the new system of transferring limited rights over revenues from the land worked smoothly, it created a new discipline over the soil which replaced the discipline provided under the prebendal system. Discipline of one kind or another, either prebendal or contractual, was necessary to prevent peasants from abandoning holdings and reestablishing themselves on unclaimed, perhaps marginal land – in the interstices of the system, so to speak. Under the prebendal system, the dispersal of genuine *sipahis* across the land, and the legal measures taken by the state to bring wanderers under *sipahi* control and to reward *sipahis* for bringing marginal land under cultivation, provided the necessary incentives for discipline. Under the legal regime which displaced the prebendal system, or coexisted with it during its decline, a comparable discipline was provided by the creation and transfer of quasi-property rights over empty or abandoned land (*mevat*) which the 'title' holder need not himself cultivate personally. The land lost to the prebendal system was brought to heel by the judiciary. This closed off the routes of escape for the fleeing peasant, obliging him to submit ultimately to one master or another. This whole development awaits further research.

At this point it is important to distinguish between titular displacement of the peasant, which is one form of usurpation as outlined above, and actual physical dispossession. The decision to take over the 'deed' (*tapu*) of the cultivator, in order to dispossess him of his customary rights under the prebendal system, is one thing. It is quite another matter physically to dispossess the peasant, drive him off the land and replace him with a sharecropper or a wage laborer.[73] It is the latter type of dispossession which is associated with the *chiftlik* formation process.

Why dispossess? According to Busch-Zantner, in a memorable half-truth, it was in order to be able to command the labor of the peasantry rather than be dependent upon their willingness to work.[74] Yet never, in the passage of the land system from its classic to its decadent form, was there any question of whether the *reaya* was obliged to pay up. He was.

The question rather concerned the degree of control of the use of the land which was thought to be desirable. In Serbia, some *sipahis* at least were satisfied with something resembling the classic arrangement two centuries after its disintegration had begun. In other places the advantages of physical dispossession were felt immediately. There was quite a difference as it happened, between the amount of profit one might derive from customary dues compared to the amount one might derive (as Bloch emphasized for a French context) by taking over completely and directly, by dictating conditions, by changing them arbitrarily to suit changing conditions and by using the power to hire and fire. These different responses by landholders were not random but were dictated in large part by economic factors (to be discussed in the final section of this study).

Physical dispossession was associated above all with movement, i.e. voluntary abandonment because of intolerable conditions. When peasants returned or others came for the first time, they were confronted by someone who already claimed superior rights over the land and had new arrangements in mind for its use. The first massive instance of this occurred in connection with the Anatolian uproar at the end of the sixteenth century. One of the 'justice decrees' published by Inalcık, dated 1609, laments the usurpation of abandoned holdings by influential military men who then settled slaves or hirelings on them and turned them over to livestock raising. This particular decree pertained to Rumelia.[75] One can infer from it that there was a reasonably good market in animal fibers, meat, or both, and that it was quickly discovered under the new conditions how the 'sheep's foot turns the sand to gold.' Around the middle of the seventeenth century, a law drafted for Hatvan in Hungary admits that a majority of the peasants had fled as a result of *sipahi* abuses.[76] At the end of the seventeenth century, the great Serbian migration from the Kosovo-Metohija area into Hungary, and the emptying out of parts of decimated Bosnia owing to the long war, were also the cause for considerable resettlement, presumably under new agreements.[77] Sarı Mehmet Pasha, in his well known treatise written in the same period, stresses the urgency of restoring to their places peasants who had fled. Yet even where there were no mass migrations the experience of many other post-feudal situations suggests that physical dispossession is not difficult if desired by the landlord, given a little time. Only an extraordinary judicial system could slow down such a conversion. There is no evidence yet to suggest that the Ottoman judiciary did anything to prevent dispossessions.

Titular dispossession, as opposed to physical dispossession, leaves the cultivator in place but generally imposes new and harsher conditions upon him. The most general and effective instrument in producing this effect (where outright coercion is not practicable) is to initiate a debt cycle by lending to the cultivator, then threatening him with breach of contract and bringing him more or less totally under control, unable even to relocate (legally). The name for this very widespread practice is peonage. The Ottoman state itself made it easy to initiate a debt cycle in any number of places (1) by overtaxing and (2) eventually by assigning tax-farming leases to provincial figures in the area of their perennial influence, and (3) probably also by failing to instruct the judiciary to do anything about peasant debts unless to ensure that their collection was enforced. But the logic of peonage does not demand full collection; instead the debt is used to hold the peon perennially in his place. Thus it would not be surprising if the matter of foreclosure on peasant debts was little represented in judges' records, even though some recent research indicates that the debts of town dwellers were a very frequent subject for litigation.[78]

The sudden growth of usury in the Ottoman empire dates from the last decades of the sixteenth century. The same decades saw peasants beginning to uproot themselves to escape tax arrears.[79] By the early seventeenth century, whether because of usury, tax arrears or the beginnings of peonage, or all of these combined, the subject of peasant debt – or to be more accurate, the effect of peasant debt upon the integrity of their holdings – had become a matter of imperial concern. According to a law for Ohrid (Macedonia) dated 1613:

Many peasant holdings (*bashtinas*) have been lost and their hearth taxes (*jizyes*) and their household taxes (*ispenjes*) swallowed up because a *reaya* has died and his son, overtaken by destitution, out of extreme hardship has separated a field or a certain amount of land from the holding and has either sold it to another or has put it up as a pledge on a loan. Henceforth this practice must be eliminated and holdings no longer broken up. . . . The *sipahi* should recover the entire holding from the seller and buyer, reconsolidate it, and give it to someone who wants it so that the imperial hearth tax and the *sipahi*'s household tax (*ispenje*) should not be lost.[80]

The multiplication of taxes, particularly during the long Candian War against Venice (1645–69) greatly facilitated the processes of usurpation and dispossession of both types, especially in Macedonia. There taxes and debts, combined with the coercive power which the state could bring to bear in support of debt contracts, appear to have been the engine with which the region was transformed.[81] The life-lease holders created after 1695 in Anatolia, and then elsewhere, were in a particularly good position, because of the relative size and security of their holdings (and presumably their alienability if loans were obtained by using them as security) to extend petty loans to the peasantry with peonage in mind.[82] In Syria, around Aleppo and Damascus, spheres of protective relationships binding villager to urban notable existed in the eighteenth century, though the precise origin of these spheres of protection remains to be explored.[83]

It can easily be seen that the fiscal position of peasants who lost their titular status as *chiftlik* holders but remained on their land was not the same as that of peasants who resettled under agreements so exploitative that even the actual landholder recognized that they could pay nothing in taxes beyond what they paid over to him. The cultivator who remained on his land was still part of an *avarızhane* ('tax house') and responsible for paying the head tax to the state. The physically dispossessed person was presumably often lost to the fisc after his resettlement, in a pattern which is an echo of late Byzantine times. Hypothetically at least the difference in situation can be represented as shown in Figure 5, though allowance for local variations must be made.[84]

Chiftlik *formation* Having an estate of one's own to supervise was not nearly so popular an idea in the Ottoman middle period as it became in later years. Mutafčieva's study of military *chiftliks* of the middle centuries shows that quite frequently *timars* seemed to have no *hassa* (*chiftlik*) section at all even though every prebendary was entitled to have one, at least until their suppression in the late sixteenth century. She finds that they were alienated by lease by the *timar* holders, who were either too occupied or too uninterested to cultivate land themselves, or to supervise its cultivation. Thus what should have formed the *hassa*, or personal section of the *timar* of the middle period, very frequently was assimilated to peasant holdings, contrary to the intentions of the architects of the system.[85]

By contrast, the later centuries witnessed the reconstruction of the lapsed *chiftliks* of the prebendal class as well as the appearance of other, newer *chiftliks* which were no longer directly connected with the *timar* system. This was an uneven development which was evident earlier in some places, later in other places, and in still other places never. Various ways of achieving a *chiftlik* were open when and as it seemed desirable to have one. Very often the would-be *chiftlik* 'owner' already had control of former *reaya* land (having usurped the position of the *reaya* on it) and had only to drive the cultivator from it, or to impose new arrangements upon him, thus transforming the cultivator into a dependant, a laborer with no legal right to the land he occupied and no recourse against the arrangements imposed by the *chiftlik* 'owner' besides flight. Other would-be *chiftlik* 'owners' did not take over the *reaya*'s position in the system but instead remained in the prebendary role or initiated a position parallel to that of the prebendaries – masters of land but without prebendal responsibilities. With the gradual demise of the *timar* system, not finally pronounced dead until 1834, the non-*timar* *chiftlik* holders came to predominate. Among the many

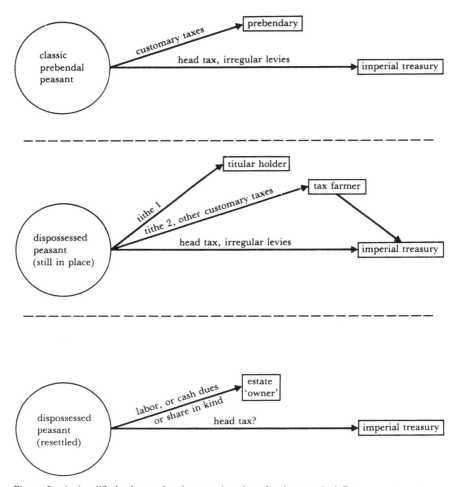

Figure 5   A simplified scheme showing tax situations for three typical Ottoman peasants

means employed to bring about this transformation were: to establish a right to a *has* object, such as a mill, or apiary, then gradually to claim the fields in its vicinity;[86] to take advantage of the imprecision of the original description of the *timar chiftlik* in some document, then gradually add land to it while taking full advantage of a superior social position if this came to a dispute with the dispossessed; leaving to one's heirs, with or without the *kadi*'s certificate (*hüjjet*), a *chiftlik* which had been awarded as *arpalik* (a holding awarded to military officers in order to maintain them between successive assignments);[87] to take a long lease on a *mukataa* holding offered by the treasury and to turn it into a perpetual lease;[88] to seize the common pasture used by villagers, especially if they had fled or were reduced in numbers;[89] to take over holdings after occupants had fled – a very frequent means;[90] to keep a field given in pledge for a debt, even though pledging and mortgaging was not officially permitted.[91] A more detailed discussion of the actual means used in *chiftlik* building appears below, on pp. 135–41. In any case the difficulty of forming a *chiftlik* – in terms of amassing the land – should not be overrated. At least until the Napoleonic period arable land was *not* very valuable in Ottoman Europe. In western Macedonia of the seventeenth century arable was worth less than meadow. The values recorded in the few such transactions that have been found varied so much that no going rate can be identified.

Besides the relative abundance of land, a second reason can be named which made all the officially disapproved land transactions easier; whether sale, pledge, mortgage or some other mode, many citations confirm that the overriding principle recognized by the government which made permissible transactions which were officially in disfavor, was the knowledge and permission of the prebendary (the *marifet-i sahib-i arz*).[92] Moreover if we cast our eyes towards numerous parallel non-Ottoman examples of decaying feudal situations – where was it ever difficult for a socially superior class to lay claim to land when it was determined to do so in circumstances of strong incentives offered by market demand? For it was not only general opportunity of a random sort which determined the rise of market oriented *chiftlik* agriculture in the Balkan peninsula but also special incentives transmitted by market demand. The pattern with which international commodity hunger manifested itself in sub-Danubian Europe of the seventeenth and eighteenth centuries will be the subject of the following section.

A far greater concern to the would-be *chiftlik* holder than the amassing of land was the problem of whom to put on it as cultivator and under what arrangements. In the later Ottoman centuries there reawakened the same labor hunger which had been a theme of the later Byzantine centuries – and on the same soil![93] Where market incentives were strong the search for labor became imperative, and some direct participation of the landholder in the supervision of his labor was the prudent course. Where this happened, traditional rents in cash or in kind were often replaced by privately arranged labor rents, or, to use more universal terms, enclaves of *Gutsherrschaft* arose within the matrix of traditionally sanctioned *Grundherrschaft*.

The *Gutsherrschaft* game could be played either by those who were in the ex-*sipahi*'s or a parallel position, or could be played by those who had usurped the *reaya*'s position as 'interested parties' (*ashab-i alaka*). The original fairness of the Ottoman system – relative to other neighboring land systems of the age – was partly to blame for the *reaya*'s dilemma. Since the original tax/rent burden had usually been bearable, with even the possibility of a slight surplus, this surplus became first the target, then the spoils of those who usurped the *reaya*'s legal position. And even in areas where this did not happen, the original tithe could be manipulated to mean substantially more. Thus the hazards of war and plague, in the seventeenth century particularly, were exacerbated by the increasingly marginal incomes of the peasantry.

Their reduced numbers were reduced further still by flight. In the eighteenth century peasants left the region entirely, settling in Hungary or the Ukraine. At the end of that century they began to hide in towns, a development which had its parallel in Anatolia.[94] The old *chift bozan* fines could not hold them in place since these were cast in the now devalued coinage of the prior era. The sanction attempted, unsuccessfully as Matkovski's exhaustive study of the question shows, was to stiffen the statute of limitations on the return of fugitive *reaya*, lengthening their liability to forcible return from ten, to twenty, thirty, even forty years. Ultimately this was futile, and in the nineteenth century few attempts at return were made, except occasionally to pious (*vakıf*) estates.[95]

Dispossession and flight became the gout and dropsy of an aging system. The government's response was twofold. First it tried to indemnify the treasury, as early as the first years of the seventeenth century,[96] by shifting tax status to the soil. One of the most common harangues found in Ottoman judicial records is the demand by the central government that all individuals – regardless of their personal status – who lay claim to land formerly worked by *reaya* (and still therefore *mirî*) would have to pay the taxes incumbent upon the land, particularly those collected through the tax house system and destined for the central treasury or for the provincial governor. (Whether the rents paid to *sipahis* were also insisted upon is less clear, the government being far more interested in the needs of the imperial treasury than in buttressing the ailing *sipahi* class.)

A second response of the government was to register as *reaya* even the landless unfortunates who had been dispossessed. Thus the government tried to have it both ways, extending tax status to the land, but also maintaining tax status for those who no longer enjoyed the security of tenure which *reaya* were originally entitled to have. This matter of registration became a very serious business since only by registration and reregistration could the integrity of the tax house system be maintained. Matkovski has held that the very definition of who was or was not a *reaya* was thereby altered. The *reaya* in the eighteenth century became someone who was registered as a *reaya* in a tax house register; he could be returned to his original place only if he became registered in a new place.[97] (Thus, insofar as record-keeping is concerned, did tax house registers assume a part of the function of the old revenue surveys which had been one of the main instruments of the sixteenth-century system. The emergent role of these registers helps to explain how administrators were able to get along without the old surveys.)

The judiciary which ignored the usurpation of *reaya* tenures, and which appears to have maintained almost a conspiracy of silence about land transactions between persons, also ignored the economic and contractual arrangements between *chiftlik* holders and *chiftlik* cultivators (*chiftchis*). These became in effect private arrangements, seemingly beyond the concern of the government or its agents.[98] Relations between the two strata were increasingly outside older institutional arrangements, and reflected typical economic behavior for which many parallels could be drawn in other parts of the world. The asymmetry in the withdrawal of institutional protection was striking. Whereas the peasant often lost his right to tenure, the *chiftlik* holder almost never lost his. The aging land regime would invariably protect the title of the usurper (a *hüjjet*, a *tapu*, etc.), who was almost always a Muslim, and not so rarely a current or former judge.

An anomalous situation arose with respect to the basic ratio between men and land. There were many landless. In Bulgaria as much as

40 per cent of the peasantry was landless in the early nineteenth century.[99] Yet the impressions of foreign observers, such as Beaujour, Pouqeville and Leake, were not mistaken – there was also a shortage of people to work the land. If men lived in a state of nature this would be absurd. The explanation is simply that all good land was under legal control, whether cultivated or not, while at the same time many good men had no land and were obliged to labor, wherever they might flee, under whatever conditions prevailed in this or that neighborhood.[100]

Studies of late Macedonian conditions[101] show that, first, although there were some medium and large *chiftliks*, most *chiftliks* were small, 25 to 50 hectares being typical (the earlier data of the next section support this impression); secondly, share tenancy (*métayage*) predominated, as it did all over Southern Europe; and, thirdly, year round wage labor existed side by side with share tenancy. Much ink has flowed over the issue of share tenancy and its apparent popularity as a mode for deploying labor.[102] The mystery of its popularity disappears when the size of the holding is taken into consideration. Share tenancy is most suitable and requires least supervision for the smaller *chiftliks* which were typical in the Balkan peninsula. Wage labor was practicable when in the same district and under the same market conditions there existed holdings large enough to justify the trouble and cost of continuous supervision. (Seasonal gang labor was also employed on larger holdings, but this is of a different nature from the perennial year round wage labor.)

In a labor-starved world without free land, control over land and laws often leads to peonage.[103] In common with landholders in many parts of the world many Ottoman *chiftlik* holders deliberately kept their tenants in their debt ('peonage of the stick') and at the same time allowed them to develop an interest in the plot of ground allowed to them as a garden ('peonage of the carrot'). In return they exacted as much of the crop as they thought the ex-*reaya* could tolerate. (The writer was pleased to have had an opportunity to interview an aged Macedonian pensioner who had spent his early youth on a *chiftlik* at Bidjevo. 'You could cultivate as much land as you wanted,' said Dimitri Tankoski, 'but come what may you split 50–50 with the *bey* at harvest time.'[104]

Although Ottoman conservatism, indifference and inaction can be indicted for the fact that little or nothing was done to protect the dispossessed from the new possessors, that conservatism had its positive side. Ottoman government did *not* erect a second serfdom, as

Braudel had supposed. It had no interest in doing so, since the government was not simply the instrument of a landholding class and had nothing to gain, as a corporation, from the degradation of the peasantry. Spiesz's differentiation is relevant here:

the decisive factor whether conditions that might be called second villeinage did or did not prevail – is not only the farming of the feudal lords on their own accounts nor the existence of *corvée* in itself, as both of these conditions can also be found in countries where the second villeinage did never exist – but it is the social and legal status of the peasants as a base the feudal lords built their farms on.[105]

The importance of the attitude of government becomes more apparent when conditions south of the Danube are compared with those in Romania. Putting it briefly, the peculiar political conditions of the Romanian principalities, both before and during the period of Ottoman suzerainty did not encourage the degree of concentration of political authority which was characteristic of the Ottoman state. Thus the *hospodars* and *boyars* were locked in a long struggle over the revenues which could be gotten from the peasantry. Once the Straits were opened so that European demand pressure was felt along the Danube there was no saving the Romanian peasantry. The government of the *hospodars* collaborated with the *boyars* to bring almost the entire peasant class, the *clacaşi*, into complete subjection, legislating progressively more oppressive corvée requirements. The year 1805 has been named as the time when the new harsher course was definitely set, only two decades after the opening of the Straits, or, at latest, the Code of Caragea (1818), which undermined all earlier attempts by *hospodars* such as Mavrocordatos and Ypsilanti to lighten the burden on the shoulders of the villagers.[106]

Two waves of chiftlik *formation in Ottoman Europe*

There is a lesson to be learned from the work of Polish historians in recent decades. Poland's provinces, like Ottoman provinces outside the Straits, were much affected by foreign economic demand in the early modern period, being the main suppliers of the Baltic trade in grain. Much patient work by the Poles has led to a consensus that location must always be taken into close consideration when studying the effects of the trade upon rural life in Poland.[107] The most affected zones were invariably near waterways, with the size, intensity and profitability of demesne farming all influenced by the availability of water transport in their immediate vicinity. The mode of deploying labor was also correlated, so that wage labor is associated with the largest holdings in the most intensively exploited zones – Pomerania and the vicinity of the Vistula mouth.

The Ottoman case also demands a location-specific approach. One generalization common among those who have written on the subject has been that the Ottoman *chiftliks* tended to be located on the best available land, usually on coastal plains and in river valleys.[108] The writer's own study of *chiftlik* location in the Manastir district certainly does not upset that generalization – the *chiftliks* of Manastir were almost all crowded near the Crna River banks (see Map 16). But not all river valleys or coastal plains were equally or simultaneously affected. An appreciation of the timing, scale and location of the entire *chiftlik* episode in Ottoman Europe requires a perspective upon the region as a whole, and a thoroughly empirical spirit.

The Ottoman fiscal records consulted in order to obtain the needed perspective unfortunately do not distinguish between *chiftliks* which were *chiftliks* cultivated on their own behalf by Muslims (whether *reaya* or military) and *chiftliks* which were cultivated by dependent cultivators on someone else's behalf. Seemingly the Ottoman treasury men were simply not interested in making that distinction. A close look sometimes allows the researcher to draw some conclusion regarding the type of *chiftlik* involved but often does not.

In order to make some preliminary overall generalizations about the development of *chiftliks* cultivated by dependent tenants throughout the entire region, a special technique was devised. It was a crude sampling technique which leaves much to be desired. Nonetheless certain results were obtained. Data sampling was done from three kinds of fiscal records: revenue surveys (for the early seventeenth century); province-scale tax house records; and, in one exceptional case, a suitable list from a Manastir judicial register. No attempt was made to distinguish between independently cultivated *chiftliks* and dependent two or three party *chiftliks* on the basis of a close reading of names, context, etc. Instead all *chiftliks* were disregarded which were no larger than standard *chiftlik* size (i.e. 100 *dönüms* = 25 acres = 10 hectares). Only *chiftliks* over that size were counted in sampling. Then a ratio was established for each zone on which data were available between 'Ç', a figure representing all 100 *dönüm* units of *chiftlik* after subtraction of all normal-sized *chiftliks* (e.g. a three unit *chiftlik* would be counted as 3) and H, the number of households, or heads of households in the same district. Often there was uncertainty about what the size of the *chiftlik* actually was and whether a '*zimmi*,' '*reaya*,' '*nefer*' or '*haymana*' was actually a head of household. The results must be regarded as a crude first attempt to grapple with the problem of *chiftlik* distribution on the basis of Ottoman fiscal records.

Three grades of *chiftlik* presence were established. The 0.2 Ç/H ratio (which is the threshold of the highest grade) means that, roughly speaking, for every five *village* households in a district there was one 'extra' unit of *chiftlik* (i.e. approximately 100 *dönüms*, or one '*chift*' of *chiftlik*, a '*chift*' or 'pair' being about the amount of land which one man, using one team of draught animals could be expected to cultivate in the course of a year using the preexisting three field techniques). Districts with a larger share of *chiftliks*, such as Karaferye[109] (modern Verroia, west of Salonica), Manastir (modern Bitola in western Macedonia), and Bergos and Varna on the Bulgarian Black Sea coast received Ç/H ratios of about 0.4 before the mid-eighteenth century. Curiously Siroz (modern Seres), a well known cotton district, received only 0.2. Certainly higher ratios will be obtained from later fiscal records where suitable ones can be found. The results as shown on the Maps 7 and 8 are simply approximations and obviously tell an incomplete story, nonetheless not without interest.

As expected, the early seventeenth century shows no very significant development of *chiftliks* in the few places where data were available. However, data for the next century (roughly 1650–1750) reveal some surprises. The concentration of *chiftliks* on the Albanian coast near Durazzo, in Thessaly, and in the Salonica hinterland are all to be expected. But moving eastward it is surprising that there were relatively few *chiftliks* on the north Aegean shore (too close to the Istanbul zone of control?). It is also surprising – to the writer at least – that the Bulgarian Black Sea coast and Dobrudja had so many *chiftliks* at this early stage. This *seems* to upset the idea that production for the Istanbul market was not profitable. Along the Danube, as expected, and in the Bulgarian interior, again as expected, the development is weak. The light Morean ratio may really result from the fact that Morea's *chiftliks* were averaged for the zone as a whole, including the presumably less developed interior. (It is likely that some larger estates were omitted from the tax house records used for the later estimates, even though all estates were decreed to be included. To the extent that this was so, the estimates offered here are low.)

These crude data may be combined with statements in the related literature on various zones (usually based on quite different sources,

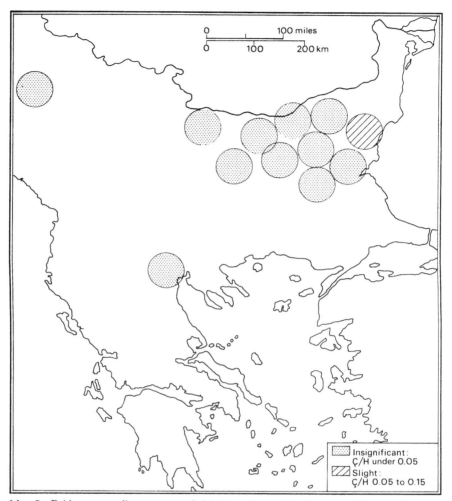

Map 7   Evidence regarding presence of *chiftliks*, early seventeenth-century Ottoman Europe

Sources for the Maps 7 and 8, showing the relative presence of *chiftlik* agriculture based on Ç/H* ratios:

Early seventeenth century: BVA Tapu Defter 695: Tirhala, 1010н; BVA Tapu Defter 722: Manastir 1022н; BVA Tapu Defter 771: Silistre 1052н; BVA Tapu Defter 718: Niğbolu 1022н; BVA Tapu Defter 742: Bosna 1033н; BVA Tapu Defter 723: Karaferye 1022н.

Late seventeenth to mid-eighteenth century: BVA MM3440: Tirhala, 1105н; BVA KK 2702: Tirhala 1094н; DAM Manastir Sicil #34 (*tevzi*): 1121н; BVA KK 2912: Varna, Silistre 1164н; BVA KK 2840: Bergos 1124н; BVA KK 2790: Şumni 1109н; BVA KK 2915: Niğbolu 1165н; BVA KK 2873: Nevrekop 1136н; BVA KK 2831: Paşa 1122н; BVA KK 2855: Mora 1128н; BVA KK 2876: Ohri 1137н; BVA KK 2825: Gümülcine 1121н; BVA KK 2869: Selanik and Paşa 1134н; BVA KK 2869: Siroz 1134н; BVA KK 2786: Siroz 1109н; BVA KK 2890: Karaferye 1147н.

* *Definition of Ç/H ratio (see opposite)*

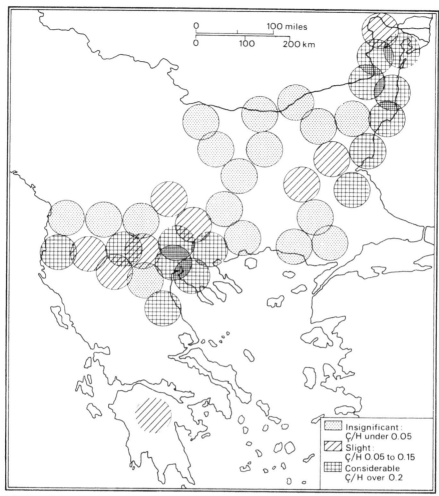

Map 8   Evidence regarding presence of *chiftliks*, late seventeenth- to mid-eighteenth-century Ottoman Europe

Ç = number of *chifts* (100 *dönüms*) of *chiftlik* after all *chiftliks* of 100 *dönüms* and less have been subtracted (i.e. all of normal size). Reasoning: *chiftliks* of 100 *dönüms* or less are probably *reaya chiftliks*, but a *chiftlik* of 2,3,4 *chifts* (i.e. 200, 300, 400 *dönüms*) must be cultivated not by one *reaya* on his own behalf, but by more than one *reaya* (one dependent cultivator) on behalf of someone else. One *dönüm* = 940m², about four to an acre, or ten to a hectare.

H = number of *reaya* households (*hanes*), or heads of household (i.e. *zimmis* or *haymanas*, etc.) associated with the *chiftliks* in the same district.

Ç/H then is the ratio of larger than normal *chiftliks* to the number of households in a particular district, a crude but helpful indicator.

BVA   =   Prime Minister's Archive, Istanbul
DAM   =   State Archive of Macedonia
MM   =   Maliyeden Müdevver Collection (BVA)
KK   =   Kâmil Kepeci Collection (BVA)

consular and travelers' reports, etc.) to arrive at certain generalizations. First, location near to the sea was as critical a factor in southeastern Europe as in Poland, or anywhere else. Secondly, zones located near the Aegean, Adriatic and Black Sea shores had their *chiftliks* long before the opening of the Straits. Thirdly, the entire northern tier, comprising Danubian Bulgaria (and parallel with it to the north, Wallachia and Moldavia), as well as Serbia and Bosnia, were not much developed for other than pastoral exports (also referred to earlier as 'fallow products') until after the opening of the Straits and the associated development of traffic on the Danube or, in the case of Bosnia, until the demand peak of the Napoleonic period. All in all, it is defensible to speak of the turn towards market oriented agriculture in south-eastern Europe as a two tier development – first in the south, later in the north.

There will be no argument about the southern tier from those familiar with the literature relating to it since, even where specific statements on *chiftliks* are lacking, the export record strongly suggests their presence in the seventeenth century, at least near the coasts.[110]

Among Bulgarian scholars, although little work seems to have been done so far on coastal development, there is general agreement that, aside from the late eighteenth-century development in the Vidin area explored by Gandev, *chiftliks* appeared in numbers only at Ruse (where Dimitrov's study shows them to have reached a plateau of development in the seventeenth century[111]) and near Sofia, as a matter of conjecture. A consensus accepts that nineteenth-century Bulgaria as a whole was not typified by large *chiftliks* but rather by small and medium peasant holdings.[112] In the Balkan interior at Kosovo, Kaleši informs us that, as one might expect, *chiftliks* did not develop until the early nineteenth century.[113]

Some difference of opinion can be anticipated regarding Serbia and Bosnia. Tričković for Serbia and Sućeska for Bosnia have reported a considerable development of *chiftliks* in the course of the eighteenth century.[114] But this picture is not supported by export figures. Bosnia does not seem to have exported much by way of vegetable products until the Napoleonic boom period,[115] which brought prosperity as well to Ali Pasha of Yanina, the holder of many *chiftliks*, and to Pazvantoğlu on the Danube, likewise the master of many *chiftliks*. Belgrade meanwhile continued to receive grain from Habsburg provinces rather than from Serbia, though Serbia returned livestock. The *chiftlik*, in the sense usually meant by the term, is an agricultural, not a pastoral, production unit. Although some *chiftliks* served an interior market provided by this or that town, the really considerable developments of *chiftlik* agriculture of the later Ottoman centuries are almost always linked (the Bulgarian Black Sea coast excepted) with foreign trade in commodities.

This is where the analytic categories established earlier become useful. The sources used by Tričković and Sućeska are doubtless teeming with references to *chiftliks*. Contemporaries like Prota Matija Nenadović, the Serbian bishop, mention them too. But knowing that Ottoman usage makes no distinction between types of usage for this term should put us on guard. This writer believes that for the most part eighteenth-century *chiftliks* claimed by janissaries in Serbia, and by the entire surviving Muslim populace in Bosnia, represent usurpations, not *chiftliks* in our conventional sense, their masters being receivers of rents, not entrepreneurs. In this they were no different from the majority of the so-called *chiftlik* holders (*sahibis*) throughout Ottoman Europe in the two century span under examination. For aside from the question of location, data on *chiftliks* so far show that the typical *chiftlik* was small, usually no more than two to three units in size (i.e. 50–75 acres). Although large *chiftliks* do occur in export oriented zones (some as large as 80–100 units) these are most untypical. The average Balkan *chiftlik* was a rental operation, far closer in its character and its scale to the *Grundherrschaft* past from which it evolved, than to the *Gutsherrschaft* character which has frequently been imagined for it.

3 ❧ Head tax data for Ottoman Europe, 1700–1815*

Population estimates for periods before the nineteenth century have almost always relied upon tax records, particularly hearth tax records, since the hearth, or unified dwelling, has so often been preferred historically as the unit of taxation. The main reason for this widespread reliance upon hearth taxes – as opposed to poll taxes – has been relative ease of collection. Unfortunately for historians, ease of collection has not resulted in easy interpretation of the records which survive. It has usually been impossible to be certain regarding the average household size underlying hearth tax totals; this might vary from two and a half to ten persons per hearth, depending upon the period and the place.[1] Data on groups of whole families, from which household size and other demographic generalities might be abstracted, seem in general to be sadly rare, although the determination of modern demographic historians has overturned many neglected stones and has led to a surprising amount of progress.

The Ottoman hearth tax reform of 1691

Before 1691, Ottoman population estimates also rest largely upon tax records in which the household, or hearth, is the predominant counting unit (though exceptional provincial surveys contained the names not only of heads of households, but of all adult males). Thus Ö. L. Barkan's pioneering work on the growth of Ottoman population during the sixteenth century, like most other estimates based upon premodern tax records, rests upon a regrettably unsteady foundation. Barkan was obliged to use a single household multiplier (five), so that

*This research was carried out with support from the Faculty Fulbright Program at the University of Michigan.

although there is little doubt about the upward trend that he was investigating, there does remain some question about the multiplier he used, and consequently about the absolute size of the population being investigated.[2]

In 1691, however, a significant reform took place, at that time important because of the immediate relief that it brought to the Ottoman treasury, but today important for historians as well – enabling us to place population estimates, at least in Europe south of the Danube, upon a more solid footing. Before 1691, the 'poll tax,' or *jizye*, which Islamic law and custom prescribed as an annual tax to be collected from all non-Muslim subjects living under Muslim rule, was collected on a household basis. Therefore, until 1691 a population estimate based on Ottoman *jizye* records could hardly yield a better result than an estimate based on other Ottoman fiscal records, such as the provincial revenue surveys (the *tahrirs*). But collection of the *jizye* on a household basis was not what the *Shar'iah* (the Muslim Holy Law) actually prescribed; it was simply a convenient basis for collection which had until that time been tolerated under Ottoman government.

For reasons which may have been partly religious and partly fiscal, household collection of the *jizye* was overturned by the Ottomans in 1691, and replaced by a new method of collection on the basis of individual receipts which every adult non-Muslim male would be expected to renew annually. Thus in the midst of a long and strenuous war with the Holy League following unprecedented fiscal emergencies, the Ottoman treasury, acting upon an imperial directive which was essentially repeated in many subsequent *fermans* dealing with the proper collection of the *jizye*, returned to the basis of collection actually prescribed by the *Shar'iah*.[3]

For the purpose of making long term comparisons, it would be extremely gratifying if the pre-1691 Ottoman *jizye* records could be rationally related to the post-1691 *jizye* records. Examples of seventeenth-century central *jizye* registers do in fact survive at the Prime Minister's Archive (Başvekâlet Arşivi, abbr. B V A) in Istanbul. But these registers do not inspire confidence: the necessary continuity of territorial units is missing and the figures cited in them are sporadic and irregular.[4]

By contrast, the *jizye* registers housed at the B V A which pertain to the period following the 1691 reform are remarkably regular, both from the territorial point of view, since one is able to follow single judicial districts or blocs of judicial districts through the whole series of registers, and from the statistical point of view, since the figures they present are regular (within plausible limits) and show plausible and gradual long term trends. After a few years of uncertainty and relative disorder following the original reform decree, the Ottoman *jizye* registers settle down to a pattern of presentation which must have been as useful to the treasury men who had to keep track of so many local situations as it is to the historian trying to generalize about them.

The reliability question

The *jizye* registers of the period 1700–1815 tell a striking story. According to these registers, the number of *jizye*-liable non-Muslims of southeastern Europe below the Danube–Sava line increased by half in the course of a century. Unless it can be shown that the definition of the adult male, or the threshold age of collection, or collection methods changed substantially during that period, we must conclude that the size of the total population from whom the *jizye* payers were drawn *also* increased at the same rate and to the same extent. Whereas household size can change radically in a century, the ratio of an adult male population (e.g. all males over 15 years) to the rest of the population from which they are drawn will change significantly only if there is a dramatic change in birth rate over a long period. Even if a radical change in birth rate could be shown to have taken place in the eighteenth-century Balkans, the ratio of adult males to the rest of a population, which in pre-industrial societies tends to be about one to three, cannot vary over time nearly as much as can household size. Therefore generalizations based on the newer *jizye* data are far more dependable for the purpose of estimating the absolute size of the non-Muslim populace covered by these statistics than household figures could possibly be.

To claim complete reliability for the post-1691 *jizye* records would be going too far. Certainly there were abuses in the collection of the *jizye* under the new rules, just as there were in other centrally prescribed collections[5] (though it is worth pointing out that the *jizye* collections were not ordinarily farmed out under the *iltizam* system and therefore not subject to the extreme distortions of *iltizam* collections). But if there were abuses, we can be confident that their effect would be to depress the official figures, not to inflate them. The interests of the collector and of local figures with whom collectors might collude would dictate that new *jizye* payers be hidden from the treasury and the difference pocketed. Thus, the substantial increases recorded in the eighteenth-century *jizye* registers (see the Appendix below, pp. 95–103) can be taken to be possibly understatements of real population growth, but not overstatements.

Another consideration which points towards rough reliability for the post-1691 *jizye* records is the fact that adjacent groups of districts (usually judicial districts, but sometimes whole provinces) tend to move together but never with a uniformity that suggests an across-the-board rigidity. In fact, the statistical whole does not move together. Thus, the investigator found it advisable to divide the sub-Danubian whole into different zones characterized by different trends – these appear in the Appendix and Maps 9–13 as the north-west, near north-east, far north-east, south-west and south-east zones. These variations within the statistical whole add a certain air of plausibility to the record, although there are, admittedly, occasionally instances where a subtotal is repeated at an interval of decades without any change whatsoever (see the Albanian entries, for instance).

Interpreting the head tax figures

Looking back to earlier times, one is struck by the low European head tax figures of 1700 compared with those of the same area a century or two earlier. From the Appendix the reader will see that in 1700 the total number of males on the European side liable to pay the *jizye* was 635,835 (this includes a very conservative extrapolation backwards from the 1720 figures to fill in the blank for Morea, which in 1700 was under Venetian occupation). As explained above, we can reasonably multiply this number by three to find the total population. If we compare the resultant 2 million with the *jizye* figures offered by Nikolai Todorov for the same territories in 1490 we are driven to conclude that there must have taken place a great fall-off in population during the intervening centuries.[6] Todorov's total of approximately 600,000 was taken from a *jizye* register (now housed at Sofia) in which the basis for collection was the household; therefore his total can reasonably be multiplied by the conventional household multiplier of five to arrive at a total of 3 million – half again as many non-Muslims as the 1700 register suggests. The contrast is even more dramatic if one takes into account Barkan's estimates for the late sixteenth century. Barkan thought Braudel's estimates for the population of Ottoman Europe (though not for the empire generally) were too high for the early sixteenth century. For the period around 1530 he suggests a total population for sub-Danubian Europe of just over 5 million (Istanbul and the islands excluded) in contrast to the 8 million suggested by Braudel. One million of these are being accounted Muslims, leaving a balance of four million – a credible increase of one-third over Todorov's non-Muslim total for 1490. Barkan's study of town population figures led him to agree that half a century later Braudel's figures for Europe were plausible since town populations exhibited substantial growth. If so, the non-Muslim populace of Europe, excluding the Hungarian and Romanian territories, may have amounted to $5\frac{1}{2}$ or 6 million – two to three times the 1700 total suggested in this study.

Looking forward to the first nineteenth-century figures which we can feel confident about, one is again struck by the seemingly diminutive eighteenth-century *jizye* totals. To the 1831 Ottoman census total for the remaining European provinces south of the Danube, Todorov has juxtaposed contemporaneous Greek and Serbian census figures for an inferred total of 4,321,282 *non*-Muslims in the same territories covered by the eighteenth-century *jizye* figures.[7] Multiplying the 1815 *jizye* figures by three gives us a non-Muslim total of close to 3 million, half again as much as the 1700 figure but far short of the over 4 million suggested by Todorov's figures only fifteen years later. Such spectacular growth does not seem possible during those troubled years. The most likely explanation would seem to be that the *jizye* figures for some

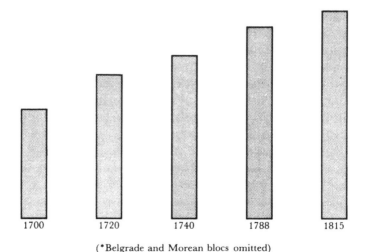

(*Belgrade and Morean blocs omitted)

Figure 6   Head tax receipts from Ottoman Europe,* 1700–1815

zones were not up-to-date in 1815. The figures for the southernmost districts are particularly suspect when one compares Todorov's figures for Greece with the last *jizye* totals.

The census figures cited by Todorov show Muslims accounting for portions of the totals shown for Ottoman European provinces ranging from 33 to 42 per cent. If one includes Muslims, the total population on the European side in those territories covered by the *jizye* figures in 1831 was 5,770,380, with the proportion of Muslims being demonstrably higher in many areas, such as Albania, than during earlier centuries. This is still at least two million short of the 8 million suggested by Braudel for Ottoman Europe in the sixteenth century and accepted by Barkan for the late sixteenth.

South-eastern Europe in the eighteenth century: recovering from catastrophe?

Accepting the eighteenth-century *jizye* figures as roughly reliable, and placing them in a context of much higher population levels in the sixteenth and nineteenth centuries, we are confronted by a disturbing appearance. How can we explain this deep trough if not as the result of the trends and events of the seventeenth century? Easy to accept (if not to explain) are the evidences of growth in the sixteenth, eighteenth and nineteenth centuries – these trends place the Ottoman provinces inside trends which encompassed most parts of Europe. Nor would a faltering population be difficult to accept for the seventeenth century – this too was a widespread phenomenon with specifically Spanish and Italian versions.[8] But the *jizye* totals of 1700 do not suggest faltering. They suggest a demographic catastrophe for which no serious explanation has yet been attempted.

The evidence of travelers' accounts has always been taken with a grain of salt. It was a commonplace observation on the part of foreigners that the Ottoman provinces through which they traveled looked deserted. Thus an impression of depopulation was created which seemed equally valid for either the seventeenth or eighteenth centuries, an impression vividly recapitulated by Beaujour's memoir of the late eighteenth. These accounts have been somewhat discounted for the simple reason that travelers seldom had occasion to stray from the road. And that the roads had a devastating effect upon nearby settlements was never in doubt.[9] Thus a grudging acceptance of depressed rural conditions throughout south-eastern Europe may have flattened out a reality far more dramatic, in that the loss of population was much greater than suspected until now, and that these losses were concentrated in the seventeenth century, with the eighteenth marked by gradual recovery.

Explanations for the apparent demographic catastrophe of the seventeenth century are for the present simply hypothetical since no hard evidence has yet been developed.[10] That the century was hounded by war and brigandage is not in dispute. That overtaxation, born of a lack of governmental efficiency and concern, also took a toll is also apparent. Another explanation, at present still hypothetical, is that the Ottoman domains, like many other parts of Europe, experienced in that century the full virulence of the typhus mechanism, a mechanism still sporadically present in south-eastern Europe, which goes into action under conditions which can be linked both to famine and to war. Demographic historians for a long time have noticed that there was a connection not only between disease and war (which was obvious even to contemporary observers) but also between disease and famine. Contemporary observers until very recent times tended to be vague in their descriptions of epidemic diseases. And in Ottoman and Balkan records, though mentions of bad harvests and attendant hunger and pestilence are not difficult to find, their seriousness and the extent of consequent loss of life is usually impossible to measure. Only with the development of modern epidemiology has the typhus mechanism been identified, as well as its now endemic presence in south-eastern Europe.

Typhus,[11] which in Germany was known as 'the Hungarian disease,' lay in wait for every military expedition headed in the direction of the Balkans. The 'murine' form of this disease is normally communicated between rats, the carrier being rat fleas. But when food supplies fail because of famine or war, rats, like humans, suffer – and so do rat fleas. Some rat fleas abandon their failing hosts and resort to human hosts, not, apparently their preferred fare but tolerable in time of need. Typhus passed on to human hosts by rat fleas can then be communicated from one human to another not by rat fleas but by body or head lice. This is especially liable to happen under insanitary and crowded conditions – in armies, in towns, and of course fortresses and towns under siege. The resultant epidemic may then travel far if local conditions encourage it. If the new human hosts are weakened by hunger, typhus (whether of the 'murine' or 'human' type) may kill them. And though a population such as that of the Balkans may eventually develop a certain resistance to the disease, such resistance has never been enough to prevent the sporadic outbreak of the epidemic under wartime conditions, as, for instance, among the Yugoslav partisans of the Second World War. It seems likely in retrospect that this killing combination – hunger and typhus – was in its heyday in the seventeenth century, and nowhere more at home than in Ottoman Europe. However, this explanation is still hypothetical and to accept it wholeheartedly for the seventeenth century means to reject it for the eighteenth, whereas we know in fact that typhus remained a major hazard, particularly for military operations.[12]

Equally plausible, but still unproven is the hypothesis that the Balkan peninsula, like the rest of southern Europe, may have experienced an abnormal (or at least changed) climate during the seventeenth century. There appears to be a growing consensus that solar and planetary periodicities combine and interfere with one another to produce secular climatic variation. Certainly glacial advances have been linked persuasively to sunspot activity. For the seventeenth century, there is general agreement that most of Europe was experiencing generally cooler weather, and perhaps the shorter growing season which that implies. This of itself would not seem to matter much in the Mediterranean climatic zone, where the great danger arises not from coolness but from dessication. But the cooler weather to the north may have been immediately linked to altered patterns of atmospheric circulation, which in turn may have caused drier weather to the south, and the lighter harvests which that implies. An equally likely hazard would have been greater variability, which would be especially hard on populations which were overtaxed.

Eventually an accumulation of dendrochronological and other evidence will remove this question from the realm of hypothesis. But for the time being the climatic explanation can neither be proven nor disproven. Le Roy Ladurie, who undertook a thorough study of the question of climatic variance over a decade ago, ended by pleading for a suspension of judgment until more evidence accumulates. That judgment still seems appropriate.[13]

Abandoning all further hypothetical explanations for the apparently profound demographic retrenchment which took place in Ottoman Europe during the seventeenth century, let us examine more closely the different experience of the zones abstracted from the head tax data of the following century.

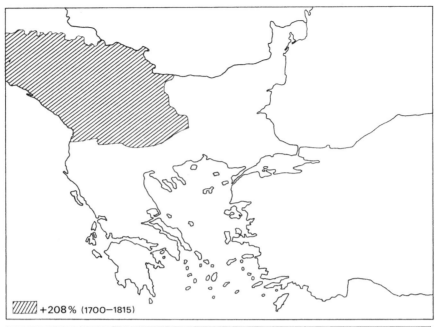

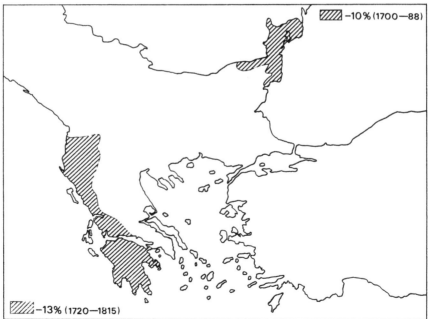

Maps 9–12 Statistically coherent subdivisions of Ottoman Europe as abstracted from head tax figures, 1700–1815

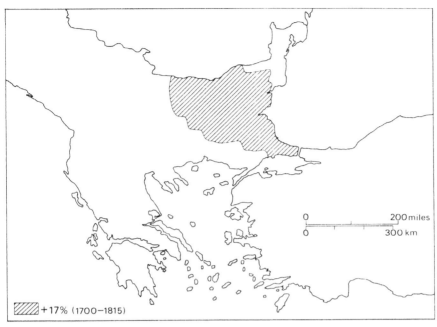

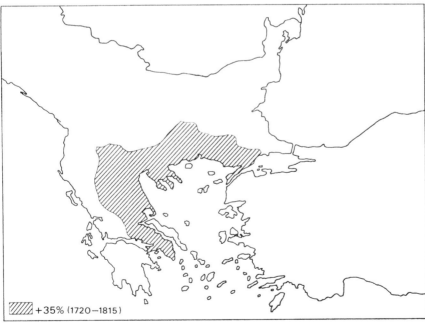

+17% (1700–1815)

+35% (1720–1815)

89

The north-west zone

The marked upswing in *jizye* figures recorded for Serbia and Bosnia are at least partly due to the recruitment of areas which lost heavily during the long war with the Holy League which ended in 1699, though from the tables it will be apparent that the rise of *jizye* payers was gradual throughout the eighteenth century, and did not take place only in the first decades of the century. A considerable exodus of Serbs (and Macedonians) took place at the time of the so-called Great Resettlement which saw as many as 200,000 Austrian sympathizers abandon Kosovo and northern Macedonia in 1690 for new homes across the Habsburg borders. Bosnia also was much exhausted by the long war with the Holy League and lost some of its Catholic population, which withdrew north across the Sava with the forces of Prince Eugene of Savoy returning from the expedition to Sarajevo in 1697.[14] According to Branislav Djurdjev, 'the long wars left an epidemic of plague in their trail.'[15]

Yugoslav scholars have followed the work of Dušan Popović, based on Austrian sources, in believing that the population of Serbia expanded greatly in the eighteenth century, especially in the final decades before the 1804 insurrection. If in fact their assumption of a threefold increase between 1740 and 1804 is justified, then the Ottoman head tax figures for 'Belgrad and its dependencies' are very deficient indeed since these give the impression of little change after 1740. But perhaps the *en bloc* treatment of northern Serbia in the head tax registers should be taken as an indication that control had slipped away from Ottoman government authorities, i.e. that the *oborknez* institution which was a leftover of the Austrian administration of the area was depriving them of direct knowledge. (If so, we may be right to suspect a similar effect in Morea which also tended to be treated *en bloc* by the registers.) In Bosnia, by contrast, the head tax data of 1815 seems to harmonize well with the later data offered by Todorov.

The north-west's gains would doubtless have been greater still if it were not for the loss of more thousands of Christians who withdrew north down the Drina and across the Sava with the retreating Austrians in 1737 (followed by a 'plague') and again in 1788, when as many as 50,000 Serbian refugees, who had been cooperating with the Austrian offensive, left their homes in Serbia and crossed north into the Vojvodina. Figures for the north-west zone were also held down by the fact that the Kosovo area was refilled mostly by Albanian tribesmen who had accepted Islam; some Serbs in Novi Pazar and Macedonians in the Šar Planina vicinity also accepted Islam in the eighteenth century.

It is believed by Yugoslav scholars that the eighteenth century witnessed the continuation of a process which had been going on more or less ceaselessly since the fifteenth century – the steady trickle northward into Bosnia and Serbia of families from the mountainous zones to the south-west where frequently insufficient food supplies prompted migration.[16] Thus the growth reflected in the *jizye* figures may be partly the result of northward migration, as well as natural increase.

Because of the relatively greater increase of *jizye* payers in the northwest Bosnia–Serbian zone, the share of this zone in the totals for all of sub-Danubian Europe rises from 15 per cent in 1700 to about 33 per cent in 1815.[17]

The south-west and far north-east zones

Jizye figures indicate that these peripheral zones lost some of their non-Muslim population in the course of the eighteenth century. However, the losses were not great, conceivably the result of imperfect collection rather than real population loss. If the losses are accepted as real the explanations which come to mind are as follows.

The south-west, Morea in particular, was badly devastated during the war between the Ottomans and the Holy League; Cornoro, the first Venetian governor of the Morea, reported 86,468 survivors from a supposed pre-war total of 200,000. Yet Venetian figures indicate that by 1708 the population of the Morea had shot up to 250,000, which if believed, must be the result of immigration from other areas.[18] This recrudescence seems to have collapsed with the return of this region to Ottoman rule after 1715. It is known that Morea suffered greatly from the depredations of Albanian irregulars during the 1770s.[19]

In the far north-east, the Dobrudja and the lower Danube, foreign troops were not active until the first of Catherine's wars, 1771–4 (though General Rönne's troops had sacked İbrail in the campaign of 1711).[20] Yet the figures indicate that most of the *jizye* loss there took place between 1700 and 1720. Possibly the concentrations of Ottoman soldiery at Ismail and Baba Dağ and of Tatars elsewhere in the Dobrudja played a role in the apparent decline of *jizye* payers in this zone. Certainly by Rumelian standards the relative strength of Muslims here was unusually great.

Map 13 Judicial districts of Ottoman Europe, seventeenth and eighteenth centuries

92

28°E
İbrail İsakçi Geçidi
Maçin Tulçi
Çardak
Baba Dağı
Hırsova

32°E
44°N

Silistre
Rusçuk Mangaliya
hova Niğbolu Zıştovi Hacıoğlu
Pılevna EskiCuma Hezargrad Pazarı
Hotaliç Şumni Yeni Balçık
Pazar Varna
Etrapoli Tırnovi Pravadi
Lofça Osman Bazar
Aydos
Akçe Kazanlik Islimye Karinabad Misivri
zladi Yanbolu Rusikasrı Ahyolu
htiman Zagra-i Atik Seferköy Bergos
Uzunca Ova Zagra-i Cedid Umur Fakiye
Filibe Çerpan Yenice
ar Havas-i Mahmud Paşa
zarı Cisr-i Mustafa Paşa
vrekop Çirmen Edirne Kirk Kilise
Ahi Çelebi Bunar Hisar
Karadağ Dimetoka Baba-i Atik Vize
Dırama Yenice-i Hayrıbolu Saray
Kara Ağaç Gümülcine Ergene Çorlu
Çağlayık Firecik Keşan Tekfurdağı
işte Kavala Megri İpsala Miğalkara Aynacık
İnoz Şarköy
Avrasa
Gelibolu

40°N

RIBOZ

36°N
28°E
32°E

93

The near north-east zone

The Bulgarian zone, which by 1815 accounted for 23 per cent of the *jizye* payers of the sub-Danubian total, at first lost *jizye* payers (before 1720, apparently as the result of the same causes which operated in the Dobrudja), then began to gain, so that the increase between 1720 and 1815 is actually 25 per cent. This zone was not, as far as one can tell, as much affected by immigration or emigration as was the north-west zone, though some movement of Macedonians into Bulgaria is believed to have taken place.[21] Throughout this zone, and particularly at the eastern and south-eastern extremities, the density of Muslims was higher in the eighteenth century than it was in most other parts of the Balkans (with the possible exception of Kosovo, the Vardar valley and parts of Bosnia). This is in keeping with the marked west-to-east gradient of Muslim settlement which is already apparent in the early sixteenth century on Barkan's map of the Balkans.

The south-east zone

Gains in *jizye* payers in the south-eastern zone were higher than in the north-east zone but lower than in the north-west. Once again the tables show that the gains were gradual throughout the century, the zone representing in 1815 about 30 per cent of the sub-Danubian total. The fact that heavily chiftlicized zones (i.e. zones characterized by export-oriented agriculture) such as Seres, Tirhala, Yenishehir and Karaferye exhibited more or less average growth in number of *jizye* receipts is cause for reflection. If the *chiftlik* owners and *kojabashis* of the southern zones worked in concert to bring down the number of tax houses allotted by the treasury to their zones (see the following study), then why were they not equally successful in hiding demographic strength? This is only one of the enigmas arising from the data offered by the Ottoman head tax figures of the eighteenth century.

Appendix: Official totals of head tax receipts held by the non-Muslim population of Ottoman Europe, 1700–1815

The five zones (NW, near NE, far NE, SW, SE) do not appear in the head tax (*jizye*) registers selected for this study. They were abstracted from the data in an effort to group together districts which seem to have been moving together statistically. These zones are identical with those on the accompanying maps. Four larger zones appear in the registers (and on the maps) as usually undivided collectivities: BOSNA, BELGRAD, MORA and AGRIBOZ. Except for a few totals taken from other registers as noted, the data for these tables come from the following registers in the Kâmil Kepeci collection at the Istanbul BVA. The Muslim (*hijri*) dates of these registers are followed by the Christian dates with which they roughly correspond.

KK 3541	1112H/1700 A.D.
KK 3560	1133H/1720 A.D.
KK 3559 (sometimes used as a supplement to 3560)	1130H/1718 A.D.
KK 3580	1153H/1740 A.D.
KK 3662	1202H/1788 A.D.
KK 3732	1230H/1815 A.D.

Occasional extrapolations were thought to be admissible in order to generalize about trends within zones, and also within sub-Danubian Europe as a whole. Thus the final table includes extrapolated totals for Mora (Morea) and Belgrade (northern Serbia) at dates when foreign occupation or war prevented their appearing in the Ottoman registers as usual. In a few cases a missing total was supplied from another register from roughly the same period, as noted.

North-western zone

Üsküb, Kalkandelen, Kırçova, Köprülü, Samokov, Ihtiman, Razlog, Köstendil, Egri Dere, Kıratova, Dupniça, Kumanova, Radomir, Siresnik, Ivranye, Radovişte, Iştip, Petriç, Ustrumca, Tikveş, Doyran

1112H (incl. Koçane)	33,000
1130H (incl. Manastir list)	49,800
1133H (incl. Ohri list)	47,770
1153H (as above)	40,050
1202H (incl. Samokov, Ihtiman listed separately, also رجمة)	57,651
1230H (minus Ihtiman, but incl. رجمة)	63,004

Niş, Ürgüp, Leskofça, Alacahisar, Ujiçe, Çaçka, Sokol, ‏سر ها ع‏

1112H (as above)	4090
1133H (Niş, ve tevabii)	12,100
1153H (as above)	17,500
1202H (only four names listed (Niş, Ürgüp, Leskofça, Alacahisar – but figures suggest that the other four districts are still included)	20,950
1230H (four names, as in 1202H)	22,969

Belgrad ve Tevabii

1112H ('Belgrad, Havale-i hod der liva-i Semendire, ve Sirem – but Sirem is already under Habsburg occupation)	12,000
1130H (as 1112H but incl. Niş, Ürgüp, Leskofça, Alacahisar = 23,000)	10,900
1153H (as above)	20,000
1202H (as above)	19,935
1230H (as above, but without any total offered)	—

Sofya, Şehirköy, Iznepol, Bireznik, Berkofça, Izladi

1112H (as above)	16,300
1130H (as above)	19,500
1153H (as above)	21,509
1202H (minus Şehirköy, listed separately without a total offered, but incl. a new name next to Şehirköy: ‏حاك› سو مان‏)	23,831
1230H (incl. ‏حاك› سو مان‏)	33,620

Bosna ve tevabii

1112H (incl. Hersek, Izvornik)	12,500
1130H (as 1112H, but without Hersek)	39,200
1153H (as above)	63,440
1202H (incl. Hersek, liva-i ‏سلم‏ ‏سرى‏ Seri Selim?)	98,329
1230H (as above)	103,883

Istari Eflak, Yeni Pazar

1112H (minus Yeni Pazar)	600
1202H (as above)	9797
1230H (as above)	10,347

Vidin, Kolotina, Isferlik, Bane, Timok, Feth-i Islam

1112H (as above)	7300
1133H ('Liva-i Vidin' but apparently intending all districts listed above)	16,600
1153H (as above)	21,500
1202H (minus Feth-i Islam)	22,236
1230H (incl. Feth-i Islam, listed separately)	27,792

Trepçe, Morava, Vılçıtırn, Nova Bırda, Yanova-i Kadim, Piriştina ma Lap, Palasniça, Koznik

1112H (minus Morava)	3000
1133H (minus Trepçe, Palasniça)	4700
1153H (as above)	5000
1202H (as above)	8587
1230H (as above)	8363

Iskenderiye, Dukagin, Pirzrin

1112H (as above)	5680
1133H (as above)	14,550
1153H (as above)	14,550
1202H (as above)	16,680
1230H (incl. ود ملی or ود د ملی)	17,429

Near north-eastern zone

Tırnovi, Eski Cuma, Ala Kilise, Osman Bazar

1112H (combined with Niğbolu list)	—
1133H (as above)	13,800
1153H (as above)	14,730
1202H (as above)	14,718
1230H (as above)	16,188

Niğbolu, Pılevna, Hass Kale, Rahova, Lofça ma Etrapoli, Ivraçe

1112H (incl. Tırnovi, Eski Cuma, Ziştovi, Ala Kilise, Rusçuk, Seferköy)	55,335
1133H (as above)	23,175
1153H (as above)	25,880
1202H (incl. Hotaliç)	28,571
1230H (incl. Hotaliç)	32,668

Şumni, Hezargrad, Hotaliç, Yeni Pazar, Umur Fakiye

1112H (as above)	10,785
1133H (as above)	7600
1153H (as above)	8300
1202H (minus Hotaliç)	6810
1230H (minus Hotaliç)	7359

Rusçuk

1112H (included with Niğbolu *et al.*)	—
1133H (as above)	11,900
1153H (as above)	13,575
1202H (as above)	14,385
1230H (as above)	14,405

Ziştovi

1112н (combined with Niğbolu list)	—
1133н	4600
1153н	4400
1202н	5288
1230н	5624

Ahyolu, Aydos, Misivri, Karinabad, Rusikasri, Hatuneli

1112н (divided into two separate groups)	11,168
1133н (as above)	11,512
1153н (as above)	12,100
1202н (as above)	13,444
1230н (as above)	14,060

Ergene

1112н	5300
1133н	5700
1153н	6550
1202н	6731
1230н	7073

Filibe, Tatar Pazarı

1112н (as above)	32,944
1130н (as above)	32,250
1153н (as above)	31,250
1202н (as above)	33,476
1230н (as above)	35,410

Bunar Hisar, Kirk Kilise, Vize, Saray

1112н (as above)	8508
1133н (as above)	7200
1153н (as above)	7270
1202н (as above)	8650
1230н (as above)	9603

Edirne ma tevabii, Havas-i Mahmud Paşa, Cisr-i Mustafa Paşa, Yanbolu, Islimye, Yenice-i Kara Ağaç, Zagra-i Atik, Akçe Kazanlık, Çerpan, Zagra-i Cedid, Çirmen, Uzunca Il Hassköy, Hayribolu, Bergos, Çorlu, Baba-i Atik

1112н (incl. Yanbolu, Islimye, Yenice-i Kara Ağaç, Zagra-i Cedid, separately listed)	53,559
1133н (Total of two separate lists, incl. Çirmen and Uzunca Il Hassköy totals from 1130н)	51,375
1153н (as above)	56,788
1202н (as above)	61,778
1230н (as above)	69,546

Far north-eastern zone

Baba Dağı, Çardak, Mangaliya

1112H (as above)	6400
1133H (as above)	4900
1153H (as above)	5000
1202H (as above)	5050
1230H (minus Mangaliya)	4520

İsakçi

1112H	3134
1133H	5477
1153H	3050
1202H	1861
1230H	3050

İsmail Geçidi

1112H	2665
1130H (incl. İbrail and İsakçi)	8260
1153H	3060
1202H	3060
1230H (no total given)	—

İbrail

1112H	1449
1130H (combined with İsmail Geçidi)	—
1153H	3323
1202H	3533
1230H	3554

Pravadi, Varna, Balçık, Hacıoğlu Pazarı

1112H (as above)	8715
1133H (as above)	8300
1153H (as above)	8000
1202H (as above)	8010
1230H (incl. Mangaliya)	8598

Silistre, Hırsova, Karasu, Tulçi, Maçin

1112H (as above)	15,500
1133H (as above)	12,200
1153H (as above)	12,550
1202H (minus Tulçi)	12,410
1230H (minus Tulçi)	12,410

South-western zone

Inebahtı, Karli Eli

1112H (combined with Yenişehir list)	—
1133H (as above)	18,250
1153H (as above)	19,270
1202H (as above)	20,460
1230H (incl. Olonderek, a separately listed judicial district, usually part of Inebahtı)	20,581

Delvine, Mezarak, Ayadonyat, Kurveles, Debedelen

1112H (minus Debedelen which at this date is included in the Avlonya list)	5900
1133H (as above)	5800
1153H (as above)	5860
1202H (as above)	5920
1230H (as above)	5919

Avlonya, Iskrapar, Goriçe, Belgrad-i Arvanid, ملا قا ص , Müzakiye, İlbasan, İşpat, Silva, Dırac ma مكره or كره, Koriçe, Upar

1112H (minus İşpat, Silva, Diraç, Koriça, Upar which appear on Yenişehir list)	11,241
1130H (as above incl. Premedi listed separately)	12,200
1153H (as above)	11,400
1202H (incl. Premedi)	11,830
1230H (incl. Premedi)	11,830

Ohri (d), Istarova, Akçehisar ma İşem, Dibri, Mat

1112H (combined with Yenişehir list)	—
1130H (minus Mat)	9500
1153H (as above)	6288
1202H (incl. ودعلى , separately listed)	6246
1230H (as above)	5536

Mora ve tevabii

1112H (under Venetian rule)	—
1133H (as above)	78,754
1153H (as above)	70,650
1202H (as above)	62,969
1230H (as above)	61,906

South-eastern zone

Manastir, Florina, Pirlepe, Morihova

1112H (included under Yenişehir list)	—
1133H (as above)	12,680

1153н (as above)	14,500
1202н (as above)	17,404
1230н (as above)	18,934

Atina ve tevabii

1103н (this total is taken from KK 3532)	3500
1133н (as above)	2263
1153н (as above)	2300
1202н (as above)	2689
1230н (as above)	3094

Argalasti

1112н	2102
1133н	2230
1153н	2460
1202н	2732
1230н	3083

Yanya, Girebene ma Vinçe, Koniçe, Narde

1112н (as above)	16,000
1130н (as above)	18,400
1153н (incl. Narde, which is listed separately)	19,800
1202н (incl. Narde, which is listed separately)	22,272
1230н (incl. Narde, which is listed separately)	24,184

Armiya, Velestina

1112н (combined with Yenişehir list)	—
1133н (as above)	3550
1153н (as above)	4071
1202н (incl. Kufos)	4243
1230н (incl. Kufos)	4539

Elasonya, İzdin, Hassköyler-i Yenişehir, Hassköyler-i Izdin

1112н (as above)	4800
1133н (as inferred from Yanya lists)	5320
1153н (as above)	6450
1202н (as above)	7046
1230н (Elasonya, İzdin, Köleler)	7821

Kesriye, Nasliç, Sarıgöl, Cuma Pazarı, Bihlişte, Ergirikasri, Horpişte, Serfice, Egri
Bucak, Ostrova, Kolonya, Pogonya

1112н Kesriye, Horpişte, Nasliç (remainder under Yenisehir)	4977
1133н (as above)	16,300
1153н (as above)	17,525
1202н (incl. Horpişte, listed separately)	20,091
1230н (as above plus Kozane)	21,254

Yenişehir, Tırhala, Çatalca, Pılatomona, Dominik ma ولمشد

1102н (as above, from KK 3531)	30,985
1112н (as above, plus Velestina, Armiya, Manastir, Florina, Pirlepe, Morihova, Köprülü, Serfice, Sarıgöl, Egri Bucak, Ostrova, Cuma Pazari, Koriçe, Upar, Bihlişte, Prespa, Kolonya, Ohri, Dibri, Istarova, Akçehisar ma Işem, Ilbasan, Işpat, Silva, Diraç ma – – –?, Liva-i Inebahtı, Liva-i Karli Eli, Kızılhisar, Olonderek der Liva-i Agriboz)	97,366
1133н (as above)	40,639
1153н (as above)	43,240
1202н (as above, plus Gulos an ifrazi Yenişehir)	49,348
1230н (as above plus Gulos)	50,860

Prespa ve tevabii

1112н (listed with Yenişehir)	—
1133н (as above)	1150
1153н (as above)	1370
1202н (as above)	1100
1230н (as above)	1192

Livadya ve tevabii

1112н (as above)	1901
1133н (as above)	2596
1153н (as above)	3175
1202н (as above)	3447
1230н (as above)	3780

Agriboz, Kızılhisar, Modenç, Istifa, Salona, Esedabad? الاب‍ا or ىاب | ‍ا‍, Talenda

1112н (as above)	10,000
1133н (as above)	11,042
1153н (as above)	—
1202н (minus Istifa)	11,423
1230н (as above)	14,674

Dimetoka, Firecik, Megri

1112н (as above)	7550
1133н (as above)	7500
1153н (as above)	7500
1202н (as above)	8799
1230н (as above)	9772

Gelibolu, Şarköy, Avrasa, Keşan, İpsala, İnoz, Tekfurdaği, Miğalkara, Aynacık

1112н (as above)	17,762
1133н (as above)	18,000
1153н (as above)	19,815

| 1202н (as above) | 22,653 |
| 1230н (as above) | 27,125 |

Gümülcine, Çağlayık, Ahi Çelebi, Yenice-i Karasu

1113н (as above, from KK 3543)	2800
1133н (as above)	3300
1153н (as above)	4095
1202н (as above)	4839
1230н (as above)	4886

Selanik, Avrethisar, Yenice-i Vardar, Vodena, Karaferye, Aganos

1112н (as above)	35,400
1133н (as above)	35,800
1153н (as above)	41,953
1202н (as above)	44,207
1230н (as above)	45,668

Siroz, Timurhisar, Menlik, Karadağ, Zihna, Dırama, Nevrekop, Pravişte, Kavala, Bereketli

1112н (as above)	20,304
1133н (as above)	21,400
1153н (as above)	24,900
1202н (as above)	31,140
1230н (as above)	31,209

Zone totals

(Note: Italic totals incorporate extrapolations)

	NW	NE	FNE	SW	SE	*Total*
c.1112н	94,470	182,199	37,863	321,303[b]		*635,835*
				Combined SW–SE total		
c.1130н	154,670	169,112	33,660	*123,704*	202,170	*683,316*
c.1153н	203,549	180,843	34,893	113,468	224,196	756,949
c.1202н	280,015	*193,851*	33,924	*107,425*	*253,433*	*868,648*
c.1230н	*307,407*[a]	*211,936*	*35,132*[c]	105,772	272,075	*932,322*

[a] includes an extrapolated 20,000 for Belgrad
[b] includes an extrapolated 80,000 for Mora, 3000 for Atina, 3000 for Gümülcine
[c] includes an extrapolated 3000 for İsmail Geçidi

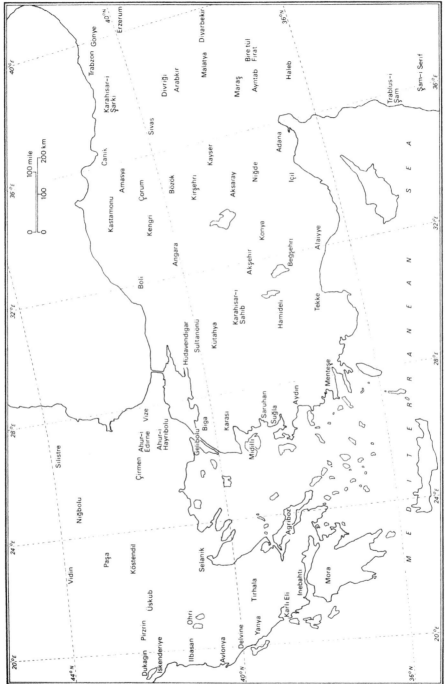

Mpa 14 Provinces of the Ottoman tax house system, 1630–1834 (including Rumeli, Anadolu, eastern Anatolia and Syria)

104

4 ❧ A look at Ottoman fiscal geography: the tax house (avarız–nüzül) system, 1641–1834*

Ottoman *timar* prebendalism rested on two major institutional bases. One was the legal binding of the cultivator to the soil in a manner reminiscent of the late Roman colonate. The other was the *mirî* principle through which the state maintained its claim to eminent domain, by right of conquest, over most cultivated land. The binding institution finally disappeared with the formal abrogation of the *timar* system. But the tradition of eminent domain was never given up.

To protect its right of eminent domain, and at the same time to maintain its control over the prebendal system it had created, the Ottoman state continually exercised a superior right of taxation over all its subjects, including those living on *timars*, and even those living on pious estates. In theory these direct collections were not a threat to *timar* incomes, since these incomes were fixed by patents. But in fact, as direct state collections became excessive in the seventeenth and eighteenth centuries, they partially subverted the *timar* system, and even the pious (*vakıf*) estates, by reducing the cultivators' capacity to pay over to the superior tenant even those dues which were prescribed by law and custom.

The collection of the head or hearth tax known as the *jizye*, sanctioned from the outset by Muslim law, was perhaps the earliest exercise of this right of fiscal interference by the Ottoman state. One other traditional tax, which like the *jizye* was collected for the central treasury on an annual basis, was the tax on sheep, the *adet-i ağnam*. Well before the sixteenth century Ottoman central authorities were also levying other village level taxes and services on an irregular basis. Among these

*Research for this study was done with financial assistance from the Council on Research in Economic History and from the Rackham Grant Program at the University of Michigan, Ann Arbor.

were the *avarız*[1] and, at least from the early sixteenth century onward, the *nüzül*.

Establishment of a system for irregular taxes

One difference between regular and irregular taxes was the method by which they were collected. Instead of falling with equal weight on each household regardless of its size or relative prosperity, the irregular taxes were levied upon tiny fiscal divisions consisting of a few households each, known as *hanes* (hence 'tax houses,' as they are called here). This method introduced a superior degree of equitability by deliberately varying the number of real households in each tiny division according to circumstances which affected their ability to pay. As to the number of real households, or adult males constituting a typical tax house, Ö. L. Barkan has ventured to suggest 3 to 15 married persons, and Mustafa Akdağ 9 adult males.[2] A matching of two almost simultaneous lists found in the records of Manastir (one of them enumerating households for hearth tax purposes, the other enumerating 'tax houses') yields an average of 3.8 real households in each 'tax house,' c. 1640. At Karaferye, in 1734, a more complicated calculation is required since 'tax houses' are there allocated at three different rates for three different categories. There the average number of households to constitute one tax house was 2.7. The average number of *chifts* to constitute one tax house was 2. (Since Karaferye was heavily chiftlicized, the tax authorities were also levying taxes upon *chiftliks* – the unit of measurement for *chiftliks* being the *chift*, a standard holding of about 25 acres of land.) The average number of *haymana* (unregistered, usually landless) households to constitute a tax house was 4.3; obviously a *haymana* household was thought to be less capable of sacrifice than the ordinary household of the villages. As we shall see, the aging of the tax house system in the eighteenth and nineteenth centuries brought changes which would make later estimates progressively doubtful.

In the sixteenth century the *avarız* appears irregularly as a cash tax, whereas the *nüzül*, though formally assigned a value in cash, was for the better part of the century levied mostly in kind – usually barley, or meal needed for a military campaign being planned, or already in progress. The occasions which called for the levying of either tax in that century were much the same; invariably they were military campaigns. In general it was the form of the assistance needed – cash or kind – which determined what the tax would be called. The *avarız* was the surrogate for the *nüzül*, and vice versa, which is why until the late sixteenth century these taxes were levied alternatively, rather than simultaneously, on the same tax houses. If the *nüzül* was proposed, it would fall on some districts as a levy in kind, and perhaps on other districts more distant from the locus of action as the equivalent in cash, as the *avarız*. This convertibility is expressed in a decree of 1579 addressed to the governor of Aleppo. Because of poor harvests in that area an earlier demand for a *nüzül* in kind was converted to an *avarız* in cash (*'avarıza tebdil üzerine'*), cash which was then to be used for the purchase of sacks and for the rental of camels.[3]

No example of the conversion of *avarız* into a *nüzül* has yet been uncovered, probably because the *nüzül* was itself, at certain times and places, a cash tax. The way in which this worked is clear from three *nüzül* registers which remain from the sixteenth century.[4] As is clear from these registers, the collections from the tax houses (which in one of them are referred to as the *'pahahanes'*[5]) are clearly divided with respect to their eventual destinations among various military and household divisions, as well as among fortress garrisons. The cash values of the grain and flour required are consistently recorded in tandem with the quantities required. The reason for this was apparently so that when the needs of the various groups and garrisons for grain or meal had been fully met, the remainder of the *nüzül* could then be collected and delivered in the form of cash. Therefore the *nüzül* was in general a tax in kind but not always, or everywhere. From the same registers it is clear that the judges of each district were the responsible parties for overseeing the collection and delivery of *nüzül* levies in the sixteenth century, although later in the century there are entries in the *mühimme* registers which also show that *sipahis* must have been frequently required to bring their *nüzüls*, i.e. the *nüzüls* of their districts, with them on campaign.[6]

The infrequent appearance in the sixteenth century of the term *bedel-i avarız* (*'avarız* surrogate') in place of *avarız* must be interpreted differently. There is no indication in the earliest evidence on the Ottoman *avarız* that its collection was in any other form but cash. Yet, as Barkan has suggested, the original collections of the *avarız* probably were in kind.[7] The conversion of the *avarız* to a cash tax would have accompanied the rise of the alternative irregular tax to be collected largely in kind – the *nüzül*. By the period in which we first find mention of the *avarız* in the statutes for Karaman (1518) and Aydin (1528–9), the Ottoman *nüzül* also already exists.[8] Therefore the sixteenth-century term *bedel–i avarız* signals a substitution of cash for kind, i.e. a change from the way in which it was originally collected before the advent of the *nüzül*. Later, at the end of the sixteenth century, when the *nüzül* also began to be collected largely as a cash tax, the need was felt for a new term to designate occasional levies of grain: hence the appearance of the *sürsat* so frequently mentioned in the Ottoman records of the seventeenth and eighteenth centuries.[9]

There is scant basis on which to generalize about the relative importance of the *avarız* and the *nüzül* in the sixteenth century. The *avarız* is more noticeable in the provincial statutes but this is because it received explicit mention as the *avarız-i divaniye*, whereas the *nüzül* was subsumed under the term *tekalif-i örfiye* in the common formula for creating partial tax exemptions for service groups and villages: '*avarız-i divaniye ve tekalif-i örfiyeden muafiyet.*'[10] Occasionally, however, the *nüzül* also received explicit mention, as in an exemption formula from the district of Sirem, c. 1570: '*avarız-i divaniye ve tekalif-i örfiye ve nüzül ve jerehor ve sair kara kulluklardan muaf.*'[11] Another, much longer exemption formula for 1543 runs as follows: '*mademki hizmet-i padishahi eda ederler ulakdan ve jerehordan ve doğanjidan ve sekbandan ve arpa ve saman ve otluk* salgınından ve *nüzül tahılından ve hisar yapmasından ve kürekchiden ve azabdan ve biljumle avarız-i divaniye ve tekalif-i örfiyeden muaf ve müsellem olalar.*'[12] The last example is especially interesting since it not only gives a full list of what may be subsumed besides the *nüzül* under the term *tekalif-i örfiye*, but also suggests that not all levies in kind at mid-century were called *nüzül*. The impression left by this sort of formula is that many situations were thought to call for ad hoc solutions, with terminology and classification being of rather little concern, or alternatively, that the *nüzül* may have gone under other, customary names in certain localities where a precedent existed for such collections.

Annualization of the *avarız* and *nüzül* taxes

With the passage of time these two taxes were elevated into the small family of annual direct state taxes. Once they became annual cash taxes, they began to be collected together as the dual components of a merged system which endured through two of the over three centuries through which their linked careers can be followed (i.e. from the 1630s to the 1830s). Four stages to their long term development and interrelationship can be posited on the basis of evidence uncovered so far.

(1)   [Hypothetical] The *avarız* an occasional tax in kind, the *nüzül* non-existent.

(2)   The *avarız* an occasional cash tax, the *nüzül* an occasional tax in kind, collected as alternatives.

(3)   The monetization of the *nüzül* and the introduction of simultaneous collections.

(4)   The annualization of both taxes at established rates and their collection in tandem.

Stages 3 and 4, the transition of the two irregular taxes into the family of annualized cash taxes, took place largely within the framework of the inflation of the period 1585–1625. Drawing on the indices offered by Halil Sahillioğlu and Ö. L. Barkan, both of the Economic History Institute in Istanbul,[13] we see that price levels expressed in *akches* – responding both to the all-European silver inflation and to the Ottoman government's ill-advised efforts to combat inflation by debasing the *akche* – rose swiftly after 1585 before reaching a plateau between 1608 and 1625. *Akche* prices in the plateau period were 2 to 4 times what they had been in 1585. *Akche* prices then moved downward to a more moderate plateau between 1635 and 1655 during which period prices in *akches* were still some two and a half times as high as their 1585 level.

Belatedly, but inevitably, Ottoman governments were forced to make upward adjustments on both sides of the ledger to meet the inflation emergency. Wages and salaries were allowed to move upward so that, for instance, when in the seventeenth century Ali Chavush of Sofia wrote a treatise on the *timar* system, one sees that the minimum *timar* income on the Rumeli side of the empire had moved upward to 6000 *akches*, which was twice the sixteenth-century level.[14] On the revenue side of the ledger one important response is found in the level of *jizye* collected: whereas 75 *akches* is the *jizye* level recorded at Požega upon the accession of Murat III in 1574, by the end of the reign of the warlike Murat IV in 1640 the *jizye* level stood at 333 *akche* in most of the European districts.[15] (In fact the *jizye* had gone on rising even after the inflation had begun to diminish – in 1622 and 1633 the *jizye* level at Manastir stood at 222 *akches* and 232 *akches* respectively.[16]

Of at least equal importance to the upward adjustment of the *jizye*, with respect to its impact upon the *reaya*, was the monetization of the *nüzül*, its definite linkage to the *avarız*, and the annualization of their collections at rates which were *10 to 15 times as high* as the mid-sixteenth-century rates. Whereas in the mid-sixteenth century typical *avarız* rates were 30 or 40 *akches* per tax house (as were *nüzül* rates when monetized), by the time they had both reached formal stability in the mid-seventeenth century the formal *avarız* level was 325 *akches* per tax house, the *nüzül* 600.

In the transition to a merged and stabilized system the *avarız* led the way, being the first to be annualized and the first (by 1622 at the latest) to reach its long term stabilized level.[17] The *nüzül* appears to have followed a more irregular course. Pressures brought about by the long war with Austria from 1593 to 1606, exacerbating pressures already created by the swift inflationary escalation after 1585, resulted in *nüzül* rates which in places quickly reached what was to be their eventual long term level of about 600 *akches* per tax house, as, for instance, at Güzelhisar in 1598–9.[18] Most *nüzül* collections seem in this period to have been collected in cash. But *nüzül* collections in kind continued to appear as an alternative throughout the seventeenth century. In the reign of Murat IV the cash level of the *nüzül* was still unsteady. In 1634 a decree registered at Manastir informs us that the *nüzül* for that year shall be collected at the rate of 300 *akches* from each tax house (here called *avarızhanes*) and that because of war needs the *nüzül* will be accompanied by another special collection of 80 *akches* per *hane*. (Since the campaign was far to the east the treasury wanted cash.)[19] In 1636 Murat proposed a *nüzül* which was apparently thought unbearable: an earlier decree for that year requiring twelve *gurush* per tax house was rescinded and replaced by a new decree authorizing a collection of five *gurush*, which at 80 *akches* per *gurush* would yield 400 *akches*.[20] But by the end of Murat's reign the *nüzül* was well on the way to being annualized, like the *avarız*, and stabilized at the formal level of 600 *akches* per tax house, though Barkan gives several examples in the 1630s and 1640s of what are apparently *nüzül* collections of 1000 *akches* and over.[21]

The descriptive potential of the tax house records

The historical interest of *avarız–nüzül* combination is not simply a matter of the importance of these two taxes within total imperial revenues.[22] The greater interest for the historian lies in the 'tax house' system of allocation and in the administration of that system. Since tax houses were set up in such a way as to reflect the demographic and economic strength of the villages of each district through the uniform application of universal criteria, the district subtotals can be used by the historian as a rough indicator – at least until better indicators are developed – of the relative economic importance of the districts included in the system. Moreover with respect to their movement over a long period the pattern of change observed in tax house totals must reveal something about economic or demographic changes in the districts to which they refer.

Although there are some puzzling aspects about the pattern with which tax house totals changed, these changes nonetheless have a story to tell, a story which should become increasingly comprehensible as other data are brought to bear. Fiscal geography can hardly be unrelated to human geography in an agrarian society.

Unfortunately provincial subtotals survive in archival records on a continuous basis only after about the mid-seventeenth century. However, from about 1640 onward on the European side, and from about 1650 onward on the Anadolu side (Anadolu meaning here what is now western Anatolia) a virtually unbroken stream of registers survives in the Kâmil Kepeci and Maliyeden Müdevver sections of Istanbul's Prime Minister's Archive, which offer an orderly view of the distribution of the *avarız–nüzül* system as a whole during its seventeenth-century apogee and during its long decline, ending about 1833–4.[23] One cannot be certain that this remarkable series of registers is not truncated and that many earlier registers will not in time be discovered in the Istanbul archive's less-explored warehouses; however the irregular order of entries and incompleteness observed in the earliest registers in this series is quickly succeeded by much greater uniformity, so that the impression given is that the series was initiated more or less simultaneously with the completion of the annualization and stabilization of the *nüzül* and its long term coupling with the *avarız* (stage 4 above, see the accompanying tables). The registers in this continuous series contain either tax house totals for the entire system on *one* side of the Bosporus, most often for Rumeli (the European side) or else contain totals on *both* sides of the Bosporus, revealing a system which stretched from the Bosnian border and the Danube all the way to Damascus. The sequence of the provinces as they appear in the registers is largely fixed. There are three large divisions, each with its components in much the same order from one register to another: Rumeli, Anadolu (western Anatolia), and the Eyalat-i Saire (eastern Anatolia and Syria). Obviously the system did not encompass the entire empire since peripheral areas are excluded: everything north of the Danube, Bosnia, and all the Arab provinces except Syria. The reader will note from the table that an exceptional register or two does exist which encompasses the Hungarian districts; these were apparently generated in a moment of great desperation, since Hungary was not part of the regular system. A decree of 1595 to the Bosnian governor makes it clear that Bosnia, because of its position facing the enemy border, was to be exempted from the *avarız–nüzül* system, as well as from other irregular taxes applied in the central provinces.[24] It would appear that all irregular taxes were levied more frequently, if not exclusively, away from the border zones. The numbers of tax houses which are occasionally encountered in these registers for the central cities – Istanbul, Edirne and Bursa – are so low that it can be said that the central cities are effectually excluded from the system, or only included under different criteria, so that they are also excluded from the tables on tax house totals which follow.

In contrast to registers summarizing tax house totals for the entire system there also survive from the seventeenth century a number of more detailed registers pertaining to only one province or even less. These detailed registers played a key role in the seventeenth and eighteenth centuries in determining who was to be regarded as *reaya* and therefore subject to the laws which bound the *reaya* to their place of registry, and who was not so regarded.[25] To be registered in one of these detailed '*avarız*' registers as tied to a particular tax house meant to be bound to the place, so that registers of this sort were the chief written

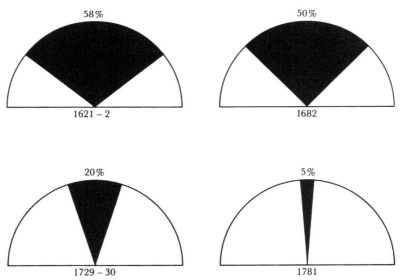

Figure 7 Proportion of the *avarız–nüzül* within total collections in the Manastir district of western Macedonia

evidence considered by the local judge when such an identification was at issue.[26] Because *tahrir* (survey) registers were so seldom drawn up in the centuries following the sixteenth, it is these detailed tax house registers therefore which offer the best opportunity to follow demographic and other changes in a particular province. It is to be expected that subsequent studies attempting to follow a single province over a period of centuries will begin with survey registers and, in lieu of later surveys, will then exploit these detailed tax house registers when they are available for the same province.

Generally speaking, there is almost no difference between the total of *nüzül* 'houses' shown in tax house registers and the total of *avarız* 'houses' shown since the two units were identical, as is seen in the phrase '*nüzül* and *avarız* house' found in a justice decree of 1609.[27] Occasionally a slight difference in their numbers is found, as in the Manastir district, where a part of the local tax houses have been exempted from regular *nüzül* payments, but not regular *avarız* payments, in return for their obligatory delivery of something badly wanted by the government, as in this case saltpetre used in making gunpowder. But over the long run, and for the system as a whole, the *avarız–nüzül* tax house and the *nüzül* tax house may be accepted as virtually identical entities.

The importance of the contribution of the *avarız–nüzül* tax combination to imperial revenues can be grasped from Figure 8 based on figures culled from the local judicial registers of Manastir, in western Macedo-

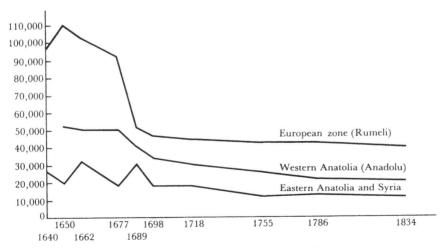

Figure 8   Number of tax houses in three Ottoman zones, 1640–1834

nia. At Manastir the proportion of the combined *avarız–nüzül* tax load within total direct tax collections in this district in 1621–2 was fully 58 per cent, in 1633–4 about 36 per cent, 1662–3 again back to 56 per cent, in 1682 around 50 per cent, in 1729 only 20 per cent, and in 1781 a mere 5 per cent.[28] Thus from being a very important tax in the seventeenth century, the *avarız–nüzül* combination was allowed to decline to insignificance in the eighteenth, pushed aside by burgeoning provincial levies.[29]

Tables 2, 3, and 4 (following) reveal the descriptive potential of the tax house system itself, the spatial distribution of implied economic and demographic strength throughout the European and Asiatic provinces. Among the most obvious features of the tables constructed from the tax house registers is the relative importance of the European provinces in contributing to total tax house revenues (see Fig. 8 and Table 2).[30] Since each tax house was supposed to be capable of bearing a burden equal to that of all the others, the preponderant number of tax houses on the European (Rumeli) side of the Bosporus implies either a greater degree of prosperity or a denser population, or both. Also interesting is the proportionate contribution of certain provinces as, for instance on the European side, the heavy preponderance of Pasha province and of Morea among the other provinces.

We are left to wonder at the swift fall in the overall number of tax houses in the period 1650–1700, particularly on the European (Rumeli) side. Surely the fall in total tax houses accords with the demographic trough implied by comparing the eighteenth-century head tax figures for Ottoman Europe with population estimates of the sixteenth and nineteenth centuries. Is not this pattern what we would expect to find during a period of severe population loss? Even if we hypothesize that the average size of the tax house was allowed to grow, we must then explain why the European totals fall so much further and faster. Also puzzling is the fact that figures for the most heavily chiftlicized zones of the latter seventeenth century – Thessaly (Tirhala) and Salonica (Selanik) – fell the furthest. What does this imply?

Appendix: Statistical digest of the tax house system of Ottoman Europe, 1641–1834

Table 1: *Avarızhane* (AH) and *bedel-i nüzül* (BN)
registers housed at the Prime Minister's Archive (Istanbul)

[Symbols: Kâmil Kepecı classification = KK; Maliyeden Müdevver classification = MM;
registers used for this study = *; Rumeli and Anadolu = R/A; Rumeli only = R/. *Liva* scale
registers are omitted from this list.]

H Year	General no.	Type	H Year	General no.	Type
1029	MM2447	(AH) R/A (incomplete)	1068	MM3187	(AH) R/
1036	MM3096	(AH) R/	1069	MM3855	(BN) R/
1038	MM3831	(AH) R/	1070	MM3810	(AH) R/A
1038	MM15972	(AH) R/A	1073	MM3157	(AH) R/
1041	MM7176	(AH) R/	1073*	KK2635	(AH) R/A
1046	MM2786	(AH) R/	1075	MM2783	(AH) Budun,
1049	MM3839	(AH) R/			Bosna, Temişvar, *et al*.
1051*	MM3845	(AH) R/A	1078	MM3352	(AH) Budun,
1051	MM3093	(AH) R/			Egri, Temişvar, Sirem, *et al*.
1053	MM2604	(AH) R/	1078	MM3874	(AH) R/
1055	MM2808	(AH) R/A	1079	MM3350	(AH) R/A
1056	KK2613	(BN) R/A	1079	MM15973	(AH) R/
1057	KK2614	(AH) R/	1080	MM3382	(AH) R/A
1058	MM3832	(AH) R/	1080	KK2651	(AH) R/A
1058	MM2907	(AH) R/	1081	KK2653	(AH) R/A
1059	MM3835	(AH) R/	1081	KK252	(AH/BN) R/A
1060*	KK2618	(BN) R/A	1081	MM16118	(AH/BN) R/A
1060	MM4950	(AH) R/	1081	MM3834	(AH) R/A
1061	MM1980	(AH) R/A	1081	MM3003	(AH) R/A
1061	MM2787	(AH) R/A	1082	KK2654	(BN) ?
1062	MM3844	(AH) R/	1082	MM2790	(AH) R/A
1064	MM2989	(AH) R/	1083	KK2657	(BN) R/A
1064	KK2621	(AH) R/	1083	MM2412	(AH) R/
1064	MM7120	(AH) R/A	1084	MM3354	(AH) R/
1065	KK2623	(AH) R/	1084	KK2659	(AH) R/A
1066	MM16215	(AH/BN) R/	1085	MM2505	(AH) R/
1066	MM16120	(AH/BN) R/	1085	KK2662	(BN) R/A
1066	MM3847	(AH) R/	1085	MM1487	(AH/BN) R/A
1067	MM3850	(AH) R/A	1086	KK2668	(BN) R/A
1068	MM2749	(AH) R/A	1086	KK2665	(AH) R/A
1068	KK2627	(AH) R/	1088*	MM3837	(AH) R/A

115

Table 1 continued

н Year	General no.	Type	н Year	General no.	Type
1088	MM3841	(AH) R/	1133	MM3964	(AH) R/
1088	KK2681	(BN/AH) R/	1133	MM2761	(AH) R/A
1089	MM3809	(AH) R/	1134	MM3828	(AH) R/
1089	KK2688	(BN/AH) R/A	1134	MM3209	(AH/BN) R/
1091	MM3830	(AH) R/A	1135	MM3970	(AH) R/
1095	MM2414	(AH) R/	1135	MM2757	(AH) R/A
1095	MM3852	(AH) R/A	1136	MM3822	(AH) R/
1096	MM2446	(AH) R/	1137	MM2978	(AH) R/
1097	MM3231	(AH) R/	1138	MM2501	(AH) R/
1097	MM2805	(AH) R/A	1138	KK2877	(BN) R/A
1098	MM3839	(AH) R/	1139	MM3151	(AH) R/
1100*	MM3167	(AH) R/	1140	MM2472	(AH) R/
1100	KK2728	(BN) R/A	1141	KK2878	(AH) R/A
1100	MM3318	(AH) R/	1143	MM2504	(AH) R/
1102	MM16085	(AH/BN) R/A	1144	KK2885	(BN) R/A
1103	MM3152	(AH) R/	1145	MM2502	(AH) R/
1103	KK2744	(AH/BN) R/A	1146	MM2788	(AH) R/
1103	MM2793	(AH) R/A	1146	MM2796	(AH) R/A
1104	MM2471	(AH) R/	1148	KK2892	(AH) R/A
1106	KK2766	(AH) R/A	1149	MM3871	(AH) R/
1106	KK2762	(BN(R/A	1150	MM3815	(AH) R/
1106	MM9480	(AH) R/	1151	MM3015	(AH) R/
1106	MM2987	(AH) R/A	1151	MM1985	(AH) R/A
1107	MM2500	(AH) R/A	1152	MM3825	(AH) R/
1107	MM3829	(AH) R/	1152	MM5548	(AH) R/A
1108	MM3807	(AH) R/	1154	MM2993	(AH) R/A
1110	MM5330	(AH) R/A	1154	KK2902	(BN) R/A
1110	MM3974	(AH) R/	1155	MM2879	(AH) R/
1111	MM3820	(AH) R/	1155	MM15630	(AH) R/A
1111*	MM3204	(AH) R/A	1155	MM3092	(AH) R/A
1112	MM3826	(AH) R/	1156	MM3219	(AH) R/
1113	MM2779	(AH/BN) R/A	1156	KK2904	(BN) R/A
1113	MM3091	(AH) R/	1157	MM3817	(AH) R/
1114	KK2807	(AH) R/A	1159	MM3153	(AH) R/
1115	MM2412	(AH) R/A	1160	MM6486	(AH/BN) R/
1116	MM3833	(AH) R/	1160	MM2887	(AH) R/
1117	KK2819	(BN) R/A	1161	MM2890	(AH) R/
1118	MM3808	(AH) R/	1162	MM3972	(AH) R/
1118	MM3846	(AH) R/	1163	MM2863	(AH) R/
1118	MM1984	(AH) R/	1164	MM2855	(AH) R/
1123	MM3811	(AH) R/	1164	KK2914	(BN) R/A
1124	MM3155	(AH) R/	1165	MM2875	(AH) R/
1124	KK2842	(BN) R/A	1166	MM20957	(AH/BN) R/A
1124	MM3199	(AH) R/A	1167	MM3148	(AH) R/
1124	MM3843	(AH) R/A	1167	MM19323	(AH/BN) R/A
1125	KK2845	(BN) R/A	1168*	MM3816	(AH) R/A
1125	MM2470	(AH) R/A	1168	MM2741	(AH) R/A
1127	MM3823	(AH) R/	1169	KK2919	(BN) R/A
1127	KK2852	(BN) R/A	1170	MM2892	(AH) R/
1128	MM3812	(AH) R/	1171	MM3158	(AH) R/
1128	MM3818	(AH) R/	1172	MM2988	(AH) R/A
1129	MM2984	(AH) R/	1172	MM3980	(AH) R/
1130*	MM2759	(AH) R/	1173	KK2922	(AH) R/A

Table 1 continued

H Year	General no.	Type		H Year	General no.	Type
1174	MM3067	(AH) R/		1190	MM2991	(AH) R/
1174	KK2923	(AH) R/A		1192	MM2890	(AH) R/
1174	MM3973	(AH) R/		1194	MM5661	(AH) R/
1175	MM6426	(AH/BN) R/A		1194	MM2983	(AH) R/
1176	MM2888	(AH) R/		1195	MM1959	(AH) R/A
1178	MM3968	(AH) R/		1195	MM2712	(AH) R/
1180	MM3813	(AH) R/A		1196	MM4119	(AH) R/
1180	MM3819	(AH) R/		1197	MM2800	(AH) R/A
1181	MM2797	(AH) R/		1199	MM3824	(AH) R/A
1182	MM2986	(AH) R/		1199	KK2948	(AH) R/
1183	MM2852	(AH) R/		1200*	MM2891	(AH) R/
1184	MM2981	(AH) R/		1201	MM2802	(AH) R/
1185	MM2992	(AH) R/A		1203	MM2884	(AH) R/
1185	MM1961	(AH) R/A		1204	MM2746	(AH) R/
1186	MM2803	(AH) R/A		1210	MM2503	(AH) R/A
1187	MM2861	(AH) R/		1212	MM19252	(BN) R/A
1188	MM2436	(AH) R/		1213	MM2801	(AH) R/A
1188	KK2937	(AH) R/A		1234	KK2972	(BN) R/A
1189	KK2939	(AH) R/A		1249*	MM2872	(AH) R/

Note: Those who have not used the Istanbul Archives should be warned that registers and documents do not always conform in reality to their descriptions in the catalogs. The writer does not guarantee that each of the registers listed here is accurately described; except for those used in the study, he has relied on the catalogs in compiling this list.

Table 2: The *avarızhanes* of Rumeli by hijri year and by *liva*

[The number of judicial districts (*kazas*) into which each *liva* is divided appears in parentheses after the number of *avarızhanes*. Those *kazas* which are for one reason or another exempt from the system are indicated separately following the total number of *kazas* in that *liva*, e.g. (36/4).]

	1051 (1640)	1060 (1650)	1073 (1662)	1088 (1677)	1100 (1688)	1109 (1698)	1130 (1718)	1168 (1755)	1200 (1786)	1249 (1834)
Paşa	24,713 (31)	26,185 (37)	24,912 (44)	23,763 (43)	17,251 (31)	11,223 (35)	14,613 (36)	10,269 (36/4)	10,082 (36/4)	10,762 (36/2)
Vize	58 (2)	702 (8)	812 (8)	812 (8)	166 (4)	153 (4)	365 (4)	212 (4/2)	214 (4/2)	214 (4/2)
Cirmen	477 (1)	2,109 (6)	1,951 (5)	1,735 (4)	857 (1)	800 (1)	785 (1)	734 (2)	613 (1)	612 (2/1)
Köstendil	5,967 (12)	4,582 (12)	4,168 (12)	3,818 (12)	3,580 (12)	1,947 (10)	1,623 (12)	2,409 (12)	2,447 (12)	2,361 (14)
Üsküb	4,925 (5)	4,350 (5)	4,066 (6)	3,700 (6)	1,682 (6)	1,274 (6)	1,078 (6)	1,155 (5)	1,154 (6)	1,187 (6/1)
Agrıboz	2,645 (6)	4,485 (12)	4,125 (14)	4,096 (14)	1,249 (7)	1,292 (7)	1,348 (12)	1,391 (12)	1,364 (12)	—
Tırhala	6,976 (8)	11,323 (8)	9,506 (8)	9,999 (8)	4,440 (8)	2,790 (8)	2,344 (8)	2,299 (8)	2,439 (8)	2,439 (8/1)
Avlonya	2,426 (6)	3,565 (8)	3,023 (9)	2,374 (9)	1,529 (9)	1,794 (9)	1,686 (9)	1,144 (9)	1,144 (8)	1,603 (9)
Delvine	2,062 (6)	1,940 (3)	2,017 (4)	1,097 (4)	1,043 (4)	738 (4)	922 (4)	586 (4)	571 (4)	571 (4/1)
Selanik	5,884 (5)	5,827 (6)	5,817 (6)	4,844 (6)	3,335 (6)	1,722 (6)	2,830 (6)	1,780 (6)	1,761 (6)	3,606 (6)
Niğbolu	3,509 (10)	7,524 (15)	7,119 (16)	7,111 (15)	3,538 (9)	3,493 (9)	2,249 (9)	2,903 (15/1)	5,146 (15/1)	5,129 (15/1)
Silistre	549 (6)	6,399 (28)	5,849 (25)	5,291 (26)	294 (6)	394 (6)	565 (6)	2,817 (20/2)	2,773 (20/2)	2,692 (20/2)
Yanya	4,529 (8)	4,398 (6)	3,606 (5)	4,024 (5)	2,547 (6)	2,823 (5)	2,442 (5)	1,900 (6/1)	1,491 (5/1)	1,566 (6)
İlbasan	836 (5)	872 (5)	939 (5)	704 (5)	699 (5)	778 (5)	747 (5)	741 (5)	741 (5)	741 (5)
Karli Eli	2,612 (6)	2,612 (6)	2,163 (6)	1,855 (6)	1,388 (6)	1,388 (6)	841 (6)	751 (6/1)	633 (6)	—
İnebahtı	1,109 (6)	1,331 (6)	1,325 (6)	1,321 (6)	1,298 (6)	1,298 (6)	963 (6)	675 (6/1)	353 (6/2)	—
Ohri	2,448 (6)	2,132 (6)	2,069 (6)	2,090 (6)	1,385 (5)	1,386 (5)	1,476 (5)	992 (6/2)	999 (6/3)	—
Pirzrin	818 (4)	996 (6)	995 (6)	995 (6)	995 (6)	995 (6)	626 (6)	955 (6)	955 (6)	955 (6)
Dukakin							306 (2)	306 (2)	306 (2)	306 (2)
İskenderiye	1,013 (4)	998 (4)	826 (4)	837 (4)	837 (4)	837 (4)	540 (2)	590 (2)	250 (2)	250 (2/1)
Midilli	2,456 (3)	2,450 (3)	2,456 (3)	—	2,456 (3)	2,454 (3)	—	—	—	—
Vidin		1,609 (5)	1,588 (5)	1,589 (5)	227 (4)	1,589 (5)	—	—	—	—
Mora	18,066 (17)	11,545 (17)	11,194 (23)	9,984 (23)	831 (4)	—	—	3,422 (26/4)	3,049 (27/4)	—
Kefe	2,678 (4)	3,068 (8)	2,574 (8)	—	1,490 (2)	811 (4)	801 (5)	811 (5/1)	(5)	—
Gelibolu								415 (4)	415 (4)	298 (4/3)
Ahur-i Edirne						2,228 (10)	3,016 (10)	2,848 (11)	2,547 (12/1)	2,849 (11)
Ahur-i Hayrıbolu						728 (6)	746 (6)	630 (5)	575 (5)	608 (5)
Ahur-i Yanbolu						770 (6)	870 (6)	604 (5)	592 (5)	592 (5)
Ahur-i Zagora						872 (4)	613 (4)	—	841 (4)	841 (4)
Totals	96,756 (159)	110,901 (220)	103,100 (234)	92,274 (221)	53,122 (154)	46,498 (180)	44,426 (181)	43,345 (228)	43,455 (232)	40,182 (185)

Table 3: The *avarizhanes* of Anadolu (western Anatolia)

[The number of *kazas* into which each *eyalet* or *liva* is divided appears in parentheses after the number of *avarizhanes*. Those *kazas* exempted from the system are indicated separately following the total number of *kazas* in that *liva*, e.g (36/4).]

	1060 (1650)	1073 (1662)	1088 (1677)	1100 (1688)	1109 (1698)	1130 (1718)	1168 (1755)	1200 (1786)	1249 (1834)
Aydın	8,059 (20)	6,825 (20)	5,100 (20)	4,731 (19)	4,107 (19)	3,560 (19)	2,840 (19)	2,100 (18/3)	2,499 (19/5)
Saruhan	4,355 (16)	4,823 (16)	4,462 (14)	3,534 (16)	3,358 (16)	2,644 (16)	2,258 (17)	1,899 (16/5)	1,899 (22/4)
Menteşe	5,333 (32)	4,797 (33)	3,670 (32)	3,306 (32)	3,024 (32)	2,817 (32)	2,769 (32)	2,473 (35/2)	2,474 (29)
Suğla	4,721 (9)	2,853 (9)	4,195 (9)	3,840 (9)	3,348 (9)	2,670 (9)	2,595 (8)	1,844 (8)	2,293 (9)
Hamideli	1,749 (21)	1,591 (21)	1,758 (21)	1,908 (21)	1,773 (21)	1,733 (21)	1,753 (21)	1,753 (21)	1,746 (21)
Karasi	2,526 (10)	2,425 (10)	2,358 (10)	2,203 (10)	2,126 (10)	1,926 (10)	1,913 (9)	1,664 (11)	—
Biga	1,381 (8)	1,355 (8)	1,357 (9)	1,319 (8)	881 (9)	913 (8)	899 (9)	895 (9)	895 (9)
Tekke	1,132 (8)	1,142 (8)	1,142 (8)	1,142 (8)	1,162 (8)	968 (7)	938 (8)	938 (8)	938 (8)
Alaiyye	323 (5)	327 (5)	325 (5)	320 (5)	320 (5)	316 (5)	318 (5)	317 (6)	317 (5)
Kütahya	4,166 (27)	4,177 (27)	4,107 (26)	3,587 (24)	3,308 (26)	3,154 (24)	2,676 (28)	2,654 (26/5)	2,642 (26)
Hüdavendigar (minus Bursa)	4,180 (23)	4,204 (21)	3,888 (21)	3,729 (20)	3,255 (21)	2,206 (23)	1,121 (21)	1,121 (21/9)	1,005 (5)
Karahisar-i Sahib		806 (10)	810 (10)	873 (10)	836 (11)	698 (10)	679 (10)	679 (10/2)	—
Angara	1,499 (9)	1,509 (9)	1,613 (9)	1,562 (9)	1,356 (9)	1,273 (9)	1,274 (10)	1,274 (10/2)	—
Sultanönü	547 (5)	550 (5)	581 (5)	556 (5)	450 (5)	465 (5)	—	(5)	—
Kengri	1,280 (17)	1,204 (17)	5,020 (17)	1,139 (17)	1,070 (17)	1,003 (17)	927 (17)	925 (17/1)	925 (17)
Boli	6,838 (33)	7,234 (33)	6,347 (33)	3,729 (34)	2,167 (34)	2,003 (34)	1,364 (36)	— (36/9)	1,248 (36/3)
Kastamonu	4,428 (32)	4,562 (32)	4,559 (32)	4,211 (32)	2,159 (34)	2,024 (34)	2,036 (39)	2,025 (34)	2,025 (34/2)
Totals	52,519 (275)	50,384 (284)	51,292 (281)	41,689 (279)	34,700 (288)	30,373 (283)	26,360 (289)	22,561 (291)	20,906 (240)

Table 4: The *avarızhanes* of eastern Anatolia and Ottoman Syria

[The number of *kazas* into which each *vilayet* or *liva* is divided appears in parentheses after the number of *avarızhanes*. Those *kazas* exempted from the system are indicated separately following the total number of *kazas* indicated for that *eyalet* or *liva*, e.g. (36/4).]

	1051 (1640)	1060 (1650)	1073 (1662)	1088 (1677)	1100 (1688)	1109 (1698)	1130 (1718)	1168 (1755)	1200 (1786)	1249 (1834)
Sivas	682 (21)	1,550 (20)	1,447 (20)	1,438 (20)	1,410 (20)	1,247 (20)	1,194 (20)	1,196 (20)	1,198 (20/4)	1,193 (20/1)
Amasya	583 (11)	1,195 (10)	703 (10)	674 (10)	632 (9)	558 (9)	373 (10)	373 (10)	373 (10/3)	311 (10/2)
Çorum	328 (8)	389 (9)	377 (9)	372 (9)	356 (9)	280 (8)	278 (8)	278 (8)	278 (8/5)	287 (8/2)
Bozok	287 (8)	372 (9)	322 (9)	321 (9)	321 (9)	171 (9)	(9)	(9)	(9)	—
Canik	330 (10)	349 (10)	206 (10)	346 (10)	346 (10)	346 (10)				
Arabkir	234 (2)	311 (2)	279 (2)	279 (2)	272 (2)	180 (2)	138 (2)	138 (2)	135 (2)	126 (2)
Divriği	128 (2)	180 (2)	184 (2)	184 (2)	184 (2)	168 (2)	149 (2)	149 (2)	149 (2)	149 (2)
Konya	656 (10)	911 (10)	821 (10)	820 (10)	810 (10)	723 (10)	324 (10)	199 (10)	199 (10/4)	179 (10/4)
Niğde	445 (6)	544 (8)	404 (5)	—	408 (5)	470 (5)	514 (7)	376 (7)	355 (6/1)	355 (7/1)
Beğşehri	420 (6)	492 (6)	485 (6)	485 (6)	482 (6)	471 (6)	462 (6)	461 (6)	462 (6)	66 (6/5)
Akşehir	269 (4)	—	385 (4)	384 (4)	374 (4)	171 (4)	336 (4)	43 (4)	43 (4/3)	(4/4)
Kayseri	372 (2)	409 (2)	511 (2)	463 (4)	499 (2)	451 (4)	419 (4)	331 (2)	328 (2)	315 (3)
Aksaray	91 (2)	259 (3)	253 (3)	253 (3)	230 (3)	227 (3)	221 (3)	179 (3)	179 (3/1)	171 (3)
Kırşehri	181 (5)	182 (5)	184 (5)	185 (5)	185 (5)	143 (5)	141 (5)	139 (5)	132 (5)	132 (5)
İçil	201 (9)	201 (12)	211 (12)	201 (12)	201 (12)	201 (12)	309 (12)	290 (12)	290 (12/1)	290 (12)
Adana	466 (9)	472 (9)	503 (6)	474 (9)	468 (7)	443 (6)			(8)	(8)
Trablus-i Şam	1,059 (15)	1,058 (15)	1,058 (15)	1,100 (15)	1,058 (15)	1,060 (15)			1,060 (15)	
Şam-i Şerif	9,520 (11)	—	13,236 (9)	—	7,974 (9)	4,307 (8)	4,411 (8)			
Haleb	4,471 (14)	4,458 (14)	4,817 (14)	4,136 (14)	7,894 (18)		2,789 (14)	2,797 (15)	2,756 (14)	2,756 (14/4)
Bire 'tül Fırat	114 (3)	413 (3)	425 (3)	425 (4)	425 (4)	425 (4)	326 (4)			
Maraş	679 (4)	676 (4)	611 (4)	611 (4)	611 (4)	523 (4)	522 (4)	408 (4)	408 (4)	408 (7)
Malatya	1,012 (7)	1,016 (7)	967 (7)	229 (7)	960 (7)	919 (7)	919 (7)	919 (7)	919 (7)	919 (7)
Ayntab	510 (2)	505 (2)	503 (2)	503 (2)	503 (2)	487 (2)	381 (2)	372 (2)	372 (2)	382 (2)
Diyarbekir	2,565 (17)	2,929 (22)	2,814 (22)	2,813 (21)	2,045 (16)	2,032 (16)	2,016 (16)	1,808 (16)	1,808 (16)	1,808 (16/2)
Erzerum	920 (14)	1,041 (12)	835 (13)	811 (13)	775 (13)	686 (13)	507 (14)	493 (15)	490 (14)	487 (16)
Karahisar-i Şarki	625 (13)	757 (15)	739 (15)	735 (15)	735 (15)	725 (15)	644 (14)	637 (15)	644 (15)	
Trabzon	625 (9)	622 (9)	—	580 (9)	512 (10)	512 (10)	452 (10)	389 (11)	389 (11)	389 (12)
Gönye					89 (4)	89 (4)	89 (4)		(4)	—
Totals	27,773 (224)	21,291 (220)	33,280 (219)	18,822 (219)	30,759 (232)	18,015 (213)	18,490 (205)	11,975 (185)	12,967 (209)	10,723 (166)

5 ❧ *Chiftlik* agriculture and fiscal practice in western Macedonia, 1620–1830*

The four preceding chapters have concentrated on various circumstances surrounding the trend toward commercialized agriculture in south-eastern Europe, and have offered a theoretical framework for studying and quantifying that overall trend. This chapter satisfies a keenly felt need to provide as much detail as possible on that trend in agriculture at one locality, in this case the judicial district of Manastir (today's Bitolj, or Bitola) in western Macedonia. Two special circumstances recommend Manastir as a zone to be studied. First, there is the fact that *chiftlik* agriculture was rather well developed there; the Ç/H ratio for this district was at or near 0.6 throughout the eighteenth century.[1] Secondly, Manastir was the single locality of the Balkans for which there still survives a complete (or almost complete) series of judicial records (*sijils*) which could yield, if not all the information desired on this subject, then certainly a great deal.

Examining the voluminous records of Manastir, the reader's attention is quickly captured on the one hand, by the striking connection between the rise of *chiftliks* in this judicial district (*kaza*), and on the other the evolution of fiscal and administrative practices intended to cope with their rise. It seems likely that judicial records surviving from other Ottoman districts where *chiftlik* formation became a problem from a local administrative point of view will also contain evidence of shifts in fiscal and administrative practices intended as compensating devices to deal with the shrinking tax base caused by the rise of the latterday *chiftliks*. Therefore, although the present study has a limited scope, and deals with a single judicial district in western Macedonia, it

*Research for this study was funded by the International Research Exchange (IREX, New York). This organization also provided indispensable help in arranging for an extended period of study at the Macedonian National Archives at Skopje. I owe thanks to the Archive personnel, and also for their advice and hospitality to my colleagues in Skopje at the National History Institute.

121

is to be expected that many of its chief findings will have precise or proximate parallels in other districts of the aging empire.

The term *chiftlik* is used here with a special meaning. No single definition for this term exists since it was employed in several ways in Ottoman usage, with meanings which generally can be differentiated by reference to the period to which they pertain and the context in which they appear. The reader will understand from what has already been said that the term *chiftlik*, as used here, can be taken to mean an arable holding, sometimes extensive, which is being cultivated to produce a commodity which is readily saleable in near or distant markets. The *reaya* of every period was wont to sell something – often livestock – at a local market, if for no other reason than to raise the cash to pay his annual head tax and to pay other incidental cash taxes. But the latter-day *chiftlik* dealt with here was devoted to a single crop – a monoculture – which would be marketed to obtain a profit, not for the cultivator, but for another individual, one who held a legal or at least technically defensible claim upon the land worked by the cultivator, a claim distinct in character from the tradition and limited prebendal rights inherent in the traditional and moribund *timar* system. Here then are the key properties of the term *chiftlik* as used in this study: (1) a tendency to monoculture aimed at the market, and (2) a claim resembling ownership over the arable land constituting the *chiftlik* enjoyed by a person other than the cultivator, a claim distinct from that of the *timarlı* (i.e. the traditional prebendal cavalryman). No precise criterion of size is intended, primarily because the *sijils* themselves do not use the term in such a way as to differentiate between large *chiftliks* and small ones. An ad hoc criterion of size would perhaps be conceivable; but a criterion which shut out the smaller *chiftlik* (as defined above) would be shutting out a large part of what became typical on the late Ottoman rural scene.

The need for a revised view of the Macedonian *chiftlik*

Macedonia has often been labeled as the classic *chiftlik* zone. This is partly due to the intensity of *chiftlik* formation in that part of the Ottoman world. But the label also reflects the fact that Macedonia remained in Ottoman hands until the Balkan Wars and thus offered latterday diplomatic observers and turn-of-the-century scholars an opportunity to observe the *chiftlik* phenomenon first hand in an Ottoman environment and to report upon it. Both the intensity of the *chiftlik* development in Macedonia and the relative availability of literature pertaining to this region were factors which influenced the choice of a Macedonian district as the subject for the present inquiry.

The time span covered by the study and the fact that it ends on the eve of the Tanzimat reforms was determined by the changing nature of the *sijils* themselves. The *tevzi* lists found in the *sijils*, whose importance for our subject will soon be demonstrated, become less descriptive after 1824 because of their own evolution in form. This accident of coverage is fortuitous since much less has been known heretofore about *chiftlik* development in this region in the two centuries preceding the Tanzimat than in the period following it, since supplementary non-Ottoman sources are increasingly abundant in the final decades of Ottoman rule. The attention here to the earlier portion of the *chiftlik* story in the Manastir district can be taken therefore as an antidote to the decided latterday bias of existing literature on the subject of *chiftlik* agriculture in Macedonia.

Because existing literature on this subject has drawn very largely upon latterday and non-Ottoman sources there has been until now a general tendency to sketch a fairly static portrait of Macedonian *chiftliks* as they appeared in the final decades of Ottoman rule and then to project that portrait backward upon the distant past. Each of the typical concerns of the extant literature on Macedonian *chiftliks* has been to some degree affected by this latterday and to some degree unhistoric bias: the legal categories dominating *chiftlik* life,[2] typical contractual relationship imbedded in the cluster of institutions associated with the name *chiftlik*,[3] typical forms of land use associated with *chiftliks*,[4] causal mechanisms which gave rise to *chiftliks*,[5] and, unavoidably, the concurrence between *chiftlik* development, as perceived, and general categories of historical development as laid out in Marxist theory.[6]

Despite the longstanding tendency towards a latterday bias, some recent writings about Macedonian *chiftliks* have indeed attempted to push the origins of *chiftlik* agriculture backward in time. No doubt partly because of an increasing awareness of the contents of the Manastir *sijils* themselves and because of an accumulating literature on the subject of *chiftliks* in other regions besides Macedonia,[7] more recent writings on Macedonia have (though with a degree of vagueness) placed the beginnings of *chiftlik* development there in the seventeenth century,[8] or have emphasized the eighteenth century as a whole,[9] or the last decades of the eighteenth century,[10] or the Tanzimat decades, or the Crimean War years, as the cradle of their wholesale rise.[11] Others have expressed uncertainty regarding the origins of the subject in Macedonia while stressing the lack of research or the lack of sources.[12]

The *sijils* of Manastir

The age, continuity and official character of the Manastir *sijils* enable us to complete and correct in at least three respects impressions about *chiftlik* development arising from an overreliance upon non-Ottoman sources: with regard to the time and the rhythm of their rise, at least in western Macedonia; in casting doubt upon the causal primacy previously lent to the methods employed in the *chiftlik*-building process; and in testing the validity of latterday *chiftlik* norms as a guide to the shifting reality of earlier periods.

The *sijils* of Manastir (known today as the *sijils* of Bitola) were housed before the Second World War at the Vakıf Library (Vakufska Biblioteka) at Bitola. After the war they were transferred to their present location in the Macedonian State Archive at Skopje where they now form the principal holdings remaining from the Ottoman period. The earliest entries in the *sijils* date from 1604, though the series becomes fully continuous only after 1632. The main series contains 178 *sijils*, ending in 1865. Although additional *sijils* exist for the period 1865–1912, their character, evidently because of legislated changes in provincial administrative practice, is much impoverished, since after 1865 they contain only cases involving the personal and familial aspects of *sher'i* law. After 1865, therefore, the *sijils* lose most of their interest for the historian.

It is difficult to be precise about the character of the law as administered at Manastir during the period covered by the main series (1604–1865). Some cases, especially those involving family matters among the Muslim community and interpersonal contracts among individuals of all faiths, are resolved in accordance with the prescriptive norms of the Hanefî school of *sher'i* law. A larger class of litigation is resolved in accordance with Ottoman positive law, secular in spirit and embodied either in the original provincial and imperial law codes or, increasingly as time goes on, resting upon the ad hoc authority of imperial decrees (*fermans*). Thus *sher'i* law constitutes the lesser vessel, carried within the greater vessel formed by the totality of Ottoman law. And, in harmony with Uriel Heyd's illuminating findings on the question of the relation between the two bodies of law,[13] it is the secular spirit which seems

generally to have dominated at Manastir. Although references to opinion (*fetva*) collections are not unknown,[14] they are extremely rare. The
loose and generous use of the terms *sher'i* and *sher'an*, both in decrees and
by the court itself, in order to give authority to decisions clearly falling
under the purview of Ottoman secular law, cannot be taken to mean
that the legal questions involved had been assimilated to *sher'i* law;
rather this usage dilutes and confuses the distinction between two
bodies of law while attempting to extend over all the local courts'
decisions the *sher'i* authority of the Sultan/Caliph. Indeed, certain essential aspects of *sher'i* law had been subverted by the Ottoman sultans
long before the Manastir record begins, one pragmatic departure being
the *mirî* principle upon which the Ottoman state's fiscal and military
strength was built, a principle which permeated most land questions in
the Manastir district during most of the two and a half centuries which
the court's records cover.

A third portion of the entries in the *sijils* of Manastir, by far the
largest portion, is not concerned with litigation at all. These entries
either notarize contracts and private acts; or record verbatim the
contents of decrees and patents originating in Istanbul; or the patents
of the governor presiding at Sofia; or are records of local administrative
acts, especially those dealing with taxation and the administration of
prices. Thus to characterize the *sijils* simply as 'judicial' records is not,
strictly speaking, correct. The *sijils* are much wider than that, containing even many matters which were not the responsibility of the judge to
oversee, but only to record in his secondary role as the notary of his *kaza*
(i.e. his judicial–administrative district).

The *sijils* are also somewhat difficult to characterize in terms of
topical content, since their content shifts and becomes narrower over
the period covered by the Manastir series. Below are three lists of the
most typical entries found in the *sijils*. The first list contains topics
which are typical of the seventeenth century but increasingly rare
thereafter. The second list contains topics typical of both the seventeenth and eighteenth centuries but rare later. The third list contains
topics common in all three centuries.

Seventeenth-century concerns

Authorizations of agents as collectors of leased rents and leased taxes
Suits over debts
Loan contracts and guarantees for loans (both sureties and securities)
Guarantees of good character in connection with banditry and other wrongdoing

Complaints involving assault, murder, robbery
Vakıf (pious estate) lists of assets, debtors
Miscellaneous notarizations – taxes paid, prebendal deliveries, etc.
Appointment of guardians for orphans, widows

Seventeenth- and eighteenth-century concerns

Timar affairs (diminishing in the eighteenth century)
Sales of houses, gardens, vineyards (diminishing in the eighteenth century)
Emancipation of individual slaves
Suits over the return of fugitive *reaya*
Disposal of assets of fugitive *reaya*
Complaints about prostitution and immorality
Suits over ownership of real estate (diminishing in the eighteenth century)
Sentencing for crimes, especially banditry
Infringements of pastures and woods
Appointments of village guards and mutual guarantees against banditry (especially in
    the eighteenth century)

Seventeenth-, eighteenth- and nineteenth-century concerns

Transfers of *mirî* revenues
Collection of *mirî* revenues, provincial revenues
Distribution of tax obligations throughout the district
Complaints over abuses in tax and rent collections
Divorces and divorce settlements
Estates of deceased persons, inherited debts
Charitable dispensations, allowances for orphans and other helpless dependents
Complaints about banditry and measures taken against bandits
Levies associated with visiting dignitaries and their entourages
Administration of prices, coinage
Measures associated with military mobilizations, especially requisitions

A close inspection of these lists will suggest that the volume of interpersonal, local and small scale transactions diminished over time. This impression is correct. Manastir *sijils* of the last century are quite different in character from the earliest one – less heterogeneous, and, from some points of view, less interesting. Although all the *sijils* share certain undying concerns, those of the nineteenth century are more public in character, and vastly more concerned with overriding imperial concerns – especially those connected with taxation and military mobilizations.

Most imperial concerns are embodied in *fermans* (easily spotted in the *sijils* because of their appearance – *fermans* almost invariably originated from '*Konstantiniyye-i mahrusa,*' written with a characteristic flourish). Answers to petitions (and there were many),[15] almost all complaints of abuses, and virtually all matters of taxation are either embodied in *fermans* or dealt with in texts which appear in close association with *fermans*, such as allocation lists, to be discussed below. This association between *fermans* and taxation was quite convenient to the investigation since it was further discovered that evidence on *chiftlik* formation was intimately intertwined with taxation, and therefore often associated with *fermans* dealing with taxation, or with tax allocations occasioned by the demands of the central government, or the governor in Sofia.

Although scholars acquainted with *sijils* have rightly emphasized their heterogeneous character (and their consequent value for the historian), clearly the *sijils* are not equally valuable for every subject. Aside from the frequent incompleteness with regard to individual transactions, which was noticed by Ronald Jennings in his work with the Kayseri *sijils*[16] (a characteristic shared by the Manastir *sijils*), they can be quite disappointing with respect to certain topics. As an example, although the Manastir *sijils* are rich with quantitative data on the numbers and magnitudes, as well as the location and 'ownership,' of *chiftliks* in that district, they contain very little data on wages, very little on land use, on crops, or on the prevailing forms of labor contracts.

The district of Manastir

When Evliya Chelebi purportedly visited the town in 1661, Manastir was said to contain 21 wards and was surrounded by heavy woods. Evliya complained of the many students who were gathered there and who led dissolute lives, consorting with all the wrong people. He also related how the outlaw Babo had raided the town with 500 men who ransacked the bazaar to the tune of 70,000 *gurush*. Yet, says Evliya, no man in town lifted a finger to resist, which the traveler found deplorable.[17] None of this seems unlikely after reading the *sijils* of that period. Indeed the seventeenth-century record as a whole is filled with stories of brigandage, murder, sexual misconduct, wild disorder and abuse of privilege. But these were only the negative aspects of life in an Ottoman town which in general functioned well enough as an administrative center and which enjoyed a reputation as a place where men of learning could be found.

From a patent (*berat*) authorizing collection of the hearth tax in the year of Evliya Chelebi's visit, we learn that the town itself was then almost wholly Muslim since only five (presumably Christian) hearth

tax payers survive in the town;[18] in addition one must make some allowance for Jews, who as a community made a single annual (and rather
modest) lump sum payment in lieu of hearth tax. (Gypsies are also
excluded from the patent since the taxes for Gypsies in this district were
farmed separately, though it seems unlikely that Gypsies lived in the
town itself.)

The administration of the town, and of the district (*kaza*) as well, was
shared among the following: the *kadi*, as the chief judicial and administrative representative of the central government; the *kethüda yeri*, a tax
farmer with some authority over the six janissary corps represented at
Manastir; the janissary commander (*serdar*); and those individuals
currently most prominent among the more prosperous and influential
men of the district (the *ayan-i vilayetin ish erleri*).[19] At certain times, as for
instance during the campaign against Ali Pasha of Yanina in 1820,
Manastir might become the temporary headquarters of the governor
(*vali*).[20] In addition, the town was often visited by *pashas* and other high
officials, whose demands for funds to cover the expenses of their visit
(always heavy and perhaps extortionate) are a frequent concern in the
pages of the *sijils*.

As was common for Ottoman towns, sources of revenue within the
town itself were reserved as *has* revenues destined for the treasuries of
the sultan, or his family, rather than for the public (*miri*) treasury.
Evliya Chelebi says that at the time of his visit (1661) the daughter of
the sultan had an income of two million *akches* from Manastir.[21] In 1694
a receipt appearing in one *sijil* indicates that all revenues from the
market at Manastir were being leased on behalf of Mustafa Pasha, the
grand *vezir* and mayor of Istanbul.[22]

Aleksander Stojanovski's study of the territorial subdivisions of
Macedonia shows that Manastir was not only the administrative center
for the district (*kaza*) of the same name but also for the district (*nahiye*)
of Demir Hisar on the north-west and part of the *nahiye* of Morihovo on
the south-east. This explains why it was the practice in the earlier *sijils*
to divide the villages administered from Manastir into two groups –
those called *nefs-i Manastir* and those called *tetimme-i Manastir*; this
practice, however, fades with the passage of years so that the villages of
both groups were eventually handled by the *sijils* as a single customary
group.

The situation of the Manastir *kaza*, together with its outlying elements was peculiar in one respect: along with several neighboring
kazas, the Manastir *kaza* lay in the isolated western wing of the giant

Pasha Liva, a province stretching all the way to the Black Sea. The creation of the province of Selanik (Salonica) in the sixteenth century had split Pasha Liva into two separated parts, so that the governor of Rumeli, who also customarily governed Pasha Liva with its capital at Sofia, had to cross other *livas* in order to reach the western end of his own.[23]

An examination of the margins of the Manastir district shown on our map leads to the conclusion that, despite the later disappearance of some of the bordering villages from the records, the boundaries of the so-called '*kaza*' of Manastir (i.e. the original *kaza* of Manastir plus its Demir Hisar and Morihovo contingents) remained substantially unchanged over the span of years covered in this study. Naturally the village constituency of the *kaza* did not remain static. Some villages disappeared entirely or reappeared. New villages were recorded. But the earlier trend in the number of villages was downward, either because of depopulation or because the population gradually redistributed itself so that a large portion of it later resettled on *chiftliks*, which sometimes were, and sometimes were not, regarded as villages. In 1641 165 villages are officially listed in the district (counting six which are apparently all-Muslim).[24] In 1694 there are 138 or so villages,[25] whereas by 1706 there are only 116.[26] Simultaneously with this fall in the number of villages there is much evidence to indicate a rise in the number of families living on *chiftliks*. Throughout the eighteenth century, however, the number of villages is fairly stable, and by 1809 the number of villages listed is 119.[27]

The 1809 list of villages is largely a remnant of the earlier lists, though some of the names on it are new. A list of the villages appearing on the 1641 list follows, which includes some names (followed by question marks) whose latinicized morphology has not been confirmed. Names from the 1641 list which survive to appear on the 1809 list are indicated by asterisks. The bulk of these surviving villages were still extant early in this century when they appeared on Jaranov's map of Macedonia,[28] which was used as the basis for the map included here. Here then is the 1641 list:[29]

Skočivir,* Streževo, Zmirnevo,* Sloestica,* Sveta,* Eflahci (modern Lahci),* Smilevo,* Ostreč,* Sveti Todor,* Sveti Petka, Slepče,* Strugovo,* Staravina, Ariljevo, Zlokučani,* Svinište, Ivanjovci, Slivica,* Presil,* Brusnik,* Bituše,* Podmol, Bazdernik,* Baldovenci,* Bratindol,* Bistrica (?), Brezovo,* Barešani,* Biljanik, Plake,* Pozdeš (?), Borakovo, Pribilci,* Babino,* Beranci (?), Porodin,* Pogošta (?),* Bela Crkva,* Paralovo, Pančar (?), Belče, Brusa (?),* Buf,* Postarka (?), Postrala (?),* Bukri (?), Pogodin,* Berlova (?), Brod (?), Brodica (?), Trnovci, Trnovo,* Trap,*

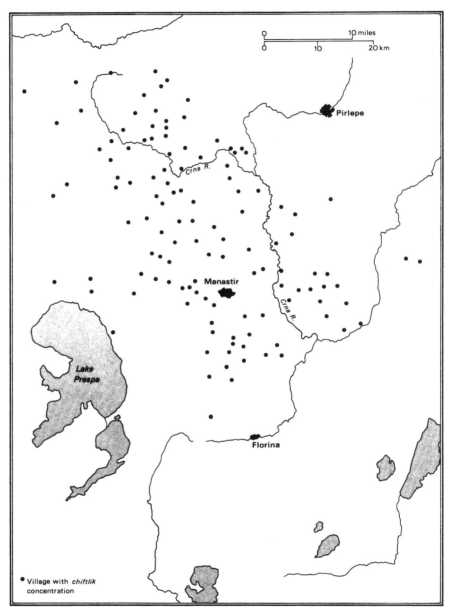

Map 15   Villages of the Manastir district, 1639

Trn,* Tepafci,* Hanali (?), Holoveni (?),* Hrastani (?),* Hrasloica (?), Čikrikči (?), Džvan,* Čagor, Čekel (?), Crnojerić (?), Čerovo,* Čer, Crnevci,* Crnobuki,* Crska Bala,* Crska zir,* Čapari,* Dolni Divjaci,* Gorni Divjaci,* Dragos,* Dolenci Demir,* Dobromir, Dobruševo, Dolenci,* Dijovo,* Demir Hisar,* Dragota (?), Dragožan (?), Drvenik (?), Dragarina (?), Dubka (?), Radevo,* Rakovo,* Rakitnica,* Ribarica,* Ramna,* Raotino, Radobor,* Ruvče, Rusna Serdek (?), Zagoriče, Žašle,* Žurče,* Žabjani, Suhodol,* Srpci,* Sopotnica,* Sekirani, Suho Grlo, Suvarok (?), Grumazi,* Gniles,* Gradešnica,* Gradišta (?),* Krkarina (?),* Klabučista,* Kostahur (?),* Karamani,* Kravci, Kukurečani,* Kočište,* Kragujeva (?), Kutretino, Kruševo,* Kišava,* Kazan,* Kanino, Kilista (?),* Lisolaj,* Laglar, Lažče, Loznani,* Leskovac, Liska, Lera,* Litvica (?), Lopatica,* Leskova,* Medžitli, Murgaš, Mramorec, Magarevo,* Mogila,* Malovište,* Majina (?), Novaselo Demir,* Novaci,* Negotin, Nižepole,* Nošpal, Negočani,* Virovo,* Vodjani, Velmeci,* Vranevci,* Velušino,* Vardino (?),* Veluj (?), Oblakova,* Orehova,* Obtičari,* Ostrilci,* Obršani, Obšireno,* Obednik,* Ednakovci,* Egri.*[30]

Demographic trends at Manastir

About demographic trends in the zone under scrutiny, one cannot speak with complete certainty. The best sources available, the head tax collection patents (the *jizye berats*), present certain problems of interpretation, the following being the most troublesome.

1. *Jizye* payment in this district was made on a household basis until the reform of the 1690s. Yet a precise definition of the pre-1690 household is lacking. There is reason to believe that, even if the definition were precise, actual household or hearth averages might nonetheless vary over time in response to factors ignored in the definition, one of them being the fact that when taxes are being collected on a household basis there exists an incentive for consolidation of households.[31]

2. When the *jizye* collection principle was changed in the early 1690s, instead of being collected on the household, *jizyes* were henceforth to be collected from adult *zimmi* (non-Muslim) males. The ratio of *jizye*-paying individuals (under the newer principle) to the number of *jizye*-paying households (under the older principle) can only be inferred from before and after totals. In this way a discontinuity is created in the record.

3. It is less likely that official tallies which appear in *jizye* patents are reliable during periods of population loss[32] than they are when population was rising, owing to reluctance to accept revenue losses.

4. The practice of lumping together *jizye* totals from three or four districts as was done in the patents and *jizye* registers of the subsequent two centuries, makes it quite impossible to isolate the totals pertaining to a single district, such as the *kaza* of Manastir.

Given these difficulties, some reserve is appropriate in using the *jizye* totals as guides to real demographic trends in a single district (though their value for wider zones is greater since the problem of isolating tallies does not arise).

The earliest *jizye* tally encountered is found in a *jizye* register now housed at the Prime Minister's Archive in Istanbul. According to this register the Manastir district (i.e. *nefs* plus *tetimme*) in 1627 contained 4328 *jizye*-paying households.[33] The earliest *jizye* tally in the *sijils* appears in a decree dated 1634 and indicates that while the Manastir district is then officially on record as containing 4207 *jizye*-paying households (*hanes*), 800 of these are by this date *gürihte*, i.e. defunct, their inhabitants having fled or otherwise disappeared.[34] As it frequently did in these circumstances, the Porte took a hard line on this occasion, insisting that *jizye* collection be made on the basis of the officially recorded total (4207) despite its admission that the total was no longer current. Although this total obviously did not include Muslim households, concentrated in the town of Manastir, nor Jews or Gypsies, who paid their *jizye* separately under special arrangements, it is unlikely that any other exclusions were intended, so far as the Christian *zimmis* were concerned. Aside from the Porte's well-known and near-universal policy of maintaining stubbornly its right to collect the *jizye* from its non-Muslim subjects, wherever they were found, including those who had semi-military functions, there were explicit directions in the *sijils* prohibiting exemption from *jizye* payment on the part of *zimmis* who lived on pious estates, sultanic estates, or on monastic lands.[35] This does not mean, however, that *jizye* collection always went smoothly, since *jizye* collection patents commonly included a warning not to allow local military personnel to interfere with *jizye* collection – obviously because they often tried to shield their own *reaya* from the collector so that they could be wrung dry by their protector rather than the man from the treasury.

By 1638 the Manastir court conceded that there were 1000 defunct households in the district.[36] Yet in 1641 the *jizyedar* was still authorized to collect 4428 *jizyes* in the district. The discrepancy was painful for all. *Jizye* payment was now carried out after a bargaining process in the presence of the *kadi* and the leading military men, with collectors on one side and representatives of the *reaya* on the other. The added burden falling upon the remaining households was to be distributed among them by village elders and priests, and the precise amounts required by Istanbul handed over to the collector.[37]

By 1662, probably as the result of reforms introduced under Mehmet Köprülü's direction, the number of *jizyes* authorized in this district was 3000.[38] Ten years later a register shows almost the same total – 3055.[39] This figure apparently holds until 1683, when *jizye* patents authorize collection of the same total of *jizyes* in the district.[40]

By 1711, the number of *jizye* receipts authorized for the district had risen just slightly, to 3201.[41] But by now the principle for the collection of the *jizye* had changed. Instead of being collected from the household, it was now being collected from each adult male, each '*nefer*.' One would have expected that this change of method would bring about a considerable expansion in the number of those liable to *jizye*. The fact that the rise over the 1683 figure is so tiny probably signifies a considerable drop in population, especially since – as we have seen – the number of villages in the district dropped substantially in the same period.

A 1740 allocation drawn up to distribute the expenses of a visit by the *vali* (governor), Osman Pashazade Ahmed Pasha, among the holders of *jizye* receipts shows a total of 4070 receipts.[42] This figure is in harmony with an upward trend shown in the *jizye* registers of Istanbul, which in that century lump the Manastir district together with Florina, Pirlepe and Morihova. The registers show that the group of four contained 11,068 *jizye* payers in 1690, 14,500 in 1740, and 17,404 in 1788.[43] Surely this reflects a real rise in population. But in the late eighteenth century a countertrend is at least possible, judging by the comments of foreign observers. Part of this would have been the result of migration into the Ukraine and Bessarabia in the decades following the Russian annexations of 1774 and 1792.[44] And in view of the protracted strain of two foreign wars and the long period of wholesale banditry which followed each, as well as the feuding between *ayan* families which became endemic in Macedonia in those decades, it would be surprising had there not been some drop in population. Thus the French diplomats Pouqueville and Beaujour, both writing around 1800, were struck by the scanty habitation of the rich Macedonian lands, particularly, says Beaujour, the northern half of Macedonia. These impressions are supported by a letter to Selim III from the governor (*beylerbey*) of Rumeli, Tatarjık Abdullah Efendi, who complains that the whole Macedonian populace including women and children work day and night just to pay taxes. Many had fled and many places were deserted.[45] But it must be admitted that the central government's *jizye* records do not support this notion: the central record for *jizye* collections indicates a rise of about 9 per cent in the number of *jizye*-payers in the four *kaza* bloc which includes Manastir, between 1788 and 1815.

In summary, considering both the changes in village totals and in the number of the *jizye*-liable, it is reasonable to generalize, as follows: (1) a considerable drop in population, perhaps 25 per cent, prior to 1641, on the basis of figures which may originate in a demographic peak period in the late sixteenth century; (2) approximate stability between 1641 and 1683; (3) a further drop in population between 1683 and 1711, probably mostly during the war years preceeding the Treaty of Carlowitz (1699); (4) a rise of as much as 50 per cent between 1711 and 1788; and (5) a debatable fall in total population at the end of that century.[46]

The economic role of the district

The economic role of the Manastir district within its Macedonian environment is a matter of inference. Macedonia as a whole, like other parts of the Balkans, exported wool, hides and skins to and through Vienna during the better part of the seventeenth century. The collapse of the German trade caused by the long war after 1683 was compensated in the south by the rise of the port of Salonica (Ottoman Selanik) through which Macedonian wool and hides moved, bound for customers in the West, especially Marseilles. The continued growth of Salonica's trade was matched, after 1718, by a revival of the German trade through Vienna and Leipzig.[47] By the 1780s the German areas again took about half Macedonia's exports, which throughout the eighteenth century were increasingly dominated by cotton, whether moving north through Zemun or south through Salonica.[48] A virtual cotton boom began with the onset of the American Revolutionary War in 1776, followed by a wheat boom beginning with the relaxation of Ottoman export controls following the French Revolution in 1789.[49] Both these booms collapsed after the Congress of Vienna, especially cotton, as the Egyptian product began to find its way to the market. By 1833 the predominance of wheat in the exports through Salonica was very marked.[50] But Macedonia also returned in the nineteenth century to pastoralism on a large scale, primarily, if we are to trust the reports of contemporary observers, because the flight of the peasantry to the towns freed vast tracts of the countryside for grazing.[51]

Sheep tax figures from seventeenth-century *sijils* do not support the idea that the Manastir area was at that time an important grazing area. In the next century there is virtually no evidence to show that the

Manastir district produced much cotton or tobacco, commodities which were concentrated in the Seres and Salonica zones respectively.[52] Again in the nineteenth century the *sijils* are of little help in determining how the land was being used in the Manastir zone, though it is known from other sources that western Macedonia (and presumably its hilly regions especially) was heavily involved in sheep raising.

What *was* raised on the north–south plain surrounding Manastir? By default it would seem that the answer was grain, primarily wheat, through all these centuries. The best evidence for this inference is the frequency with which in each.of these centuries stores of grain, led by wheat, appeared among the registered effects of deceased Muslims (the *tereke* lists), exceeding by far all other agricultural commodities. Naturally it is not usually clear whether these grain stores were intended for sale or for consumption.[53] Some of that wheat was exported through Salonica, as we can see from the fact that a ban on the sale of grain to Salonica was imposed at Manastir around 1800 in order to prevent food shortage within the district itself.[54] Certainly there were always enough caravaneers at Manastir to suggest a considerable overland trade. The Manastir district was sometimes called upon to supply the government with wheat or flour, during war time, especially if the action lay to the south, as it did in the 1820s. Therefore it seems likely that Manastir, aside from its own local needs, functioned economically within the Macedonian environment as an area which forwarded wheat surpluses to other zones, such as Seres and Salonica, which were heavily involved in producing other export commodities and where there was a need for additional wheat to supplement the local supply. The destination and content of Manastir's surpluses may in any case appear to be a secondary question when we see how closely the growth of *chiftliks* there – and the market-oriented agriculture which that implies – followed the growth of Macedonia's export trade, viewed as a whole.

Chiftlik formation at Manastir

The existence of plantation-like estates on the Ottoman scene did not always and everywhere imply a connection with foreign trade. The market sought might be a large town in the vicinity of the grower. Thus we occasionally find large *chiftliks* scattered throughout the survey registers (*tahrir defters*) of the sixteenth century.[55] Moreover, the reorganization of much land as sheep ranches in late sixteenth- and early seventeenth-century Anatolia cannot be linked to any marked trend in foreign trade. The ranches of the *jelali* era seem to have arisen because the opportunity for usurpation was there rather than because the market demanded their appearance.[56]

Many entries from Manastir *sijils* of the seventeenth century can be cited as evidence of the existence of *chiftliks* (as previously defined) in the Manastir district. Often their size is unclear. Many seem to have been small, no larger than a typical holding worked by a single man and his oxteam. But on the other hand, some of them were clearly large *chiftliks*, occasionally very large. In one case recorded in 1636, we learn that the village Krkarina (?) has been meeting interest payments on a debt of 2000 *akches*, owed to one Sheyhzade Mehmet Efendi, by providing him annually with 100 laborers (*ırgats*). In 1641 one Mehmet Ağa requested registration in the court record of the fact that he employed about 150 laborers each year from the village of Rakovo, at a wage of 10 *akches* each. In 1662, in a case similar to the first, it is recorded that the village of Podmol had for thirty years been sending 200 laborers to work on the fields of Chorlu Mustafa Ağa as payment of interest upon a loan of 4000 *akches* which he had once made them.[57] How were these laborers used? To whom were the products of their labors sold? How large were the *chiftliks* which required such large inputs of day labor? Unfortunately the *sijils* offer no help in answering these questions.

How were *chiftliks* created? If the lesser tricks and subterfuges are ignored, a basic list of ways and means emerges:

1. by expansion of the *sipahi*'s prebendal *chiftlik*, mill, apiary, etc;
2. by the seizure either of the holdings of individual villagers or, more frequently, of the pastures, woods and other lands customarily used by villagers in common;
3. by occupying land abandoned owing to overtaxation and debt;
4. by receiving land from villagers in return for protection from tax collectors and bandits, or in return for relief from deliberate terror and harassment;
5. by foreclosing on lands given in pawn by villagers seeking loans;
6. by purchase, or by transactions tantamount to purchase.

By stretching the evidence one can read each of these means into each of the later Ottoman centuries. But a close examination of the Manastir *sijils* suggests that in western Macedonia, at least, only one of these means (seizure) was a perennial theme, whereas the other means listed, which together account for a far greater part of the *chiftlik*-building story, are somewhat periodized in their impact. For good reason, certain means predominated earlier and others later. Separate consideration of each of the means cited will help clarify this assertion.

Expansion of prebendal chiftlik   The *hassa chiftlik* was a portion of the cavalry *timar* (prebend) which was intended for direct exploitation by the holder of the *timar* or by a companion in arms. *Hassa chiftliks* were of various descriptions and variable in size. During the earlier centuries it was often and at many locations unprofitable or simply inconvenient for *sipahis* to work them personally so that they often leased them out to villagers. Thus there was a strong tendency towards the assimilation of such *chiftliks* among other villagers' holdings despite laws intended to discourage such conversions. Many *timars* of the earlier centuries did not therefore contain *hassa chiftliks* at all, presumably because they had disappeared by assimilation.[58] However economic conditions were changing in the seventeenth century so that at many locations the preservation and enlargement of *hassa chiftliks* by dubious means had become profitable.

In the seventeenth century, when *chiftlik* building (using the term *chiftlik* in its latterday sense) began to spread, the government took the line that individuals who usurped land which had been held by *reaya* would have to be responsible for the same dues which had been legally incumbent upon those villagers.

As for those *sipahis* and other Muslims who have taken over Christian holdings and made use of them, then make excuses when the time comes to collect the *jizye* and *ispenje* and don't give it and have the poor indemnify them, let *jizyes* and *ispenjes* be collected from such as these without fail whether they are bailiffs, *sipahis*, or whoever they happen to be. Let the incumbent *kadi* take full payment of (both taxes) from those who would not give it, or else with the intervention of a *sipahi* take the holding out of their hands and give it to someone who will undertake to pay (these taxes).[59]

This decision was fundamental. It signified a shift of the stigma of subjection from the person (the individual *reaya*) to the land, in a process for which a parallel can be found in the late medieval West. Moreover, it represented a breach in the traditional class system of the Ottomans since it required persons of clear military status to pay taxes, which by definition they had never before had to do.

The advantage of holding and enlarging a *hassa chiftlik*, as opposed to a *chiftlik* gotten by other means, was this. The holder of the *hassa chiftlik* remained exempt from all taxation, in keeping with the norms of the classic system regarding persons of military status. Thus, for instance, in 1707 we encounter a case in which the issue of taxation hung on whether or not a *chiftlik* could be proven to be 'an old military *chiftlik*.'[60] The embellishment of 'old military *chiftliks*' was apparently a common ambition in the eighteenth century, so that well before the end of that century it is their *chiftliks*, rather than their prebends which seem to have been the foremost concern of *zaims* and *timarlıs*. This conclusion seems warranted by the wording of a *ferman* issued in 1778 and addressed to all *kadis* in the 'center band' (*orta kol*) of Rumeli. The concern of the *ferman* was malingering on the part of *zaims* and *timarlıs*, supported by local officers (*alaybeys*). The sanction proposed against malingerers who did not mobilize and proceed to Hotin was that they should have their '*chiftliks*' taken away! It seems fair to assume, therefore, that by the third quarter of the eighteenth century at the latest, the process of reconstituting and embellishing *hassa chiftliks* had reached a point where *timars* were assumed to have contained as a matter of course a *chiftlik* which apparently provided the chief part of the revenues from what may have been otherwise greatly impoverished prebends.[61]

Seizure of holdings or of village commons   The seizure of land from villagers by powerful individuals (usually military men) seems to have presented a perennial possibility. Examples can be cited from the Manastir *sijils* both early and late.[62] Yet it is hopeless to try to quantify forcible seizure with respect to its relative importance as a means of creating *chiftliks*, or with respect to its relative prevalence in particular periods. In the mid-seventeenth century *kadis* apparently often lacked the necessary backing, surprising as that may seem, in enforcing the will of the court against such seizures. By the end of the eighteenth century *kadis* seemingly no longer preferred to oppose seizures vigorously, partly perhaps because *chiftlik* building had by then become so normal that adherence to the old norms seemed like a lost cause. For the same reason one may suspect that forcible seizure was more often successful, if not more frequent, as time went on. Yet it would be presumptuous, for any period, to try to assign to seizure a rank relative to other means of building *chiftliks*.[63]

Seizure might take place upon pretext, usually the non-payment of a loan, or without pretext. But forcible seizure, indeed all means of *chiftlik* formation, did not always go unopposed. From the *sijils* it is apparent that, in the seventeenth century particularly, the *chiftliks* of powerful men were often the targets (and ironically sometimes the launching points) for bandit raids.[64]

By occupying land abandoned owing to overtaxation and debt   In the middle decades of the seventeenth century the Manastir district witnessed an epidemic of indebtedness and flight whereby whole villages fled to avoid the debts which they had collectively contracted. Judging by numerous entries the usual reason for their indebtedness was the exorbitant demands of tax collectors, or perhaps also their usual demands which had become exorbitant because of bad harvests. Flight by individual villagers is a common theme late in the eighteenth and in the early nineteenth centuries, and of course individual flight also created opportunities for would-be *chiftlik* holders. But flight by whole villages, in the manner of the Great Flight of the *jelali* era in Anatolia, seems to have been limited in the Manastir district mostly to the seventeenth century. The drop in the number of villages and in population during the seventeenth century may plausibly be linked with this cycle of overtaxation, debt and flight.

According to a *ferman* addressed in 1640 to Hadji Ahmet, surveyor for Salonica, Trikala, and the 'left wing' of Pasha Liva: 'You have reported that the *reaya* of the district which you have been appointed to survey have destroyed their houses and gone elsewhere and that certain powerful people (*bazi zi-kudret kimesneler*) have converted that land into *chiftliks*.'[65] The report of the surveyor is borne out by evidence from the *sijils*. Lists of villages which were in debt as collectivities show up in the *vakıf* audits of 1640 and 1641.[66] Over a hundred villages of the Manastir district were so encumbered, owing money both to *vakıfs* and also to individual lenders. Not all of these villages were in real danger; sometimes the amounts on loan were fairly modest. But at least two villages are known to have been emptied in the same two years: Murgaš and Baldovenci.[67]

In each of these cases, the villagers who had fled had been sought out and had apparently agreed to return providing that a one, two or three year tax holiday was offered. In the case of Murgaš we see the consequence of a situation in which each of four joint holders of a *timar* squeezed the villagers for his own advantage:

There are several joint holders at the aforementioned village. For the reason that both they themselves and their bailiffs (*subashıs*) were disturbing the *reaya* all have dispersed and fled.

The men who share the *timar* admit this:

If henceforth the *zimmis* of the aforementioned village will settle in their village again we will all authorize the Jew Menteshe to represent us. When it will be necessary to collect legally prescribed tithes and customary and other dues, let them be collected by the aforementioned Jew and be distributed as stipulated in the patent among each of us. In the aforementioned village let no one interfere either personally or by means of a collector he has authorized. We all agree that it should be this way.

And the *zimmi* Dujo says:

> If the Jew Menteshe is authorized by all the *sipahis* as collector, as declared, and if no one else interferes, I will do all I can to bring back those who have fled.[68]

Probably over the long run flight by individual families created more opportunities for usurpers than did the abandonment of whole villages. Whereas flight by whole villages seems mostly limited to the seventeenth century, flight by families was endemic throughout, certainly after the middle of the seventeenth century. But where to flee was a problem. Conversely for the usurper there was a question – who would work the land? As *chiftliks* became more numerous it was increasingly to *chiftliks* that desperate villagers fled. Perhaps they had few illusions that things would be easier in a new situation. But what better way was there to shake off an unshakeable accumulation of debts? Only when towns began to grow again in the nineteenth century did any real alternative appear. Meanwhile a tension had arisen between a dying prebendal class which would enforce the laws on fugitives and a growing class of *chiftlik* holders, many of them also *sipahis*, who wanted to ignore and subvert the fugitive laws in order to receive the fugitive labor they needed.

By receiving land from reayas in return for protection   There were two ways to flee. One was by giving up and leaving, the other was by giving up and staying. Of the two modes, the latter became more common with the passage of time. Like the man who fled to a distant *chiftlik*, the man who remained when a *chiftlik* was being formed, or who without actually fleeing very far accepted the protection of a neighbouring *chiftlik* holder, was less likely to be an easy prey either for the *mirî* tax collector or for his old *sipahi*. The labor he could provide was a limited good, which the *chiftlik* holder, if he were powerful enough, would do all he could to hoard for himself. As the *chiftlik* holders became more numerous they naturally wielded influence as a corporation to establish protective practices within their district.

In a *ferman* dated 1748 addressed to all of Rumeli, the anxiety of the central government over the debilitating effects of the protection game upon the failing *timar* system, and upon the government's own capacity to levy taxes, is apparent:

> I have issued a proclamation under which henceforth, in the provinces and districts cited, tax requirements are to be apportioned, after adjustments are made, with the full knowledge of the local judiciary; and the *reaya* of *zaims* and *timarlıs*, no matter where they may be located, are to pay their old taxes to their *sipahis*, while the abuses of *chiftlik*

holders (who say 'he's a *reaya* on our *chiftlik*') towards the people of their district are prohibited, and henceforth in this way *zaim* and *timarlı* villages are not to be sold to make *chiftliks*, and in every district *reaya* – whether belonging to villages or the *chiftliks* – are to fulfill *mirî* tax requirements on an equal basis.[69]

The protection game, as this *ferman* suggests, was linked not only to the (commendation-like) surrender of the villager's rights over his land, but also to the acquisition of land by other means, which although sale of land is specifically mentioned, can be taken to include seizure, foreclosure and the occupation of abandoned land which might then be resettled by fugitives.

By foreclosure and by purchase Of the six means of *chiftlik* building which were named, the first four were dealt with less effectively by Ottoman government, or on an ad hoc basis as they arose, since these developments had not been foreseen by those who drafted the law of the classic system. By contrast the law drafters of the classic era did realize the damage which could be done to the classic land regime, either by the use of *reaya* land as security for loans, or by the sale of such land to individuals outside of that class. As we shall see, an effort to forestall these processes had been institutionalized long before *chiftlik* formation became a serious problem. Evidence of the breach of the injunctions against pawning and sale is very rare in the Manastir *sijils*.[70] And if these injunctions weakened with time and were subverted before the end of the eighteenth century, nonetheless a holding action in their favor, especially by the *sher'i* courts, long delayed the emergence of these two processes, which otherwise would surely have quickly eroded and in effect dismantled the land regime upon which the Ottoman *timar* system had rested.

The effort to defend the crumbling regime

Opposing the usurpers were the Ottoman land laws and the Ottoman *kadi*. Various land laws, largely already extant in the sixteenth century but reconfirmed and embellished in the early seventeenth century, permitted the *kadi* to employ these lines of defending the system: (1) against transfer of *reaya* land without the *timarlı's* permission, (2) against alienation of land from the broad *mirî* category, and against the flight of the *reaya* from his land.

Defense of the timar The laws forbade that *reaya* holdings be sold, given away or willed in gift, left in trust, loaned, pawned in return for a loan, leased, exchanged or transferred to a neighbor of a deceased *reaya* on a preferential basis without the knowledge and permission of the responsible *timarlı* (often called the *sahib-i arz*) as expressed evidentially by the *timarlı's* issuance of a certificate, called the *tapu* or *tapuname*.[71] Although the automatic descent of a *reaya* holding to sons and daughters was sanctioned by law, according to an opinion (*fetva*) attributed to the Sheyhulislam Okchuzade Yahya Efendi (whose several terms in that office stretched from 1622 to 1644) the formerly automatic descent in the direct line also had to be certified by issuance of a *tapuname*.[72] If a transfer of *mirî* land with compensation was permitted by the *timarlı*, it was recorded under the law not as true sale (which was prohibited) but as a legitimate transfer only of the *reaya's* right of usufruct, not outright ownership. The cumulative effect of the laws regarding *mirî* lands was not to prohibit transfer processes altogether but rather to forbid transfer of a *reaya* holding, or even part of one, without the knowledge and approval of the *timarlı*. Thus in 1641 when Gore V'lkan of Dobromir was obliged to sell his house, his fields and his vineyard to the *kadi* himself, one Ramazan Efendi, as compensation for an unpaid loan of 4000 *akches*, the transaction cannot be branded improper since as the record states the 'sale' was done with the knowledge of the tenant-in-chief (*marifet-i sahib-i arziyle*).[73] The laws moreover specifically forbid that the *kadi's* permission and the *kadi's* certificate (*hüjjet*) be substituted for the *timarlı's*.

Obviously those who drafted the laws and opinions which comprise the *mirî* corpus were convinced that *timarlıs*, by acting in their own best interests with regard to the transfer of the *reaya's* right of usufruct, would also be acting in the state's best interest. The *reaya* was, of course, also protected under the system, which did not permit the arbitrary alienation of his holding, even as punishment for a crime. The integrity of the holding was also usually protected by provincial laws providing for its joint cultivation by all the sons working together, as well as by the widespread practice of demanding payment of primary taxes, such as the *jizye* and *ispenje*, on a household basis, thus encouraging the maintenance of consolidated households.

The *timarlıs'* role in maintaining the *mirî* character of *reaya* holdings by keeping them in *reaya* hands was obviously subverted as *timarlıs* leased out collections on their *timars* (an increasingly common practice in the seventeenth century), as their own numbers were eroded through the award of *timars* to remote and often fictitious persons, and perhaps above all as the *timarlıs* themselves, for a variety of reasons, starting with the diminution of the real income from their prebends, began to give up their military roles in favor of *chiftlik* formation. However an inspection of all the 'sale' transactions contained in one of the Manastir *sijils*, no. 8 dated 1633–5, suggests that the veto of the *timarlıs* was still in those years partly effective in preventing the transfer of *zimmi* holdings to non-*reaya* hands. Of 29 'sale' transactions in this *sijil*, 15 involved transfer of vineyards, which like houses and gardens and orchards, were exceptions to the *mirî* regime. Only 14 transactions involved transfer of *mirî* fields and pastures, or even *chiftliks* so-called. What is interesting is that whereas the vineyard transactions show little pattern with respect to the identity of buyers and sellers, the *mirî* transactions do. Of the 14 transactions five are from one military man to another (or at least from one Muslim non-*reaya* to another). Four transfers are from Muslim *reaya* to Muslim military men (or at least to non-*reaya*). One was from a military man to a Muslim *reaya*, one from a military man to a Jew, one from a Jew to a military man. In one of the two remaining transactions the seller was a Christian woman, the other parties unclear. Though this evidence is not conclusive, there is certainly reason to believe that in a predominantly Christian district one could expect more *mirî* transactions involving Christians (*zimmis*), providing there was no inhibitory factor operating to prevent them. On the other hand, it is also possible that since only the *timarlı*'s *tapuname* was required to legitimize the transfer of all or part of a *reaya* holding there was no felt need to register all such transactions with the *sher'i* court.

To sum up the seventeenth-century situation, 'sales' of land do not appear in the record with the frequency one might expect. Cases of land being held as security on loans are yet more rare. But whether this is due to a respect for the provisions of the law or to incompleteness of the record is not certain.

In the eighteenth century, as already mentioned, fewer and fewer land transactions of any sort appear in the *sijils*. O. L. Barkan has already commented upon the paucity of 'sale' transactions involving the transfer of arable land during the seventeenth century, speculating that perhaps with the increasing laxity of the land regime more and more arable land was sold under the guise of garden and vineyard.[74] Certainly the disappearance of land transactions from the Manastir *sijils* during the course of the eighteenth century cannot be taken to signify a real diminution of such transactions. Nor can the absence of *chiftliks* on the inheritance (*tereke*) lists in the seventeenth, eighteenth and nineteenth centuries be taken to mean that such *chiftliks* (almost always at least technically *mirî*) did not descend between generations. The most plausible explanation for the gradual disappearance would seem to be that Ottoman *kadis* and *naibs* simply were disinclined to record transactions which were not legitimate and while this disinclination admirably protected the propriety of their records, from the historian's point of view it is a cause for frustration and regret.

Defense of the village as a collectivity   A second mode of defense which the *kadi* might employ on behalf of villagers was to protect their prior right to the *tapu* on land left without heirs or, alternatively, to protect the villagers' right to the continued use of communal pasture or other communally held land. Ö. L. Barkan has published excerpts from general laws which deal with these rights. For instance, after exhausting a list of those eligible to assume the *tapu* one law says:

> and if there is no one of that description or if he refuses the proposal to take on the land with a *tapu*, it is given to those in that village who need land. And even if it has been given to people from another village, people from this village who need land may take it if they take it within a year's time.[75]

Barkan believed that this principle was ultimately set aside, however, and that eventually – apparently towards the end of the eighteenth century – a new principle appeared in decisions (*hüküms*) originating from the central government which dealt with land cases, namely that 'between those from within the village and those from the outside no preference exists.' (It must be admitted that no evidence was discovered in the Manastir *sijils* which demonstrates the application of either of these principles.)

Regarding the village common pasture:

> If there are pastures where the people of a village have been grazing cattle for a long time, it is not permissible for the *timarlı* to give out that pasture with a *tapu*. And if the people of a village give their consent, and he gives it out with their agreement and they cultivate it and afterwards people come forward and complain, the decision will be in favor of keeping the land pasture; there is no advantage in saying 'it has been cultivated for this much time' for pasturage has priority. Because pasturage is indispensable for villagers. It is impossible to do without pasturage.[76]

The application of this principle is seen best at Manastir in the occasional *fermans* returned to the district which deal with usurpation of pastures by powerful individuals. The outcome of such cases is seldom clear; what is usually apparent is that the people of a certain village have sent a petition to Istanbul regarding the usurpation of their pasture, obviously with the expectation that their grievance would be sympathetically received.

Defense of the mirî *status of land and the* reaya *status of the cultivator*   Mirî land was in fact frequently alienated from the *timar* system. In all such cases there was an immediate danger that the central government would lose not only the services supposedly rendered by a *sipahi* but in addition all income from such land whatsoever. Therefore the *kadis* of Manastir, like *kadis* in other districts, were frequently urged in *fermans* not to tolerate the alienation of land from the treasury but to enforce the *mirî* status of the land by obliging those who held it to continue paying taxes, or more accurately, to continue to allow *mirî* collections from the villagers who cultivated the land for them.

Just as serious as the usurpation of land was the usurpation of the labor force, that is, the alienation of cultivators from the *mirî* system by *chiftlik* owners who attracted, and then harbored fugitives, and if possible 'protected' them from the visitations of the state's tax collectors. In addition to villagers who fled to *chiftliks* there were those who changed villages, or who emigrated to Istanbul or other towns, or towards the end of the eighteenth century, into Russia's newly acquired territories. The flight of villagers was already a problem at Manastir in the 1630s around the time when the first surviving *sijils* were written, and it remained a problem, at least on *vakıf* land, as late as the 1820s.

Until the 1630s villagers who had fled were generally simply required to pay compensation to the *timarlı* from whose *timar* they had fled, in addition to taxes at their new locality. The intent was obviously to secure continuity of revenues for the *timarlı*, and the right of the man to change his place of residence was not usually questioned so long as he was willing to pay compensation. Possibly because of a general decline in population and a consequent labor hunger, a harsher rule came to prevail. Laws requiring the return of fugitives began to appear in the seventeenth century, and the *kadi* was called upon to enforce them and to help conserve the labor force of the *timarlı*, just as he helped conserve the integrity of the *timar* and the *mirî* status of the land.

The fact that tax liability had begun to shift to the land itself early in the seventeenth century (a shift which explains why *mirî* land was eventually called *veriji* land) does not mean that Ottoman governments were ready to free the *reaya* of their personal tax liability. Liability of the land had simply been intended to fill a gap created when the original cultivator disappeared and was displaced by a stranger (i.e. a person often not by status tax-liable). The test invariably applied by the *kadi* in determining who was a *reaya* and therefore tax-liable by status was to establish whether the individual concerned had been registered in an *avarız* register (i.e. a 'tax house' register) of the kind maintained by treasury officials from the early seventeenth century onward as a record of all those who were liable because of status to pay the *mirî* taxes demanded by the central treasury.[77]

The transition from the rule which demanded only compensation to a regime demanding the return of fugitives was not smooth. In 1636 there appeared an imperial rescript (*hatt-ı humayun*) requiring the return of fugitives to their villages of registration up to a limit of forty years after their flight.[78] Yet two years later there appeared a *ferman* stipulating a limitation of ten years on returns,[79] while in 1641 yet another *ferman* stipulated application of the compensation rule, an apparent reversion.[80] In fact an exhaustive study of the *reaya* institution recently completed by Aleksandar Matkovski shows that the Ottomans never fully made up their minds on the matter of limitations, so that although return of fugitive *reaya* was demanded by law for over two centuries preceding the Tanzimat, the term of limitation applied alternated between ten, twenty, thirty and forty years or, in the case of pious (*vakıf*) land, no limitation at all.[81] The most commonly applied rule, however, was the ten year rule.[82]

As is clear from surviving *fermans*, migration to towns, to Manastir itself, and particularly to Istanbul, became a problem in the eighteenth century. The central government repeatedly demanded that such migration be stopped.[83] As with inflation, the combined effects of flight and migration could go into a spiral since the burden of the taxes formerly paid by the fugitives was invariably loaded on the shoulders of those who remained behind. Such a spate of flight does seem to have taken place during the commodity boom of the Napoleonic era. After that demands for the return of fugitives are less frequent in the judicial records, probably because by that time the remnants of Manastir's *timarlıs* had set themselves up as *chiftlik* holders no longer legally in a position to demand the return of fugitives (and possibly, because of a shift in factor supply, no longer needing the return of fugitives).

Subversion of the old regime by the *timar*-holding class

The legal weapons at the disposal of the *kadi* might have been sufficient to protect a prebendal system which itself was full of vitality. But they could not adequately protect a prebendal system which was in reality dying. Given the conservatism of the Ottomans, it seemed unthinkable, at least until the Tanzimat, to abandon outright an institution thought to be indispensable to the power of the Ottoman state at the time of its sixteenth-century apogee. But an ambivalence about the *timar* system can be traced from the time of the long war against the Habsburgs at the end of the sixteenth century. Although the decline of the *timar* system is a vast development which still awaits research, there is no doubt that *timar* incomes were allowed to decline in the seventeenth century. Simultaneously the overall numerical strength of the territorial *sipahis* was allowed to decline. Judging from the Manastir situation the vast majority of *sipahis* lived in town in 1635, at a distance from the villages comprising their prebends.[84] Numerous notices make it clear that their interest in their villages was slipping since they frequently leased out their right to collect their incomes to other individuals, usually known as *jabis*.[85]

The eighteenth century saw at least four attempts at *timar* reform. The contents of the *fermans* announcing these reforms do not have anything to say about the abuses of *timarlıs* in their districts or about *timars*, perhaps because these were so common as to be thought impervious to reform. the reform *fermans* instead limit themselves largely to the appointment of *sipahis*, their place of residence and the identity of the appointing officer. A 1707 decree demands that all the *zaims* (larger landholders) and *timarlıs* of Rumeli and Anadolu, together with their helpers, as well as lesser officials and scribes holding *timars*, present themselves once a year at Istanbul.[86] The 1732 decree admits the decay of order which has taken place among the military 'since the Hungarian campaigns' (since 1718?) and demands that *zaims* and *timarlıs* reside on their livings and that they be appointed by the *alaybey*, a cavalry officer, and not by the *kadi* or anyone else.[87] The decree of 1777 also rails against the loss of discipline and character among the bulk of the *timarlıs* and *zaims*, complaining that many *timars* had been ruined out of greed. In this decree it is demanded that *sipahis* be chosen from those who lived within the province, that they be appointed by an officer and properly identified in registers to be inspected by the Grand Vezir, and that the officer himself be carefully chosen.[88] The 1792 reform decree was not found in the *sijils*, but its effect at Manastir can be seen in another *ferman* of 1795 which identifies 96 *timars* and *ziamets* at Manastir which were transferred from illegal holders following an inspection.[89] And while *timar* patents almost disappear from the late eighteenth-century *sijils*, the persistence of an interest in defending the system can be seen from a case registered in 1803. In this case the *sipahi*, Mustafa bin Abdullah, holding the village of Gabrovo as his *timar*, had complained that certain individuals were displaying a *tapu* 'deed' entitling them to his *timar*, a certificate which had apparently been sold to them by the previous *sipahi*; however since the plaintiff was shown to have been recorded as holder of that place in the *timar* register, it was decided that the encroachers must be prevented from disturbing him.

But for the most part *timar* holders were continually tempted to subvert the system one way or another so that they could slip out of the *timar* system and slip into the ranks of the *chiftlik* holders.[90] Since the *akche* depreciated while *timar* incomes failed to keep pace, probably at no time after the late sixteenth century were *sipahis* rewarded in a manner commensurate with their military responsibilities. Judging from the quantitative evidence of *chiftlik* development to be offered below, two waves of desertion must have taken place in which *timars* were abandoned, or converted into *chiftliks*, one wave culminating in the late seventeenth and the second wave culminating in the late eighteenth century.[91]

Evidence for the first wave of conversion can be seen in the spate of *fermans* in the mid-1690s which wrestle with the problem created for a treasury hard pressed by war by the behavior of many provincial *chiftlik* holders, *timarlıs* and other men of influence. The pattern of their behavior was not new, only more serious because of the dilemma brought on by the exhausting war with Austria and Venice (1683–99). Three modes of errant behavior are evident in these wartime *fermans*: (1) non-payment of *mirî* taxes by land usurpers; (2) the protection of *reaya*, i.e. hiding *reaya* from the state's collectors or preventing access by the collector; (3) the practice of *deruhdejilik*, i.e. acting as fiscal intermediary between the treasury and the state's collectors, a tolerated but objectionable development, which like the other two just mentioned had led the Ottoman state into a virtual tax base crisis (though depopulation may have contributed even more to this crisis).

Already in the Ohrid law of 1613 there had appeared the government's grievance against *sipahis* and other Muslims who had usurped *mirî* land, 'then make excuses when the time comes to collect the hearth tax and the *ispenje* and don't give it and have the poor indemnify them.' The government's solution was to transfer *reaya* liabilities onto the land, in an attempt to force usurpers to shoulder the fiscal responsibilities of the dispossessed: 'let *jizyes* and *ispenjes* be collected from such as these without fail whether they are *sipahis* or *sipahis'* agents or whoever they happen to be.'[92] A *ferman* of 1800 demonstrates that the same principle (i.e. that *mirî* land remained tax-liable regardless of who held it) was still in force, at least in theory.[93] Intermittent *fermans* issued during the course of the seventeenth century show, however, that collections from non-*reaya* were in fact very hard to carry out.[94] Not only hearth taxes such as the *jizye* and *ispenje*, but all *mirî* taxes, such as the *avarız* and *nüzül*, were evaded by the usurpers. And in 1695, according to one *ferman*, even the government's order authorizing grain purchase (*mubayaa*) at Manastir (to supply Beograd) was being evaded by, or with the help of powerful individuals, including *chiftlik* holders, who were determined to have the burden shifted to weaker shoulders.[95] The second practice, protection, arises in a *ferman* issued in 1634, the first of a series of such *fermans*: 'but *reaya* have taken shelter on the *chiftliks* of some *sipahis* and janissaries and other military men, and it has been reported that these latter have been preventing the collection of *mirî* taxes.'[96] A particularly sharp conflict surrounded the collection in connection with the new regulation of *jizye* liability, which shifted responsibility for payment from the household onto the individual adult male non-Muslim (*zimmi*) with no exceptions permitted, even for clergy. The *fermans* of these years lament the fact that many villages were deserted, their inhabitants apparently scattered by the unbearable burden placed upon them during the long war with Austria.[97] In exasperated language, a 1695 decree indicts the *kadi* of Manastir, the local men of affairs, local bailiffs, tax collectors and village elders for willful negligence and for inciting the *reaya* on their *chiftliks* and other properties to resist paying the *mirî* taxes. 'You are all,' says the *ferman*, 'deserving of punishment.'[98] This *ferman* actually asserts that a majority of the *reaya* of the district are in one way or another working for or living under the direct control of influential Muslims, but this is apparently an exaggeration. (It is probable nonetheless that the war years did witness many loan activities which would have helped drive *reaya* into the arms of the influential. In theory a priority of *mirî* collections over collections of loans (*muamele akchesi*) had already been established during the early Köprülü years,[99] but it seems unlikely that such a priority was enforced by collectors at the village level.)

A third local practice, troublesome from the Porte's point of view, was for influential individuals, often with the collusion of the *timarlıs*, to undertake to mediate between individual villages and the *mirî* collectors who embittered their existence and even endangered their survival. The entrepreneur who mediated for a village was called a *deruhdeji*. It is not clear how he was rewarded for his role or what his relationship to the villagers was other than as their *deruhdeji*. This too was obviously a form of protection, and as such a threat to the treasury's short run requirements (though not necessarily to its long run needs).[100]

Although an apparent stability between *chiftliks* and *timars* lasted through much of the eighteenth century (see *tevzi* data below) new stimuli, both negative and positive, brought about a trend towards further *chiftlik* formation in the last quarter of that century. There had always been banditry in western Macedonia, often on a large scale; the town of Manastir itself had been raided at times.[101] But the scale of the brigandage which accompanied and followed the two wars with Russia in the last quarter of the century was clearly unprecedented. Albanians used as irregulars during the war of 1768–74 rampaged in bands for years afterwards or sought employment in the retinues of the powerful. Many men were again learning how to use chaos to their own advantage. During and after the war of 1788–92, great bands of so-called *kirjalıs*, occasionally numbering in the thousands, roved across western Macedonia, destroying as they went. Epidemics born of war raged in 1772, 1778 and 1781. And throughout these decades the *beys* connived, combined and fought each other for supremacy.[102]

At this time the world's demand for cotton, wheat and other commodities rose. Though Macedonian cotton had been exported in steadily growing quantities since the early eighteenth century, the stint of supply brought on by the American Revolutionary War initiated a new upward phase which would not end for four decades. The French Revolution brought with it a long lasting boom in wheat. How powerful were these incentives to commodity production is suggested by the rise in prices commanded by wheat: in 1780 a *kile* of wheat sold at port for 12 *gurush*; in 1804 for 20; and in 1813 for 45.[103] A second price series shows a rise even more dramatic; in 1780 a *kile* of wheat sold for $1\frac{1}{2}$ piastres; in 1800 for $5\frac{1}{2}$ or 6 piastres; in 1812 for $14\frac{1}{2}$ or 15 piastres.[104] Doubtless because of Manastir's distance from the sea prices there were not as high; nonetheless between 1782 and 1802 they were partly comparable. Wheat was valued there in inheritance (*tereke*) lists of 1782 at 620 *akches* (at about 140 *akche* to the *gurush*). In 1802 wheat was at 1400 *akches* (again drawing on the *tereke* lists).[105] So there is no doubting the new and greater rewards awaiting those who succeeded in organizing land and labor for commercial commodity production in these decades, just as there is no doubting the terrible pressures created both by the continual strife of brigands and *pashas*, and by the greed of the land usurpers, in the lives of the cultivators themselves.

Neither the *chiftlik* building which led to the tax base crisis of the 1690s nor the *chiftlik* building of the profiteering decades of the Napoleonic era can be illustrated quantitatively by counting individual land transactions in the *sijils* – there simply are not enough such transactions, particularly in the late eighteenth and early nineteenth century. Hristo Gandev, working with the Vidin *sijils*, made the same discovery there. Where are the land transactions which together comprise the trends just discussed? Gandev's theory on this question is probably correct, at least in part.[106] He reasons that since every entry into the judicial record involved a fee, there would be a tendency to neglect registry unless a need for it were felt; also that the entire *chiftlik* building process could be accounted for simply by the issuance of *tapunames* by the landholder, who was often a *timarlı*. His conclusion is that the entire *chiftlik*-building process was the work of those who issued *tapunames*, a privilege which the Ottoman land laws had invested in the prebendal class but which under special circumstances might be exercised by others, such as the officials who dispensed *has* land at Vidin (and perhaps by extension whomever held the land).

Although this line of argument is in theory sufficient, there are occasional signs in the *sijils* that not only the *tapuname*, but also the *kadi*'s certificate (*hüjjet*) was used in the late eighteenth and early nineteenth century to authorize and confirm land transfers (even though the use of *hüjjets* for this purpose had been forbidden since the drafting of the first general land law corpus referred to above). One *ferman* from a Karaferye *sijil*, which was addressed in 1795 to all the *kadis* of the 'left wing' of Rumeli depicts the rural situation as follows:

1. villagers in debt to moneychangers and others were being forced to sell their fields;
2. conversion of villages into *chiftliks* had resulted in a greater burden on the remaining villages and consequent loss to the treasury;
3. no further conversions of this sort would be allowed without the express permission of the Grand Vezir;
4. *kadis* were forbidden to go on issuing *hüjjets* for land thus obtained.[107]

A second *ferman*, dated 1804, this time addressed to all *kadis* and *naibs* in the middle band of Rumeli, and issued after a representation to the Grand Vezir by the chief *kadi* of Rumeli, is a reconfirmation of the fact that it is forbidden for *kadis* to draft *hüjjets* requested by individuals who sell or give property in order to alienate it from their normal heirs.[108]

Therefore it would seem that there were at least two means for 'legalizing' land transfers in those feverish decades, one by using the 'deed' or *tapuname*, in harmony with the letter (but not the spirit) of the law, the other by eliciting the *kadi*'s *hüjjet* despite the prohibition on this procedure.

Was there any real hope at Istanbul of controlling the situation? It seems doubtful in the semi-feudal atmosphere of those times that there was. In 1780 a man who is called a brigand (*shaki*) in the record had his 69 *chiftliks* confiscated, some of them located in the Manastir district. All these *chiftliks* were then sold, for 350 *gurush*, to one Ahmet as outright property (*mülk*) and an imperial certificate (*mülkname-i humayun*) was issued. If there were any pious or prebendal holdings included among these '*chiftliks*,' they were to be returned to the original holders. Ahmet is not praised for any special service and his name appears devoid of titles. This was an absolute alienation of quite a lot of land for cash. It would be wrong to place too great a weight on a single case; yet this does not sound like the behavior of a government which felt it was in a position to make the most expedient use of land over which it claimed to have ultimate ownership.[109]

Fiscal contributions from the Manastir district

Once Ottoman coinage has been studied systematically and analyzed to construct continuous tables showing the exact content of Ottoman coins in everyday use during the seventeenth, eighteenth and nineteenth centuries it will be possible to make accurate quantitative statements about secular trends in fiscal burdens at the village level, including the burden borne by the Manastir district. At this point it is possible to say not that the provincial fiscal burden was always heavier with each passing year but rather that the total fiscal 'system' bifurcated and proliferated irrationally so that it was clearly impossible for the central government to know with certainty whether or not current fiscal demands were tolerable in any given district. It seems quite probable that it was not only the weight of the tax burden in average years which drove peasants to flight at Manastir, as in other districts, but also year to year fluctuations in that burden which had slipped from central control, coupled with the year to year fluctuations in harvests which are a natural feature of life on the Mediterranean periphery.

Under the classic system of the sixteenth century the fiscal burden of the village consisted of two main components: (1) prebendal dues in support of the *timar* system (including market dues), and (2) *mirî* taxes collected and then disbursed under control of the central treasury, including occasional levies to meet special needs, usually in wartime. But in the seventeenth and eighteenth centuries the prebendal dues supporting the *timar* system were pruned not only by preemptive increases in *mirî* burdens but also by the emergence of two new levels of taxation which were not under central control: (3) taxes raised for provincial needs, and (4) taxes raised for local district needs.[110] By sketching the shifts within and between these 'systems,' we can appreciate easily how competing fiscal demands – often out of control and without coordination – ground the *reaya* down.

The prebendal system The survival of prebendal dues under the *timar* system of the later Ottoman centuries has been studied very little. Although the introduction of new dues by the *timarlı* were not authorized by law, abuses of authority on his part were always hard to control, particularly when, as became increasingly the case in the seventeenth and eighteenth centuries, the appointing officer or the local *kadi* had profited through his appointment. Aside from applying pressure to obtain part of the *timar* for his own direct use, two other devices were probably widespread among *timarlıs*: arbitrarily raising the amounts of customary cash taxes (the *ispenje* in particular), and collection of the 'tithe' (*öshür*) in kind rather than cash, as a hedge against currency inflation. The fact that these abuses are scarcely noticeable among the complaints of *reaya* as recorded at the court in Manastir is no disproof; such practices may have been so common as to be taken for granted by all parties concerned. Thus although the face value of standard *timars* tended to freeze at levels reached in the early seventeenth century (typically 6000 to 7000 *akches*), so little is known about the real incomes of *sipahis* in the seventeenth and eighteenth centuries that it is unwarranted to assume that *sipahis* failed to compete with the treasuries of the central and provincial authorities for the benefits of the land. Be that as it may, the pattern and the levels of taxation (or 'feudal rents') authorized under the *timar* system appear to have changed little or not at all on paper during the two centuries under discussion here.

Larger prebends (*has* and *ziamet* assignments), which tended to be farmed out annually by the treasury after the late sixteenth century, also displayed the pattern of customary prebendal dues which had characterized the *timars*. But so little research has yet been done on the levels and patterns of collections under the tax farming system that it is at present impossible to generalize about the survival of the traditional prebendal dues as instruments of that system.

The mirî *tax system*   Two village level taxes were reserved under the classic system for collection directly by the central treasury, rather than being leased out as *timar* income; these were the hearth tax (*jizye* or *harach*) and the sheep tax (the *adet-i ağnam* or *resm-i ağnam*). The amount of the *jizye* was adjusted upward many times in the seventeenth and eighteenth centuries.[111] By contrast the sheep tax (which in the Manastir district was collected only from Muslims) was allowed to ossify at the original level of one *akche* per head of sheep; this tax became so insignificant owing to the degeneration of the *akche* that it appears to have gone uncollected after the first decades of the eighteenth century[112] – at least it ceases to be noticeable in the *sijils*.

The older sheep tax was replaced by a new sheep tax – the *jelepkeshan* – which came to be required annually from the Manastir district. The evolution of the *jelepkeshan* is essentially similar to that of the *mirî* taxes discussed in the preceding section, the *avarız* and the *nüzül*. The process starts as some districts (originally Bulgarian and Wallachian districts) are asked to supply Istanbul with sheep at sacrifice prices, at first irregularly. Other districts less well situated are then asked to contribute the equivalent in cash, the *jelepkeshan*, so that the burden of supplying Istanbul is not placed upon certain districts only.[113] Then the new tax is collected annually rather than irregularly, and eventually ossifies, i.e. continues to be collected long after the original cash value of the tax has lost its meaning owing to devaluation of the currency.

Another class of *mirî* taxes remained irregular.[114] These include the *mekâri*, an occasional levy to buy pack animals for transport services, and other levies for the purpose of supplying grain either for the capital complex in time of need or for garrisons or mobilized forces. This class of grain levies, variously known as *ishtira*, *mubayaa* and *sürsat*, can be regarded as the seventeenth-century surrogates for the *avarız* and *nüzül* levies of the sixteenth century. Once again the *bedel* principle can be seen in operation. If the district was fairly conveniently located it might be required to supply grain or flour in kind. If the district was too remote from the zone where the need was manifest, then a cash *bedel* was required. (A distinction has usually been made in the literature between *sürsat*, i.e. grain purchased at confiscatory prices, and *ishtira/mubayaa*, which supposedly indicated grain purchased at normal price levels. Thorough study of this question will be necessary before it can be said that this distinction was valid and enduring. (In 1776 the Manastir district was ordered to supply 10,000 additional *kile* of flour at 50 *akches* per *kile*, while a *tereke* list from the following year shows flour to be valued at 400 *akches* per *kile*. Was this a *sürsat* transaction or *ishtira*? – the enabling *ferman* does not use either term.)[115] Grain purchases were eventually made not only from the villagers but from *chiftlik* owners as well: a grain purchase *ferman* of 1788 occasioned by the campaigning against Russia authorizes purchases from 'the owners of storehouses and *chiftliks* and villagers who have grain on hand' (this *ferman* arrived in February).[116]

Taxes raised for provincial needs

Provincial governors (*valis*) and other higher officials felt a need for greater incomes long before the central government made appropriate adjustments. Like *timar* revenues, the revenues of high officials were undercut in the seventeenth century by the preemption policy of the central treasury and also squeezed by their own compelling need to maintain larger and larger retinues in the interests both of prestige and of security. Hence *valis* and *pashas* and others of their peers were forced to find new means for raising their revenues from the hard-pressed provinces. A profusion of taxes, known collectively as the *tekâlif-i shakka*, appears, especially from the time of the war for Crete (1645–69).[117] These were authorized not by the central government but by the *valis* for their own benefit. Likewise before the end of the seventeenth century it became very common, as one can see in the *sijils*, for a district to be called upon on an annual basis and sometimes more frequently, to provide entertainment funds to meet the needs or the wants of visiting dignitaries and their retinues.[118]

At first the tendency was for the central government to rail against the levying of taxes by provincial authorities. More rarely it might even demand restitution. In a letter from the steward of Rumeli governor Mehmed Pasha in 1679 we find that the Pasha was under pressure to return to the Manastir district 700 *gurush* which he had raised there under the guise of 'hat money.' But, by agreement with the district, only 400 of the 700 was actually returned.[119] In the long run the insufficiency of regular revenues could not be denied, and in 1717 by one account (or 1719 in another)[120] the institutionalization of the *tekâlif-i shakka* was authorized. However, instead of authorizing all the various forms which such provincial levies had taken, the central government specified the collection of an annual cumulative provincial tax known as the *imdad-i hazariye* (in time of peace) or as the *imdad-i seferiye* (in time of war). Since the *imdats* were collected in two semi-annual (and often unequal) installments they also became known under the name *taksit* ('installment'). This regularization did not end all provincial collections under other guises, however. In 1730 a *ferman* addressed to the Rumelian 'right wing' still condemns collections under various notorious pretexts, demanding that collections be limited to the now standard *jizye, avarız, nüzül, imdad-i hazariye* or *imdad-i seferiye* and other legal dues.[121] The persistence of these bad habits is evident from another *ferman* of 1779, addressed this time to all the *kadis* of Rumeli.[122] While Ahmed Pasha was *vali* (at Sofia), runs the *ferman*, he collected, in addition to the *imdats*, 300 purses as 'honors' (*teshrifiyye*). Although the practice of collecting the *teshrifiyye* had been forbidden by the Grand Vezir Muhsinzade Mehmed in 1773 because the populace could not bear it, other *valis* had sought to reintroduce the practice: now once again the *teshrifiyye* was forbidden. The practice of requiring districts to pay expenses for visiting dignitaries was equally stubborn. A *ferman* from the same year as that condemning the *teshrifiyye* (1779) rails against excessive demands for traveling expenses on the part of traveling *vezirs* and *mirmirans*.[123]

The fact that local figures of influence were dipping their hands into the public purse with every *mirî* collection, when there was an entertainment bill to meet or when grain collections had been authorized, did not escape notice at the center. A *ferman* from Edirne in 1695, in response to a petition by the *reaya* of the Manastir district, is aimed at abuses by local notables in general.[124] But later *fermans*, in 1729, 1740, 1779 and 1781, are aimed directly at the *kadis* and their substitutes as chief culprits in this game.[125] Perhaps it was increasingly easy for *kadis* to disguise their manipulations, for by the 1780s it had become regular practice to throw all of the province expenses together on one annual or semi-annual account, for which a joint collection was then made. The province account for 1781, for instance, combines an *imdat*, an 'oil price,' entertainment of the *vali*, and several other entertainment items such as the 'grain price.'[126]

Taxes raised for district needs

There was nothing of the welfare state about the local needs met by local taxation at Manastir. The first of these needs was the courier service. By the late seventeenth century Manastir was the site of a station (*menzilhane*) where imperial couriers could remount. The up-keep of the stable, of the shelter which presumably adjoined it, and the salary of the man in charge were met from a separate local *menzilhane* levy.[127] The second of the needs to be funded locally was the mainte-nance of a local garrison of militia, called *segbans*. The presence of the *segbans* is most noticeable in the *sijils* of the later decades of the eight-eenth century in a period when the district's need for protection was unprecedentedly great.[128] But there were also other periods earlier, as during the long war against Austria at the end of the seventeenth century, when the district had been called upon to support the recruit-ment of infantry to be stationed there.[129]

In view of these various changes in taxation at the district level, it is not surprising that the composition of the non-prebendal tax burden of the Manastir district looks different in cross-sections spanning a long period of time. Table 5 which follows indicates the composition of the non-prebendal tax burden at Manastir at several points in time (i.e. for several disparate *hijri* years). Although the table suggests long run change, it does not demonstrate adequately the year to year fluctua-tions, especially in wartime, which obviously placed a great strain on the district population in the worst years. (The fact that a particular tax does not appear on this table in a given year cannot be taken as a guarantee that the tax was not collected – only that no entry regarding that tax appears in the *sijil* pertaining to that year.)

The local tax allocation system at Manastir

Students of Ottoman government are, rightly, inclined to the view that the record-keeping of the seventeenth and eighteenth centuries was more disorderly than in the golden age of Ottoman power. At least part of the disorder arose from the reluctance of the central government to admit that the golden age had passed or, in concrete terms, to admit that depopulation and flight had taken place. Thus their *jizye* and *avarız/nüzül* registers were allowed to get sadly out of line with reality, so that these registers might go for long periods without an appropriate downward adjustment. This practice placed local administrators, above all the *kadis*, in a bind since they were obliged to supervise collections at stereotyped levels from a weakened populace which each exorbitant demand weakened further.

Table 5. Components of the non-prebendal tax burden at Manastir, 1622–1781

1031 H	(20 July 1621 – 9 July 1622):[130]
	jizye, avarız, nüzül, adet-i ağnam
1043 H	(8 July 1633 – 26 June 1634):[131]
	jizye, avarız, nüzül, adet-i ağnam
	bedel-i mekâri, bargir bahası,
	nev yafte akchesi
1073 H	(16 August 1662 – 4 August 1663):[132]
	jizye, avarız, nüzül, resm-i ganem,
	jelepkeshan, zahire bahası, sürsat
	(levied for the visit of Silahtar Mustafa Ağa)
1093 H	(10 January 1682 – 30 December 1682):[133]
	jizye, avarız, nüzül, zahire bahası,
	menzilhane
1142 H	(27 July 1729 – 16 July 1730):[134]
	jizye, avarız–nüzül, jelepkeshan,
	imdad-i hazariye, menzilhane,
	shalitre ishtira, yağ ishtira
1195 H	(28 December 1780 – 16 December 1781):[135]
	jizye, avarız, nüzül, jelepkeshan,
	imdad-i hazariye, segban, menzil,
	vilayet account (including entertainment
	of Rumeli *vali, revgan bahası*)

To a degree Ottoman villages were fiscal collectivities, as we see from the fact that they took loans as collectivities. Although little is known about distribution of tax burdens within the village by village authorities, the co-responsibility of villagers for taking up the slack in the tax burden as the result of flight was already in part articulate in one of the laws of Mehmet the Conqueror: 'And on any *timar* from which tax-liable unbelievers have fled I have ordered that (they) take half their hearth tax from the *timar* holders and half from the unbelievers who have remained in their places.'[136] However, district administrators could not afford to press so heedlessly upon the villages as the central government pressed upon the districts. Therefore they invented by stages a device for reapportionment which took into consideration real changes in fiscal strength and which could be adjusted yearly to fluctuations in local conditions at the village level. This device became known as the *tevzi*, and the unit of reapportionment the *tevzi hane*. In 1635, well before the appearance of formal *tevzi* lists in the Manastir *sijils*, one finds that the Manastir *kadi*, together with the local *timarlıs* and other peers, is already involved in a reapportionment problem – the need to readjust an (undiminished) *jizye* burden so that it would rest equally on the shoulders of those who were not either 'dead, or fled' (*güzeşte gürihteler*).

A similar session is recorded in 1638.[137] In 1640 a reapportionment session was also needed at Manastir in order to equalize the *avarız* burden.[138] The first formal *tevzi* lists found which actually show the relative burden to be borne by each of the district's villages were those of 1661, appended to a *ferman* authorizing a *sürsat* collection, and to another authorizing the annual *nüzül*.[139] The first use of the term *tevzi hane*, meaning a mini-district serving as a unit of reapportionment, was found in an entry dated 1694, at the end of a *tevzi* list dealing with a combined *avarız/nüzül* collection.[140]

The inspiration for the *tevzi* lists and the *tevzi hanes* was undoubtedly the central government's *avarız/nüzül* system which had for a long time divided Rumeli and Anatolia into tiny fiscal districts of a few households each, established for the purpose of apportioning the *mirî* taxes known under those names. But although the goal of rational apportionment was the same, the *tevzi hane* was different from *avarız/nüzül hane* in an essential aspect: whereas the *avarız/nüzül hane* was intended to constitute a stable and continuous unit of so many households (held together by registration and internal collective responsibility) the *tevzi hane* was from its first appearance a flexible unit – one of an indeterminate number of units into which a particular tax burden had been divided after consultation within the district. Whereas the number of *avarız hanes* was officially held steady, the number of *tevzi hanes* in the Manastir district was permitted to float, at one time near the number of villages in the district, in another period around a hundred (for easier arithmetic?). Probably the total of *tevzi hanes* moved involuntarily through a process which involved first a temporary conception of what the strength of one unit ought to be and, secondly, negotiation about applying that concensual conception to the circumstances of a particular year or of a particular moment in a year. The negotiators were naturally not inclined to adjust the unit value of each village simply because the burdens of one or a few villages had been changed; it was easier to adjust the face value of the collection due from each unit.

These manipulations introduced into the *sijil* record generate a multiplicity of concepts which can be a pitfall for researchers. The *sijil* reader who is following tax matters must distinguish carefully (in the seventeenth-century records particularly) between (1) the official *jizye* number, (2) the official *avarız/nüzül* (or *mevkufat*) number, (3) the current *tevzi hane* number, (4) the current number of actual households, and (5) the current actual number of adult males (*nefers*). Likewise care must be taken to distinguish official tax rates (for *jizye*, *avarız* or *nüzül*, for instance) from the rates actually applied after consultation in the district.

Reapportionment was not always on the basis of *tevzi hanes*. Sometimes reapportionment was done on the basis of households or, in the eighteenth and nineteenth centuries, on the basis of *chiftliks*, as we shall see. Sometimes two principles might be applied in the same year, or combined, as for instance in 1694 when one *ishtira* sale is arranged on a simple household basis while another is arranged on the basis of *tevzi hanes*.[141] To complicate matters further the number of villages varied slightly. This may have been done to excuse certain hard pressed villages, to excuse Muslim villages, or for some other reason. After a time *tevzi* lists contained, in addition to a greater number of villages subject to equal reapportionment, a few villages – always the same ones – which were apparently privileged in being able to pay their contributions on a fixed (*maktu*) basis. These villages were called '*tuğralı*' (signed) villages, perhaps with reference to the patents which gave them privileged status. All three of Manastir's *vakıf* villages eventually had *tuğralı* status.

A detailed *tevzi* drawn up on a household basis allows the researcher to follow changes in village size, insofar as this is reflected in numbers of households. An official list of households from 1641 (doubtless reflecting an out-of-date situation) shows an average village size of 26.7 households. A household *tevzi* drawn up forty years later, in 1682, shows an average village size of only 6.7 households![142] What conclusions are possible from this startling drop? A manifestation of depopulation; a change in the definition of the household; a real change in household size; or the result of 'protection' by influential men? Perhaps all of these explanations are partly correct. The same 1682 survey shows only one household for 18 of the 140 villages listed. Of these 18, six have disappeared completely in a comparable survey made thirty years later (in 1710),[143] while eight are accompanied by indications showing an unusually heavy concentration of *chiftliks* in their vicinity.

A contemporary account of a *tevzi* session (i.e. a session to reapportion a fiscal burden) was offered by one of the founders of modern Serbia, Prota Matija Nenadovich, who as the son of one of the leading *knezes* (native chiefs) of Serbia in the years leading up to the events of 1804 was in a good position to observe local politics. It would seem from his account, however, that the *tevzi* process in the Beograd *pashaluk* was not carried out on the basis of *tevzi hanes* but rather on the basis of adult males. (The 'legal households' referred to in the account can only be the archaic official *avarız hane* count. Also the *vezir*'s ignorance which he speaks of is a little difficult to believe; surely he had a better idea of the numerical strength of the Serbian districts than the Prota realized – though indeed the obfuscatory tendencies of the *sipahis* were real enough since every gain by the *vezir* was a loss for them.)

Those meetings that I remember were carried out thus: all three *knezes* – with a few followers, went to Valjevo and each brought with him to the courts the accounts of his own district; if, for example, any *pasha* or any other Turk had passed through for whose entertainment much had been spent, or for some building material or something else that they had paid that should have been paid for by the whole district. A number of old Turkish *ağas* presided over the court, looked at the accounts, and when they had agreed that they were in order the *kadi* confirmed them with his seal. The *knezes* then took this list of expenses and wrote an order how much should be chargeable to every married man and so, little by little, it was reckoned that every legal household would have to pay about a hundred or sometimes more *grosh* on Mitrovdan or on Djurdjevdan. But it should be known that in the Valjevo district there were only 750 of these legal households inscribed. So the *knezes* had told the first *vezir* after the German war [i.e. after 1792] and this they had ever afterwards held to, so that when they assessed the taxes among the people by married men it came to eight or at the most ten *grosh* each, since the *knezes* concealed the number from the *vezir*, and the *sipahis* and the other Turks who knew of this did not want to tell them. The *knezes*, when they went to the *vezir* in connection with the taxes, brought with them the best of the local followers whom they dressed in the very poorest clothes – and when they appeared before the *vezir* they cried out: 'Aman, aman, for the health of the Sultan! We cannot pay such heavy taxes; you see that we are naked and barefoot. . . . Who can ask a hundred or a hundred and sixty *grosh* a head[144] from such as we?' and so forth. Then the *vezir* would reduce the taxes a little.

Then our three *knezes* went into their districts and on their way told everyone to fix a day on which two or three men from each village would come to Valjevo. . . . The local *ağas* came also. After that the *kadi* would study the *vezir*'s order and would say how much the tax was to be.

Quantification of *chiftlik* agriculture at Manastir

The strain of the long war with the Holy League (1683–99) could scarcely have been surmounted at Manastir had it not been for the equitability introduced by the locally administered *tevzi* system. But the system was not without enemies. It was subverted even during the war by military men who sought either to protect *reaya* who already worked on their *chiftliks* or to bring additional villagers under their control, thus cheating the tax collectors of the contributions due from them. The frustration of the central government with this situation is given voice in a *ferman* addressed to the Manastir district (and three others) in connection with the *avarız/nüzül* collections of 1694:

when the time had come for the collection of the *avarız* and the *bedel-i nüzül* from the districts named and our collector arrived and began to make collections as required by the decree and by the [*mevkufat*] register which had been given him, some of the notables (*ayan*) of the province and *timar* holders appeared as middlemen (*deruhdeji*), and in order to mediate (*deruhte eylemek*) on behalf of various villages did not permit a *tevzi* register to be given on time, and because of the hindrance and delay of the *timar* holders they have caused difficulty for the imperial kitchen accounts, it is reported, so that my imperial decree has been requested in order that the middlemen and *timar* holders be prevented from interfering and in order that the *tevzi* register be delivered with the knowledge of the local judge, and their door opened, and the collection accomplished as soon as possible so that no shortcoming shall result for the decree and the [*mevkufat*] register entrusted to him.[145]

Not until 1709 was the *tevzi* system at Manastir reformed to adapt to a trend that must have been obvious for a long time: the growth of *chiftlik* agriculture at the expense of the local villagers. A system geared to taxing every village according to its ability to pay (*her karyenin tahmiline göre*) and to loading the taxes of the fugitives onto the shoulders of those who remained (*gürihtesin asıla zamm*)[146] was finally expanded to include the now numerous *chiftliks* which had appeared in the district.[147] That *chiftlik* holders had been for a long time among the troublemakers of the district (from the central government's point of view) is clear from a *ferman* of 1695 issued in response to a complaint of some inhabitants of the district that the burden imposed for the forced purchase of grain was not being shared equally:

reaya living in the villages of the aforesaid *kaza* have petitioned the imperial camp (*ordu*) and have reported: 'although the 2200 *kiles* of grain ordered this year for purchase from our *kaza* have been made ready nonetheless Muslim and non-Muslim townsmen and others who hold *chiftliks* (*mutasarrıf olan*) have had the support of some men of influence in not giving up their share of the grain; and *chiftlik* holders have not turned over the grain falling to each of their shares but have said, "you give all of it," and have by their misconduct caused our ruin.'[148]

All earlier references to *chiftlik* holders (*sahibs*) had failed to mention how many such individuals there were. But from the 1709 *tevzi* list, which for the first time in the Manastir district forces this favored class to share a tax burden as a group (in this case one-fifth of the currently demanded *jelepkeshan*) we learn that the district contains 419 such persons; and since their names are also given it is clear, quite unsurprisingly, that they are virtually all Muslims.[149]

From 1709 to 1823 one is able to see, in a rough sort of way, the level of *chiftlik* agriculture in the Manastir district, owing to the inclusion in the record of occasional *tevzi* lists which distribute tax burdens either partly, or upon occasion wholly, among the *chiftliks* of the district. Within the *chiftlik* group four apportionment principles were at first by turns applied: (1) an equal sum from each *chiftlik*, (2) an equal sum from each *chift*, i.e. each unit of 25 acres, (3) an equal sum from each cultivator working on a *chiftlik* (i.e. working on a holding which was legally held by someone else), and (4) a sum of money, graduated according to the size or estimated strength of the *chiftlik*.[150] Fortunately, because of the application of different apportionment principles, at least at the outset, more data on the magnitudes of *chiftliks* are available than would otherwise be the case. The principle of apportionment invariably favored after the experimentation of the first two decades was apportionment by *chifts* (item 2 above), although the reason for this preference is not clear.

The frequency of *tevzi* lists which include *chiftliks* varies, as does the extent of the burden which they were expected to carry; probably this variance, like the variance in the number of *tevzi hanes*, reflects year to year vicissitudes, making the cooperation of the politically more powerful *chiftlik* holders more urgent in some years than in others. Throughout the eighteenth century it is safe to say that the villages continue to carry the great bulk of the tax burden. This situation changed, however, in the nineteenth century (see below).

Great care is necessary in handling the numbers contained in the *tevzi* lists. Figure 9 below reveals that there were two different ways of counting *chifts*, perhaps in deference to some socioeconomic distinction among *chiftlik* holders or to spatial distribution of the *chifts*, with the large group being attached to the villages of the *tevzi* system, and a smaller group being the *chifts* belonging to outlying *chiftliks* in socially prominent hands. Great care is called for therefore in using *tevzi* data, so that different series of numbers are not confused with one another. Not all *tevzi* lists are equally revealing. Yet the best of them offer much data useful to the historian – data on the magnitudes and distribution of *chiftliks*, and on their animal and manpower requirements.

The most striking feature of the data on the number of *chiftliks* is that there is no great change over the 114 years spanned. From this one may draw at least three different conclusions: that *chiftliks* as we have defined them were already well established in the Manastir district early in the eighteenth century (and conceivably long before that), and that the stimulus to commercial agriculture did not change much during the course of that century (despite the higher prices of Napoleon's time); or that the data are not reliable, or become less reliable with the passage of time;[151] or that the stimulus to production in the later decades was answered by growth in the size of *chiftliks* rather than their numbers (though if that were the case then the growth in their size ought to be reflected in the number of *chifts* recorded – yet this number did not change drastically in the later decades either).

Magnitudes of Manastir's *chiftliks* can be inferred through three sets of data which are found in the early eighteenth-century *tevzis*: a distribution (and not merely the total number) of the adult males living on the *chiftliks*; a distribution (and not just the total number) of *chifts* (25 acre units) of *chiftlik* land, and a distribution, in one instance, of a graduated tax burden upon the *chiftliks* of the district.

Thus in 1710, whereas 2079 adult males (*nefers*) lived in villages, 1265 were living on *chiftliks*. Since the number of *chiftliks* indicated on this particular *tevzi* was 362 (rather than the 419 appearing on the graph for 1709) the mean number of adult males on one *chiftlik* was 3.5. More *chiftliks* had two *nefers*, 69 cases, than had any other number. Thirteen *chiftliks* had ten *nefers* or more living on them; of these two had 20 *nefers* and one had 85.[152]

In 1729 a *tevzi* shows 1230 *chifts* distributed among 476 *chiftliks*, an average of 2.6 *chifts* per *chiftlik*.[153] The highest number of *chifts* indicated was 12.

In 1731 a *tevzi* apportioning a tax burden (occasioned by the visit of the 'Rumeli *vezir*') upon 382 *chiftliks* in graduated 100 *akche* steps, ranging from 100 *akches* to 2200 *akches*, yields an average burden of 375 *akches* per *chiftlik*, the distribution being as follows: 100 *akches* (66 cases), 200 (66), 300 (85), 400 (59), 500 (38), 600 (30), 700 (11), 800 (10), 900 (6), 1000 (3), 1100 (1), 1200 (1), 1300 (1), 1400 (1), 1600 (2), 2100 (1), 2200 (1).[154] Perhaps it is also worth showing the distribution of Muslim titles identifying the *chiftlik* holders in this *tevzi*: *ağa* (72 cases), *sipahi* (29), *chelebi* (22), *efendi* (20), *kâhya* (9), *beyzade* (8), *efendizade* (7), *pasha* (6), *zaim* (5), *yazıjı* (5), *hoja* (5), *ağazade* (5), *hanım* (3), *bey* (2), *pashazade* (2), *kadızade* (2), *chelebizade* (1), *hazinedarzade* (1), *veznedarzade* (1), *chavushoğlu* (1) *hajızade* (1) (not all *chiftlik* holders had titles accompanying their names). Among the eight *chiftlik* holders who were apportioned more than 1000 *akches* were two *efendis*, one *efendizade*, one *hanım*, one *ağa*, two *beyzades* and one *pasha*.

From the aforegoing one can infer that the average *chiftlik* of the early eighteenth century was no great affair, though it is obvious that there were a dozen sizeable estates at the high end of the distribution. Unfortunately data on magnitudes, except for *total* numbers of *chifts*, are lacking from later *tevzis*. Possibly large *chiftlik* owners were successful in discouraging *chiftlik* censuses so that the earlier figures survive as stereotypes. In any case the impression created of modest size for the average *chiftlik* seems in harmony with one study of late nineteenth-century *chiftliks* at Polog (in Macedonia) which includes some rare data on magnitudes. At Polog 46.8 per cent of the *chiftliks* were under 25 hectares, with an average size of only 14 hectares – disposing as a group of only 10.8 per cent of the cultivated surface. In the next group, 20.2 per cent of the *chiftliks* had an average of 25–50 hectares. In the over 50 hectare group there were a few quite large holdings, topped by one *chiftlik* with 625 hectares. *Chiftliks* under 57.35 hectares comprised 75.7 per cent of the cultivated surface.[155]

As shown on Map 16, the *chiftliks* of the early eighteenth century were to a marked degree distributed along the north–south axis described by the Crna River. This preference for bottom land, land which was presumably better watered and therefore more fertile, is in keeping with the descriptions of twentieth-century geographers relying upon nineteenth-century data, such as Jovan Cvijić and Richard Busch-Zantner. But the confirmation of their generalization at Manastir does not mean that all the river basins of Rumeli were similarly infested. To the contrary, there are strong reasons to believe that the southern half of the Balkan zone, better placed with respect to international markets, witnessed an earlier and more dramatic growth of *chiftlik* agriculture than did Bosnia, Serbia and most of Bulgaria at any time.

The number of draught animals employed on the *chiftliks* of Manastir can be presumed to be closely correlated with the *chift* series shown on the figure. Thus in the 1710 *tevzi* the low series begins with 960 *chifts*, in 1748 there are 800, in 1776 either 850 or 750, in 1788 – 864, in 1813 – 934, in 1824 – 937;[156] in the higher series, 1230 in 1729, 1100 in 1788, 1060 or 1160 in 1803, 1100 in 1809 and 1144 in 1820.[157]

Although the *tevzi* lists offer nothing to explain the manner in which *chifts* were counted, one *tevzi* of 1816 does explicitly divide extant *chifts* into two groups, one a group of 896, concentrated in six villages, the other a group of 298, held by 24 Muslim notables (with a range of four to 30 *chifts*). The two groups total 1194, in other words, showing roughly the same relation that had been evident between the high and low series on *chifts* for a century.[158] Although the reason for so dividing the *chifts* into two groups remains obscure, at least it can be said that whether the high or low series is followed, the figures on *chifts*, like the figures on the *chiftliks* themselves, show much stability, moving, to the extent that they do, in somewhat the same rhythm.

Unfortunately only three *tevzis* were encountered which cite the number of cultivators working on the Muslim-held *chiftliks*, and of

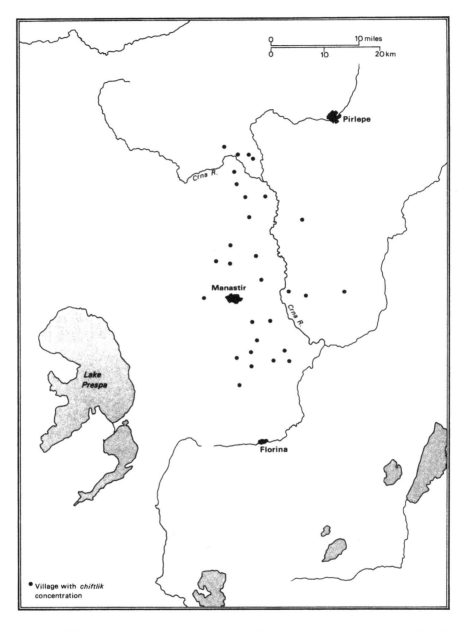

Map 16   Villages of the Manastir district where *chiftlik* agriculture was concentrated, 1710–30
Note: see text for definition of *chiftlik*.

166

these only two show their distribution. Thus from the *tevzi* of 1711 showing 1274 *reaya* living on *chiftliks* (as against 1927 living in villages) it is learned that more *chiftliks* have two cultivators than have any other number, and that the average number of *reaya* per *chiftlik* (in this *tevzi*) is 3.8.[159] The ratio between the *reaya* of this *tevzi* and the *chifts* of the 1710 *tevzi* is 1.33 to 1. In the 1788 *tevzi*, however, the number of *chiftlik* cultivators is shown as 864,[160] which is the same as the number of *chifts*. This strongly suggests a rationalized system, with each *chift* employing one man and one team.

A clearer indication of a change in the use of manpower can be seen in some *tevzis* of the Napoleonic period. In 1803, 1809 and 1814 the *tevzis* include a new tax: a tax on the 'day labor bosses' (*reis-i aylakchıs*). The amount of the so-called *aylakchı* tax is not great. What seems most interesting, aside from their very existence, is the fact that the number of such 'bosses' is close in each case to the number of villages included in the *tevzis*.[161] This can hardly be a coincidence. One is driven to

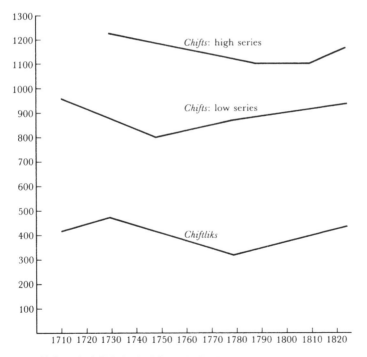

Figure 9   *Chifts* and *chiftliks* in the Manastir district, 1709–1824

Note: see text for definitions of *chift* and *chiftlik*. Low series may represent only *chifts* attached to villages of the *tevzi* system; high series may include the *chifts* of outlying *chiftliks*.

conclude that, in this period at least, each village had a day labor boss whose duty it presumably was to mobilize day laborers (i.e. Macedonian '*momaks*') from the villages for employment on nearby *chiftliks*. After 1814 this usage disappears, suggesting that the day labor phenomenon was associated with the first great surge of higher prices of the Napoleonic years. But if this is so, it is puzzling that other categories – *chiftliks, chifts* and *chiftchis* – cannot be shown to have changed very dramatically in the same period. It is possible, of course, that these latter figures were by now largely stereotyped and resistant to change, and it may be significant in this connection that the last detailed survey encountered was that of 1788.

It was the Greek War of Independence, with its constant demands for special levies in support of military operations, which seems to have finally broken the *tevzi* system in the Manastir district. From 1816 to 1822, although the proportions vary, the villages, divided as usual into *tevzi hanes*, still carry the heavier share of the burden of most of the levies.[162] Then in 1823 a *tevzi* appears in which a shift is perceptible.[163] Although the villages are still broken up into '*hanes*' they now are listed together with the number of *chifts* belonging to the village, and it is upon the *chifts* – at so much per *chift* – that the current burden is distributed. Thus there emerge two major groups of *chifts* in the Manastir district: (1) those belonging to the villagers – the so-called '*hane chifts*,' and (2) those belonging to Muslim third parties – the so-called '*kaza chifts*.'

In 1824 the shift was suddenly complete. *Tevzi hanes* are no longer relevant. The entire district was apportioned according to its *chifts* – those of the villages and those of the district. In this year the total of both groups of *chifts* is shown as 3735, 3832, 3840 and 3929.[164] The reason for this shift in practice was possibly in order to simplify and rationalize the *tevzi* process. The number of *chifts* is now close to the number of *jizye* payers. Apparently all units of cultivation are being lumped together here.[165] Most probably the landholders and other notables of the district had closed ranks in order to preserve the population from ruination under the pressure of the central government's demands, while at the same time reinforcing their own position as beneficiaries of the district's 'surplus' product. In the same year one finds in the *sijil* declarations such as that of the inhabitants of the village Malovište; according to their declaration, they renounce Rustem Bey as their middleman (*deruhdeji*) and accept Ahmet Bey as his replacement for an annual compensation of 3000 *gurush* out of which Ahmet

Bey must agree to pay their *avarız, nüzül, jelepkeshan, menzil* and 'other authorized taxes,'[166] Quite suddenly, the *chifts* of the villages (now called the '*hane chifts*' – the larger of the two groups of *chifts* under the old system?) have been thrust under the protection of the middlemen, the *deruhdejis*. A list of *chifts* from the end of 1824 shows that there are nineteen groups of *hane chifts*, all under the '*deruhde*' (responsibility) of powerful Muslims whose names all appear as holders of many *chifts* of their own.[167] In 1830 the distinction between *hane chifts* and *kaza chifts* broke down; the *chifts* under the direct control of the *deruhdejis* (i.e. the *chifts* for which they presumably held *tapus* or other evidence of 'ownership') were by then lumped together for fiscal purposes with the *chifts* under each man's *deruhde*. The largest of these *deruhdejis*, al-Seyyid Abdulkerim Bey, had at this time 1227 *chifts* – almost a third of the district's total – under his *deruhde*.[168]

The *deruhdejilik* institution undoubtedly deserves a special study. Its introduction into the Manastir district must have done much to consolidate the position of the district's men of substance during the difficult war years at the expense of the central government, and may well have been a considerable source of profit for them – conceivably more than their own personal *chiftliks*. But it is hard to imagine that the position of the villagers was thereby in any way eased. A *ferman* of 20 August 1825, cited by Matkovski, says that unless some solution were found for regularizing the payment of taxes to district authorities, the overburdening of '*chiftchis*' (i.e. cultivators) would force them to abandon their *chiftliks* and bring about their ruination.[169] But how often had the people been on the brink of ruin, or ruined? The grumbling of the *vezirs* at Istanbul is no guide in the matter.

Macedonia of the 1820s and 1830s was in fundamental ways different from the Macedonia of the preceding two centuries. The position of the villagers may have been as desperate as it had ever been. But the towns had begun to grow anew, and there were now more places to flee. Cases of fugitive returns had become rare. Were there, under the cloak of *deruhdejilik*, more *chiftliks* created than had existed before in the country districts from which some still sought escape? A quantitative answer to this question will be difficult to find. In the era of the *deruhdejis* numbers are still less to be trusted. A *buyruldu* of 1830 from the *vali* of Rumeli called for a survey of *chifts* to be made in the district.[170] But although there are indications that such a survey was in fact carried out[171] the documentary link between new *chifts* and old *chifts* was broken. The continuity of data which would allow the researcher to extrapolate lines based on data from the earlier *tevzis* does not exist. Thus in the Manastir district, at least, the *tevzi* institution and its documentary record is effectually at an end at the very moment when the *deruhdeji* institution appears in full scale.

Conclusion

At this stage of Ottoman studies, each use of the archives tends to bring to light questions which require further archival delving. Each of the general empirical conclusions which follow is therefore also a beginning which is destined to be modified by subsequent research.

1. The modest proportions of Ottoman export trade within total world trade, and its apparent lack of growth during the seventeenth and eighteenth centuries, suggest that the sector of Ottoman agriculture aimed at exporting must also have grown only slowly during this period.

2. Most *chiftliks* of south-eastern Europe were still small scale in the seventeenth and eighteenth centuries, and predominantly characterized by sharecropping (*métayage*). Although some larger estates did exist, particularly in zones where exporting was more important, such as Seres and Thessaly, the prevailing smaller size of *chiftliks* in this period suggests that *chiftliks* were not generally, or not yet, a primary means of becoming wealthy.

3. The population of south-eastern Europe seems to have fallen considerably in the seventeenth century, and to have recovered, although unevenly, in the eighteenth century. The spatial distribution of this waning and recovery awaits further explanation.

4. Tax house figures suggest that there was a great difference between the historic experience of south-eastern Europe and that of Anatolia during the late seventeenth century. This appearance also awaits explanation.

5. The Ottoman judicial system of the seventeenth and eighteenth centuries worked both for and against preservation of the old order but seemingly mostly against it, owing to the deliberate neglect of key norms of the classic land regime. The transformation thus countenanced by territorial courts became inevitable after the central government itself lost interest in defending the old regime.

The net effect of these five studies has been, in my view, to demote the importance of investigating *chiftlik* agriculture and at the same time to reassert the importance of the fiscal struggle between imperial center and periphery. A study recently published by Gilles Veinstein suggests, on the basis of the experience of the Izmir zone, that it was the fiscal domination of the peasantry and not the organization of estates to serve the export trade which was the primary rural source of power and fortune.[1] This tentative finding seems to be corroborated by recent work of Halil Inalcık, in which tax gathering, tax farming and tax allocation are emphasized as the institutional bases of the provincial *ayan* class.[2]

With respect to the exploitation of land and labor in the late Ottoman world, the following three topics also seem urgently in need of empirical study.

1. Studies of the rural rent and tax lease system (*mukataa/iltizam*) are badly needed.[3] Such studies should be aimed at the territorial distribution of tax-lease and rent-lease contracts and the quantitative trends in their contribution to imperial revenues at the expense of the crumbling *timar* regime. This will help greatly in describing the relative success of landholders in various localities in their fiscal struggle with the imperial treasury.

2. Studies of the organization of large estates in various localities are needed. Only analysis of the economy of larger estates and their masters can lead directly to conclusions about the importance of rent-taking and fiscal mediation as sources of wealth and power, compared to the profitability of organizing *chiftlik* estates as suppliers of the export trade. The right sources for such studies have still to be identified, although Yuzo Nagata has already shown the potential importance of inheritance (*tereke*) lists for this work.[4]

3. Dealings between foreign traders and their agents, on one side, and Ottoman landholders and officeholders, on the other hand, should be analyzed in order to discover the degree to which landholders involved themselves directly in trade, or conversely whether traders were deeply involved in agriculture as usurers.[5] European sources will presumably be of primary importance for this line of research.

While no one can predict the exact course of future research, it seems likely that, with respect to Ottoman rural history, archival research will provide most of the new facts and most of the surprises in the decades to come. The exploitation of the magnificent inheritance of late Ottoman documents has just begun.

Notes to the text

Notes to chapter 1, pp. 1–44

1. At the same time as I was completing this study of Ottoman exports, Traian Stoianovich was writing a fine study of his own which in some respects overlaps mine: 'Pour un modèle du commerce du Levant: économie concurrentielle et économie de bazar, 1500–1800,' *Association Internationale d'Études du Sud-est Européen, Bulletin* (Bucarest), 12/2 (1974), 61–120. Whereas the study in hand is limited to exports which affected land use, Stoianovich interested himself in imports as well, especially textiles, and gives more attention to the sixteenth century and to Persia. Stoianovich also discusses trade sectors (though his are more conceptual than spatial) and the periodization of the Levant trade. Because of major shifts in French participation, Stoianovich designates 1580–1630, 1680–1730 and 1780–1830 as periods in which the nature of the trade was significantly modified. He concurs with the writer in his finding that the total monetary value of the Levant trade, once allowances are made for inflation, was basically stable during the seventeenth and eighteenth centuries. For another recent essay dealing with the pre-Napoleonic Levant trade, see R. Mantran, 'The transformation of trade in the Ottoman Empire in the eighteenth century' in T. Naff and R. Owen (eds.), *Studies in Eighteenth Century Islamic History* (London, 1977), pp. 217–35.

2. The starting point for modern location theory, as applied to agriculture on a world-wide scale, is the pioneering work of the early nineteenth-century agricultural economist and gentleman farmer Johann Heinrich von Thünen; a recent edition of his work is P. Hall (ed.), *Von Thünen's Isolated State: An English Edition of Der Isolierte Staat* (Oxford, 1966). For various thoughts on the reapplication of von Thünen's theory on a regional or world-wide scale, the writer is indebted to J. R. Peet, 'The spatial expansion of commercial agriculture in the nineteenth century: A von Thünen interpretation,' *Economic Geography*, 45 (1969), 283–300; J. Schlembecker, 'The world metropolis and the history of American agriculture,' *Journal of Economic History*, 20 (1960), 187–208; D. Saalfeld, 'Produktion und Itensität der Landwirtschaft in Deutschland und Angrenzenden Gebieten um 1800,' *Third International Conference on Economic History: Munich, 1965* (Paris, 1969), pp. 141–8; A. Lösch, *The Economics of Location* (New Haven, 1954); R. Ely, *Land Economics* (New York, 1940); P. Lloyd and P. Dicken, *Location in Space: A Theoretical*

Approach to Economic Geography (New York, 1972); W. Warntz, *Macrogeography and Income Fronts* (Philadelphia, 1965); J. Kolars and J. Nystuen, *Geography, the Study of Location, Culture and Environment* (New York, 1974); E. F. Penrose, *Population Theories and Their Application* (Stanford, 1934); G. Rullière, *Localisations et rythmes de l'activité agricole* (Paris, 1956); R. Dodgshon 'A spatial perspective,' *Peasant Studies*, 6/1 (Jan. 1977), 8–19; M. Chisholm, *Rural Settlement and Land Use* (Chicago, 1962); M. Hurst, *A Geography of Economic Behavior* (New York, 1972), pp. 106–25.

3. With respect to Ottoman population trends in the sixteenth century, much work remains to be done. But the basic trend for the sixteenth century seems clear from the figures produced by Ö. L. Barkan, 'Essai sur les données statistiques des registres de recensement dans l'Empire Ottomane aux XVe et XVIe siècles,' *Journal of the Social and Economic History of the Orient*, i (1957–8), 9–36; other findings appear in M. A. Cook, *Population Pressure in Rural Anatolia, 1450–1600* (London, 1972). For demographic trends in various parts of Europe in the sixteenth, seventeenth and eighteenth centuries, the writer has relied upon P. Guillaume and J. P. Poussou, *Demographie historique* (Paris, 1970); M. Reinhard, A. Armengaud and J. Dupâquier, *Histoire générale de la population mondiale* (Paris, 1968); R. Mols S. J., 'Population in Europe, 1500–1700,' *Fontana Economic History of Europe*, vol. ii (London, 1972), ch. 1; and A. Armengaud, 'Population in Europe, 1700–1914,' *ibid.*, vol. iii (London, 1970), ch. 1; K. Helleiner, 'The population of Europe from the Black Death to the eve of the Vital Revolution,' in *The Cambridge Economic History of Europe* (2nd edn), iv, 1–95; D. Bogue, *Principles of Demography* (New York, 1969); and D. Glass and D. E. C. Eversley, *Population in History* (Chicago, 1965). Fortunately these various authorities are in general agreement. A map series depicting the gradual coalescence of denser populations for the period 1340–1700 along an arc stretching from northern Italy to the Low Countries appears in A. P. Usher, 'The history of population and settlement in Europe,' *The Geographical Review*, 20 (1930), 110–32, at p. 120. Relying on estimates by Mols and Barkan, the following densities have been computed for 1600: Italy 97 persons per square mile, France 86, the Low Countries 112, Britain 56, 'Turkey in Europe' 41, 'Turkey in Asia' 20.

4. Warntz, *Macrogeography*, p. 13. Ralph Davis describes the new concentration of buying power in the north-west: 'a decisive shift in economic strength towards the countries of northwestern Europe took place during the first half of the seventeenth century. It was a movement away from Italy – away from central Europe – and away from Spain. . . . It was a movement towards Holland, to which much of the old commercial and financial activity of the Low Countries had gravitated in the last years of the sixteenth century; towards England – and towards France. . . . A new international division of labor was emerging, in which the lands of the Baltic and Mediterranean, and of the Spanish Atlantic, were suppliers of primary products for the increasingly industrialised societies of northwestern Europe.' *The Rise of the Atlantic Economies* (London, 1973), p. 89.

5. E. H. Fox, *History in Geographical Perspective: The Other France* (New York, 1971), pp. 56ff. Peet and Polanyi are quoted in Dodgshon, 'Perspective,' p. 12.

6. The salt and herring which supplied a large part of the eastbound Baltic trade were exceptional in this respect.

7. A number of interesting syntheses, each with its own strengths, can be cited which treat the early modern conjuncture of higher population levels, trade and agricultural technique: E. Boserup, *The Conditions of Agricultural Growth* (Chicago, 1965); B. H. Slicher van Bath, *The Agrarian History of Western Europe, A.D. 500–1850* (London, 1963); E. L. Jones, *Agrarian Change and Economic Development* (London, 1969); J. de Vries, *Economy of Europe in an Age of Crisis, 1600–1750* (London, 1976); D. North and R. Thomas, *The Rise of the Western World: A New Economic History* (Cambridge, 1973); M. M. Postan, 'Economic relations between Eastern and Western Europe' in F. Graus *et al.* (eds.), *Eastern and Western Europe in the Middle Ages* (London, 1970); P. Earle (ed.), *Essays in European Economic History, 1500–1800* (Oxford, 1974), especially P. and H. Chaunu, 'The Atlantic economy and the world economy,' pp. 113–26 and J. Jacquart, 'French agriculture in the seventeenth century,' pp. 164–84; K. Glamann, 'European trade, 1500–1750' in C. Cipolla (ed.), *The Fontana Economic History of Europe* (London, 1971), vol. ii, ch. 2; and R. Davis, *Rise of the Atlantic Economies* (London, 1973).

8. The Levant trade benefits were perhaps less obvious to contemporaries for three reasons: (1) the trade was more variegated, (2) the destinations were more dispersed, (3) the destinations were often far short of the Amsterdam/London nexus – typically Marseilles, Livorno, Barcelona or Vienna; yet supplying these places relieved demand pressure on the entire interregional system.

9. See Davis, *Atlantic Economies*, p. 117, and Chaunu, in Earle, *Essays*, p. 120.

10. For the most precise reformulation of the von Thünen concept, see Lloyd and Dicken, *Location*, pp. 16–18, which includes a discussion of the bid rent curves created when various alternative land uses compete for space.

11. F. Braudel, *The Mediterranean and the Mediterranean World in the Age of Philip II*, i (London, 1967), 586, 588.

12. For maps of general zones of agricultural intensity and exhibiting the expected concentricity centered on north-western Europe, see S. van Valkenburg and C. Held, *Europe* (New York, 1952), pp. 101ff.; for commodity-specific maps showing intensity of inputs, see Kolars and Nystuen, *Geography*, pp. 223–4.

13. This corollary offers an area ripe for exploration, relevant for nineteenth- and twentieth-century Ottoman agriculture as well (insofar as the later commodities were not exotic specialties which had no European equivalent such as sultana grapes, etc.). A complete demonstration of the hierarchy of location rents in early modern Europe is properly a joint effort which awaits initiative. A collation of rents from the whole continent will certainly not be easy or completely satisfying though, since in many areas, the outlying Ottoman regions being a good example, an active market for land developed rather late. Thus rents from areas where a land market did exist would have to be collated with less stable rents from other areas which reflected many non-economic factors.

14. See E. Heckscher, *Mercantilism* (London, 1955, rev. 2nd edn), pp. 128–34; cf. H. Inalcık, 'The Ottoman economic mind and aspects of the Ottoman economy' in M. Cook (ed.), *Studies in the Economic History of the Ottoman Empire* (London, 1970), pp. 207–18, esp. p. 212.

15. Nistor's evidence is cited by I. Sakazov, *Bulgarische Wirtschaftsgeschichte* (Berlin, 1929), p. 250. The existence of a trade in commodities between Wallachia and the Ottomans even before the conquest of Istanbul is attested to in one of the laws of

Fatih Mehmet; cf. I. Steinherr and N. Beldiceanu, 'Acte du Règne de Selim I concernant quelques échelles danubiennes de Valachie, de Bulgarie et de Dobroudja,' *Südost Forschungen*, 23 (1964), 91–115, at 93.

16. R. Mantran and J. Sauvaget, *Reglements fiscaux ottomans: les provinces syriennes* (Beirut, 1951), p. 20.

17. The best work to date on the Ottoman policy of provision with respect to grain has been that of L. Güçer, as in this instance his article 'XVI yüzyıl sonlarında Osmanlı Imparatorluğun dahilinde hububat ticaretinin tabi olduğu kayıtlar,' *Iktisat Fakültesi Mecmuası*, 13 (1951–2), 79–98; Venetian ambassadors' observations on its operation (especially Morosini's) are found in E. Alberi, *Relazione degli ambasciatori Veneti al Senato* (Florence, 1838–63), Series III, vol. III; cf. H. Inalcık's articles in *Encyclopaedia of Islam* (2nd edn): 'Dobrudja' and 'Istanbul'; W. Hahn, *Die Verpflegung Konstantinopels durch staatliche Zwangswirtschaft* (Stuttgart, 1926); G. I. Bratianu, 'La Question de l'approvisionnement de Constantinople à l'époque Byzantine et Ottomane,' *Byzantion*, 5 (1929–30), 83–107; *idem*, 'Nouvelles contributions a l'étude de l'approvisionnement de Constantinople sous les Paléologues et les Empereurs Ottomans,' *Byzantion*, 6 (1931), 641–56; for other work on the Ottoman command economy, see the mini-bibliography offered by B. Cvetkova, 'Vie économique de villes et ports Balkaniques aux XV et XVI siècles,' *Revue des Études Islamiques*, 38 (1970), 267–355, as well as that of R. Mantran, *Istanbul dans la seconde moitié du XVIIe siècle* (Paris, 1962). The *Mühimme* citations are as follows: Register 6, item 47, p. 23, 972H; 6/472/p.220/972H; 52/316/p.126/991H; 52/367/p.146/991H; 52/710/p.268/992H; 522/680/p.258/992H; 62/184/p.83/995H; 64/304/p.112/996H; 73/867/p.396/1003H; 73/950/p.430/1003H; 73/999/p.452/1003H; 73/1067/p.485/1003H; 73/1154/p.529/1004H; 73/1003/p.454/1003H; 73/985/p.447/1003H; 73/980/p.444/1003H; 73/1041/p.472/1003H; 73/325/p.139/1003H; 73/74/p.30/1003H; 73/261/p.115/1003H; 73/1154/p.529/1004H; 73/1147/p.526/1004H. These items are merely a sampling; the registers are replete with similar items.

18. This incident, which took place in 1760, is recounted in P. Masson, *Histoire du commerce français dans le Levant au XVIIIe siècle* (Paris, 1911), pp. 613–14. For certain rare exceptions to the custom excluding Western ships, see R. Paris, *Histoire du commerce de Marseilles*, v: *de 1660 à 1789: Le Levant* (Paris, 1957), 457–8. Owing to an intensive diplomatic campaign by a series of French ambassadors, the French succeeded officially in breaching the barrier to carry on a very limited trade at Kaffa, in the Crimea, in the period 1748–68. This ended with the outbreak of the Russo-Ottoman War and was not resumed until after the Russians obtained egress in 1783. One Turkish historian cites a document indicating that merchants at Flanders were granted permission to do some business at Kaffa and Trabzon in 1646: see I. Uzunçarşılı, *Osmanlı Tarihi*, III, pt 2 (Ankara, 1954), 578. See also C. C. de Peysonnel, *Die Verfassung des Handels auf dem Schwarzen Meere* (Leipzig, 1788), pp. 353–4. Peysonnel, the fourth French consul to attempt to develop Kaffa as a port of call for the French in order to capitalize on Villeneuve's diplomatic coup of 1740, met the youngest Linchou at Bender. Never, insists Peysonnel, could the French do business in the Principalities without the protection of a consul. His own report on commercial possibilities on the Black Sea shores, based on his personal reconnaisance along these shores, includes an

interesting explanation of the way in which the Ottoman 'permit system' to channel the movement of grain actually then operated at Kaffa. Masson, *XVIIIe siècle*, p. 637, also speaks of permission to enter the Black Sea having been accorded the Dutch under their capitulatory agreement of 1678, although they seem not to have used it.

Other exceptional cases of foreign flag entries under special permit were recalled from memory by Mehmet Genç in a recent conversation. (Genç is among a handful of persons now living who can be said to be familiar with a good portion of the holdings of the Prime Minister's Archive at Istanbul.)

Venetian, Dutch and Russian attempts to break the grip of the Ottomans on Black Sea commerce also met with failure in the mid-eighteenth century: N. Kireev, 'On the history of Russian trade relations via Istanbul in the middle of the 18th century,' *AIESEE Bulletin*, 12 (Bucarest, 1974), 25–132.

19. R. Mantran, *Istanbul dans la seconde moitié du XVIIe siècle* (Paris, 1962), p. 196; Th. Thornton, *État actuel de la Turquie* (Paris, 1812), p. 144; L. Güçer, 'XVIII yüzyıl ortalarında Istanbul'un iaşesi için lüzûmlu hububatın temini meselesi,' *Iktisat Fakültesi Mecmuası*, 11 (1949–50), 397–416, at p. 406.

20. *ibid.*, p. 405.

21. M. Alexandra-Dersca, 'À propos d'un firman du Sultan Mustafa III . . .,' *Balcanica*, 7 (Bucharest, 1949), 363; and *idem*, 'Contribution a l'étude de approvisionnement en blé de Constantinople au XVIIIe siècle,' *Studia et Acta Orientalia*, ɪ (1957), 13–37, at p. 20.

22. The normal functioning of the sheep purchase system has been studied by Cvetkova ('Vie économique'), the normal functioning of the grain purchase system by Güçer, 'XVIII yüzyıl,' and R. Mantran, *Istanbul dans la seconde moitié du XVIIIe siècle* (Paris, 1962, pp. 186–200. Some interesting later aspects of the system are covered by T. Yaman, 'Istanbul'un zahire işlerine dair iki vesika,' *Tarih Vesikaları*, I (1941–2), 341–4; and by the contemporary observers, e.g. Thornton, *État*; W. Leake, *Travels in Northern Greece*, (London, 1835), ɪv, 282, 335; W. Wilkinson, *An Account of the Principalities of Wallachia and Moldavia* (London, 1820), excerpted in D. Warriner (ed.), *Contrasts in Emerging Societies* (Bloomington, 1965), pp. 74–85; Peysonnel, *Verfassung*, pp. 180–2; and G. Olivier, *Voyage dans l'Empire othoman, l'Egypte et la Perse* (Paris, 1801), p. 360.

23. In the first years of the eighteenth century, and occasionally thereafter, the Iron Gate was the site for a temporary market for the sale of grain destined for Belgrade. But the Gate was not easily passable, and by and large Belgrade was supplied from its own vicinity. See H. Gandev, *Zaraždane na Kapitalističeski otnošeniia v čifliskoto stopanstvo na severnozapadna B'lgaria prez XVIII vek* (Sofia, 1962, pp. 68–70.

24. S. Colombeanu, *Grandes exploitations dominiales en Valachie au XVIIIe siècle* (Bucharest, 1974), pp. 181, 196–9.

25. See V. Paskaleva, 'Osmanlı Balkan eyaletlerinin Avrupalı devletlerle ticaretleri tarihine katkı (1700–1850),' *Iktisat Fakültesi Mecmuası*, 27 (1967–8), 37–74, at 73.

26. B. Ohlin, *Interregional and International Trade* (Cambridge, Mass., 1957), p. 20.

27. For his discussions of the limiting role of reciprocity in the English Levant trade, see R. Davis, 'English imports from the Middle East, 1580–1780' in M. Cook

(ed.), *Studies in the Economic History of the Middle East* (London, 1970), pp. 193–206; *idem, Rise of the English Shipping Industry*, p. 247; and especially *idem, Aleppo and Devonshire Square* (London, 1967), pp. 28–32. See also J. H. Parry, 'The Mediterranean trades,' *CEHE*, IV, 155–67.

28. Especially, among the latter, the Thirty Years' War and the Seven Years' War.

29. B. Hrabak, 'Izvoz žitarica iz Bosne i Hercegovine u primorje od kraja XIII do početka XVII veka,' *Godišnjak Društva Istoričara Bosne i Hercegovine*, 14 (1963), 121–301; M. Aymard, *Venise, Raguse et le commerce de blé pendant la seconde moitié du XVIe siècle* (Paris, 1966), pp. 125–35.

30. D. Sella, 'Crisis and transformation in Venetian trade' in B. Pullan (ed.), *Crisis and Change in the Venetian Economy in the Sixteenth and Seventeenth Centuries* (London, 1968), p. 91; *idem, Commerci e industrie a Venezia nel Secolo XVII* (Venezio, 1961), p. 27; G. Tongas, *Les Relations de la France avec l'Empire Ottoman durant la première moitié du XVIIe siècle* (Toulouse, 1942), pp. 140–2. For a more detailed account of the growth of French participation at the end of the sixteenth century see Stoianovich, 'Modèle du commerce.'

31. Sella, 'Crisis,' p. 91.

32. *ibid.*, p. 97.

33. *ibid.*, pp. 93–4.

34. A graph showing the dramatic effect of Atlantic competition upon the output of the Venetian woollens industry appears in D. Sella, 'Les mouvements longs de l'industrie lainière à Venise aux XVIe et XVIIe siècles,' *Annales: économies, sociétés, civilisations*, 12 (1957), 29–45.

35. S. Woolf, 'Venice and the Terraferma: problems of the change from commercial to landed activities' in B. Pullan (ed.), *Crisis*, pp. 175–203; cf. T. Stoianovich, 'Raguse, société sans imprimerie' in Association Internationale d'Etudes du Sud-est Européen, *Structure sociale et developpement culturel des villes sud-est européennes et adriatiques aux XVIIe–XVIIIe siècles* (Bucarest, 1975), pp. 52–3.

36. Sella, *Commerci*, p. 52; Tongas, *Relations*, 209–10.

37. See V. Vinaver, 'Dubrovačka trgovina u Srbiji i Bugarskoj krajem XVII veka (1660–1700),' *Istorijski Časopis*, 12 (1963), 189–237, at pp. 212–13; N. Čolak, 'Brodovlasnici Zadarske komune između Kalovačkog i Požarevačkog mira,' *Pomorski Zbornik* (Zadar), 3 (1965), 775–808; S. Traljić, 'Izvoz Bosanske robe preko Splitske luke u XVIII stoljeću,' *ibid.*, pp. 809–27; *Historija Naroda Jugoslavije* (Zagreb, 1959), II, 517, 520, 594; for the high point of the Bosnian trade in the Napoleonic period, including figures, see M. Šamić, 'Ekonomski život Bosne i Sarajeva početkom XIX vijeka,' *Godišnjak Istoriskog Društva Bosne i Heregovine*, 9 (1960), 111–34; regarding Albania, cf. V. Paskaleva, 'Osmanlı Balkan eyaletlerinin Avrupalı devletlere ticaretleri tarihine katkı (1700–1850),' *Iktisat Fakültesi Mecmuası*, 27 (1967–8), 37–74; Z. Shkodra, 'Le marché Albanais au XVIIIe siècle,' *Actes du Premier Congrès des Études Balkaniques* (Sofia, 1969), IV, 761–74; F. Pouqueville, *Reise durch Morea und Albanien nach Konstantinopel und in Mehrere andere Theile des Ottomanischen Reichs in den Jahren 1798, 1799, 1800, und 1801* (Leipzig, 1805), III, 79; B. Hrabak, 'Albanija od konačnog pada pod Turska vlast do sredine XVIII veka' in Društvo Istoričara Srbije, *Iz Istorije Albanaca* (Beograd, 1969), pp. 45–73.

38. Ragusa's adaptation and decline as a trader is discussed by F. Carter, 'The

commerce of the Dubrovnik Republic , 1500–1700,' *Economic History Review*, 24 (1971), 370–94; also the same author's *Dubrovnik (Ragusa): A Classical City State* (London, 1972), where he speculates, perhaps rightly, that a greater arbitrariness on the part of the Balkan *pashas* may have played a role as well; cf. J. Tadić, 'Le commerce en Dalmatie et à Raguse et la decadence économique de Venise au XVIIième siècle,' *Convegno Aspetti e Cause della Decadenza Economica Veneziana nel Secolo XVII* (Venice–Rome, 1961), pp. 235–72; Vinaver, 'Dubrovačka trgovina,' pp. 213–18; and E. Georgieva, 'Dubrovniskata t'rgoviâ v severoistočna B'lgaria prez XV–XVIII v.,' *Godišnik na Sofiiskia Universitet*, 65 (1972), 269–302.

39. H. Koenigsberger, *Europe in the Sixteenth Century* (London, 1968), p. 33. Details on the Livorno traffic are given in F. Braudel and R. Romano, *Navires et marchandises à l'entrée du port de Livourne (1547–1611)* (Paris, 1951).

40. Armenian merchants with strong family connections in Ottoman territory took a leading part in this trade. Cf. Tongas, *Relations*, p. 210.

41. Sella, 'Crisis,' p. 94.

42. Regarding the use of Dutch and English ships to supply Genoa and Livorno, see H. Wätjen, *Niederländer im Mittelmeergebiet* (Berlin, 1909), p. 166. On the superiority of Dutch ships, cf. V. Barbour, 'Dutch and English maritime shipping in the seventeenth century,' *Economic History Review*, 2 (1930), 280. The great Dutch innovation was the *fluit*, a cheaper, safer, unarmed vessel built solely to do service as a freighter; but because they were unarmed the *fluits* had generally to move in convoys, a fact which helps to explain the considerable cooperation in trading which existed between the Dutch and English nations in the Mediterranean, at least in the intervals between their frequent maritime wars – 1664–7, 1672–8, 1688–97, 1701–13; see P. Cernovodeanu, 'The general condition of English trade in the second half of the 17th century and the beginning of the 18th century,' *Revue des Études du Sud-est Européen*, 5 (1967), 447–60.

43. Davis, 'English imports,' p. 193.

44. Tongas, *Relations*, pp. 208–10. These figures may be compared with a computation of the shares of the trading nations used as the basis for settling a dispute between them in 1634: France 26.6%; England 39.8%; the Dutch 7.8%; Venice 25.8%; cited in Stoianovich, 'Modèle,' p. 73.

45. E. Hobsbawm, 'The crisis of the seventeenth century' in T. Aston (ed.), *Crisis in Europe, 1560–1660* (New York, 1965), p. 10.

46. K. Glamann, *Dutch–Asiatic Trade, 1620–1740* (The Hague, 1958), p. 131.

47. Davis, *Aleppo*, pp. 29–32. Instead the English fostered a new scheme in the late seventeenth century using Armenian trade partners to move Persian silks to Bombay for resale there: Stoianovich, 'Modèle,' p. 81.

48. Tongas, *Relations*, 142–52.

49. P. Masson, *Histoire du commerce français dans le Levant au XVIIe siècle* (Paris, 1897), p. 236.

50. *ibid.*, p. 236; Tongas, *Relations*, pp. 210–11.

51. After 1683 capitulations tended to reflect *quid pro quo* rewards for assistance. Cf. H. Inalcık, 'Imtiyāzāt,' *Encyclopedia of Islam*, 2nd edn.

52. Masson, *XVIIe siècle*, pp. 286–7, 305. This concession gave rise to the so-called *caravanaire* trade carried on by the masters of small French vessels.

53. S. Clough and C. Cole, *Economic History of Europe* (Boston, 1952). For a statement

on Colbert's brand of mercantilism, cf. H. Hauser, 'The characteristic features of French economic history from the middle of the sixteenth to the middle of the eighteenth centuries,' *Economic History Review*, 1st ser., IV (1933), 257–72. For the social background of this trade recovery, cf. R. Grassby, 'Social status and commercial enterprise under Louis XIV,' *Economic History Review*, 2nd ser., 13 (1960), 19–38.

54. Davis, *Aleppo*, pp. 28–9; Masson, *XVIIIe Siècle*, p. 375; R. Paris, *Histoire du commerce de Marseilles*, V: *de 1660 à 1789: Le Levant* (Paris, 1957), 505, 510–15.

55. C. Cipolla cites this report in 'The decline of Italy: the case of a fully matured economy,' *Economic History Review*, 2nd ser., 5 (1952), 178–87, at 181.

56. Masson, *XVIIIe siècle*, p. 432. Cf. J-P. Filippini *et al.* (eds.), *Dossiers sur le commerce français en Mediterranée orientale au XVIIIe siècle* (Paris, 1976), which includes a fine bibliography on French documentary sources.

57. C. Volney, *État du commerce du Levant en 1784, d'après les registres de la chambre de commerce de Marseilles*, reprint in C. Issawi, *Economic History of the Middle East, 1800–1914* (Chicago, 1966), p. 37.

58. T. Stoianovich, 'The conquering Balkan merchant,' *Journal of Economic History*, 20 (1960), 274.

59. *ibid.* For the influence of the Passarowitz commercial agreement upon trade, see S. Gavrilović, *Prilog Istoriji Trgovine i Migracije Balkan-Podunavlije XVIII i XIX stoljeća* (Beograd, 1969), in which he draws on the original research published in M. von Herzfeld, *Zur Orienthandels politik Osterreichs unter Maria Theresa in der Zeit von 1740–1771* (Wien, 1919), and A. Beer, *Die österreichische Handelspolitik unter Maria Theresa und Josef II* (Wien, 1898).

60. For the improvement of the routes to the Adriatic, see M. Kostić, 'O dunavskoj-savskoj trgovini, lađama, lađarima, i lađarskim ćehovima u XVIII i XIX veka do pojave železnica,' *Istoriski Časopis*, IX/X (1959), 259–93; J. Kalbrunner, 'Zur Geschichte der Wirstchaft im Temeswarer Banat bis zum siebenjährigen Kriege,' *Südostdeutsche Forschungen*, I (München, 1936), 57ff.; E. Turczynski, *Die deutsch griechischen Kulturbeziehungen bis zur Berufung König Ottos* (Munich, 1959); F. Mayer, *Die Anfänge des Handels und der Industrie in Österreich und die Orientalische Compagnie* (Innsbruck, 1882).

61. See D. Zografski, *Razvitokot na Kapitalističkite elementi vo Makedonija za vreme na Turskoto Vladeenje* (Skopje, 1967), pp. 55–6; this book offers a review of the effects of the commodity trade upon Macedonian economic life. For the development of Austrian trade via the Adriatic and for trade estimates for the eighteenth century, see H. Halm, *Habsburgischer Osthandel im 18 Jahrhundert* (Munich, 1954); I. Erceg, 'Trgovina između Habsburške monarhije i Turske preko sjeverno jadranskih luka u 2 polovici 18 i 1 polovici 19 stoljeća,' *Jadranski Zbornik*, 8 (1973), 161–84; *idem*, 'Aussenhandel der Nordadriatischen Seestädte als Faktor im Entstehen der Kapi-talistischen Beziehungen in Österreich im 18 und 19 Jahrhundert,' *Vierteljahrschrift für Sozial und Wirtschaftsgeschichte*, 55 (1968–9), 464–80; W. Kaltenstadler, 'Der Österreichische Seehandel über Trieste in 18 Jahr.,' *Vierteljahrschrift für Sozial und Wirtschaftsgeschichte*, 55 (1968–9), 480–500, and *ibid.*, 56 (1970), 1–164; *Kurzgefasste Beschreibung der Handlung der vornehmsten europaischen Staaten* (Liegnitz and Leipzig, 1778–9), II, 212, quoted in N. Michoff, *Contribution à l'histoire du Commerce de la Turquie et de la Bulgarie* (Sofia, 1971), p. 31.

62. For the cattle drives of the seventeenth and eighteenth centuries, see R. Riedl, 'Der Wiener Schlachtsviehhandel in seiner geschichtlichen Entwicklungen,' *Jahrbuch für Gesetzgebung Verwaltung und Volkwirtschaft im Deutschen Reich*, 17 (Leipzig, 1893), 829–98; for the contrast of the seventeenth- with the eighteenth-century trades, see Rajko Veselinović, 'Prodiranje austrijske trgovine u Beograd u drugoj polovini XVII veka,' *Osloboďenje gradova u Srbiji od Turaka, 1862–1867* (Beograd, 1970), pp. 163–79, at 168–78. A list of the Ottoman trading colony at Vienna, dated 25 April 1766, is found in the Commerz collection of the Finanz und Hofkammer Archiv at Vienna, no. 114 in the Niederösterreich section, pp. 222–312; leaving aside non-principals, the list of 134 principals shows 82 'Greeks,' 21 Armenians, 18 Jews, and 13 Turks (obviously the Habsburg authorities at that time thought in religious categories, as did their Ottoman contemporaries); this list may be compared with remarks on the seventeenth-century trades in C. von Peez, 'Alte serbische Handelsbeziehungen zu Wien,' *Mitteilungen des Instituts für österreichische Geschichtsforschung*, 36 (1915), 498–510. Another recent article affirms the cattle trade as Hungary's most important export until the mid-eighteenth century, then to be displaced by wheat and wool: L. Makkai, 'Der Ungarische Viehhandel, 1550–1650' in I. Bog, *Der Aussenhandel Ostmitteleuropas, 1450–1650* (Vienna, 1971), pp. 483–506.
The displacement of cattle raising by wheat cultivation in later eighteenth-century Hungary is discussed by G. Benda, who states that wheat exports from Hungary into Ottoman territory comprised only a minor part of total Hungarian wheat exports in those decades: 'Production et exportation des céréales en Hongrie (1770–1870)' in B. Köpeczi and É. Balázs, *Paysannerie Française, paysannerie hongroise XVe – XXe siècle* (Budapest, 1973), p. 195.

63. For the dependence of Belgrade upon supplies from Habsburg territories, see V. Čubrilović (ed.), *Istorija Beograda*, 3 vols (Beograd, 1974), I, 686–90; for the presence of Macedonians at Leipzig, A. Matkovski, *Gurčin Kokalevski* (Skopje, 1959), p. 45. There were five Macedonians there in 1748, 12 in 1752, 34 in 1767 and 69 in 1774; the source for these figures is E. Hasse, *Geschichte der Leipziger Messen* (Leipzig, 1885); for trade on the Bulgarian–Romanian routes, see V. Paskaleva, 'Austro-b' lgarski trgovski vrzki v kraia na XVIII i načalato na XIX v.,' *Istoričeski Pregled*, 14/5 (1958), 83–92; H. Gandev, 'Trgovskata obm'na na Europa s' b'lgarski zemi prez XVIII i načalato na XIX v'k,' *Godišnik na Istoriko-Filologičeski Fakultet* (Sofia), 40 (1944), 1–36; I. Iordanov, *Istoria na B'lgarskata T'rgovia do Osvoboždenieto* (Sofia, 1938), pp. 163–4; C. Şerban, 'Le Rôle économique des villes Roumains aux XVIIe et XVIIIe siècles dans le contexte de leurs relations avec l'Europe du sud-est,' *Studia Balcanica, 3: La Ville Balkanique, XVe – XIXe ss.* (Sofia, 1970), pp. 139–53; S. Panova, 'Zur Frage der Handelsbeziehungen zwischen den Bulgarischen und den Rumanischen Landen im XVII Jahrhundert,' *Études Balkaniques*, 11 (1975), 102–14.

64. On the development of Habsburg commerce on the lower Danube, H. Halm, 'Die Entdeckung der Donau als Welthandelstrasse,' *Zeitschrift des Forschungsinstitut für Donauraum* (Vienna, 1960), pp. 92–100; *idem, Donauhandel und Schiffahrt, 1781–1787* (München, 1954); J. Grunzel, *Die Handelsbeziehungen Oesterreich – Ungarns zu den Balkanländern* (Wien, 1892); and J. Winkler, 'Wien und die Entwicklung des Donauhandels,' *Mitteilungen des Kais. und königl. geographischen Gesellschaft im Wien*,

15 (1872), 72–92. For the Polish–Ottoman exchanges, see T. Ciecerska-Chłapowa, 'Echanges commerciaux entre la Pologne et la Turquie au XVIIIe siècle,' *Folia Orientalia* (Krakow), 14 (1972–3), 261–87; J. Reychman, 'Le Commerce Polonais en Mer Noire au XVIII siècle,' *Cahiers du Monde Russe et Sovietique*, 7/2, 234–48; M. de Chemier, *Revolutions de l'Empire Ottoman* (Paris, 1789), p. 337, quoted in N. Michoff, *Contribution à l'histoire de la Turquie et la Bulgarie*, III (Svištov, 1950), 43. On the breakthrough from the Black Sea to the Mediterranean, H. Gandev, 'Obm'na,' p. 10; and H. Inalcık, 'Imtiyāzāt,' in *Encyclopedia of Islam*, 2nd edn. The sixteenth-century situation on the lower Danube is reviewed by B. Cvetkova, 'Vie économique de villes et ports Balkaniques aux XV et XVI siècle,' *Revue des Études Islamiques*, 38 (1970), 267–355.

65. Mantran, 'Transformation,' p. 229.

66. C. Issawi, 'The decline of Middle Eastern trade, 1100–1850' in D. Richards (ed.), *Islam and the Trade of Asia* (Oxford, 1970), p. 247.

67. J. Marlowe, *Perfidious Albion: the Origins of the Anglo-French Rivalry in the Levant* (London, 1971), p. 16; Davis, *Aleppo*, p. 37.

68. W. Lewis, *Levantine Adventurer: The Travels and Missions of the Chevalier d'Arvieux, 1653–1697* (New York, 1962), p. 43.

69. *Masson, p. 403.*

70. *ibid.*, p. 509.

71. *ibid.*, p. 598. Paris gives figures showing the steady diminution of Egyptian exports as a percentage of France's imports from the Levant via Marseilles: 1671–5: 28%; 1717–21: 16%; 1736–40: 14%; 1773–7: 12%; 1785–9: 7.5%. See R. Paris, *Histoire du commerce de Marseilles*, V: *de 1660 à 1789: Le Levant* (Paris, 1957), 370. Raymond has chosen the figures offered by J. B. Trecourt, *Mémoires sur l'Egypte* (Cairo, 1942), pp. 24–85, as probably more complete than those offered by the French National Archives. According to this source, Egyptian exports to Europe in 1783 amounted to 6,537,702 livres, while exports to the Ottoman empire totalled 25,369,125 livres, and to North Africa 2,420,000 livres; cited in A. Raymond, *Artisans et commerçants au Cair au XVIIIe siècle* (Damascus, 1973–4), I, 193, cf. also p. 184. For the dwindling entrepôt trade in coffee, see L. Meignen, 'Esquisse sur le commerce français du café dans le Levant au XVIIIe siècle' in J. P. Filippini (ed.), *Dossiers su le commerce français en Méditerranée orientale au XVIIIe siècle* (L'Université de droit, d'économie et de sciences sociales de Paris: séries sciences historiques, no. 10, Paris, 1976), pp. 105–50.

72. Masson, *XVIIe siècle*, p. 374.

73. F. Charles-Roux, *Les Échelles de Syrie et de la Palestine au XVIIIe siècle* (Paris, 1928), p. 7; Glamann, *Trade*, pp. 114–19.

74. Masson, *XVIIe siècle*, p. 374.

75. Masson, *XVIIIe siècle*, p. 512. Arbitrary demands by local pashas had more than once caused the displacement of one Syrian port by another: in 1612 Aleppo's port of Tripoli was abandoned in favor of Alexandretta (Iskenderun); in the eighteenth century the depredations of Ahmed Jezzar Pasha caused the replacement of Sayda by Acre as the leading port of Damascus (*ibid.*, p. 512; Masson, *XVIIe siècle*, p. 380).

76. Masson, *XVIIe siècle*, Appendix XV, Table V (but note Masson's comments in

Appendices XVI through XIX regarding the imperfections of the statistics maintained at Marseilles).

77. Masson, *XVIIe siècle*, pp. 509–626. The French in this period seem to have had two-thirds of the exports of Aleppo, and three-fifths of those of Egypt, leaving Ottoman waters. For the political background affecting the eighteenth-century trade from Ottoman Syria, cf. A. K. Rafeq, *The Province of Damascus, 1723–1783* (Beirut, 1966), esp. pp. 75–6, 178–80, 195, 315–16; *idem*, 'Changes in the relationship between the Ottoman central administration and the Syrian provinces from the sixteenth to the eighteenth centuries' in T. Naff and R. Owen (eds.), *Studies in Eighteenth Century Islamic History* (London, 1977), pp. 53–73; R. Mantran, 'The transformation of trade in the Ottoman Empire in the eighteenth century' in *ibid.* pp. 217–35; and A. Cohen, *Palestine in the Eighteenth Century – Patterns of Government and Administration* (Jerusalem, 1973).

78. Volney, *État*, p. 36.

79. Paris, *Levant*, passim; the percentages offered never total 100.

80. Stoianovich, 'Merchant,' p. 267.

81. H. Wätjen, *Niederländer im Mittelmeergebiet* (Berlin, 1909), p. 163.

82. For details, cf. Davis, *Aleppo*, pp. 36–7.

83. Masson, *XVIIIe siècle*, p. 554.

84. Masson, XVIIe siècle, p. 393.

85. By Morea, Westerners understood all of Greece south of Salonica.

86. Masson, *XVIIIe siècle*, p. 616. Paris gives the following percentages pertaining to Salonica's share in the Levantine exports passing through Marseilles: 1711–15: 1.75%; 1724–8: 4.75%; 1750–4: 6.25%; 1773–7: 14.5%; 1785–9: 7.5%: Paris, *Levant*, p. 478. N. Svoronos, *Le Commerce de Salonique au XVIIIe siècle* (Paris, 1956), p. 196, indicates that Greek traders continued to trade with the ports of Italy despite the presence of the French. Svoronos offers the following figures (in piastres) to show the growth of the trade of other nations than the French at Salonica in the eighteenth century: 1700–18; 600,000; 1722–37: 550,000; 1738–43: 800,000; 1744–9: 1,000,000; 1750–70: 2,000,000; 1771–7: 3,000,000; 1778–86: 5,000,000.

87. Masson, *XVIIe siècle*, p. 436n.

88. For the rise of the ports of the lower Adriatic, see Z. Shkodra, 'Le marché Albanaise au XVIII siècle,' *Actes du Ier Congrès International des études balkaniques et sud-est Européennes* (Sofia, 1969), pp. 761–74; B. Hrabak, 'Albanija od konačnog pada pod Turska vlast do sredine XVIII vek' in Društvo Istoričara Srbije, *Iz Istorije Albanaca* (Beograd, 1969), pp. 45–73; S. Pollo, 'Considerations sur l'essor économique et culturel de la ville de Shkodra durant la seconde moitié du XVIIIe siècle,' Association Internationale d'Études du Sud-est Européen, *Structure sociale et développement culturel des villes sud-est Européennes et Adriatiques aux XVIIe–XVIIIe siècles* (Bucharest, 1975), pp. 163–8.

89. Actually it was a trade composed of numerous Indian and Far Eastern items of high value, a trade preempted first in part by Portuguese traders in the early sixteenth century, and towards the close of the century carried in the holds of English and especially Dutch merchantmen traversing the Cape. Cf. W. Stripling, *The Ottoman Turks and the Arabs, 1511–1574* (Urbana, Ill., 1942); the pioneer effort by A. Lybyer, 'The Ottoman Turks and the routes of oriental trade,' *English Historical Review*, 30 (Oct. 1915), 577–88; F. Lane, 'Venetian shipping during the

Commercial Revolution,' *American Historical Review*, 30 (Jan. 1933), 219–39; *idem*, 'The Mediterranean spice trade,' *American Historical Review*, 45 (April 1940), 581–91; N. Mirkovich, 'Ragusa and the Portuguese spice trade,' *Slavonic and East European Review*, 21 (March 1943), 174–87; A. Hess, 'The evolution of the Ottoman seaborne empire in the age of the oceanic discoveries, 1453–1525,' *American Historical Review*, 75 (1970), 1892–1919; L. Dames, 'The Portuguese and the Turks in the Indian Ocean in the sixteenth century,' *Journal of the Royal Asiatic Society* (1921), pp. 1–28; J. Parry, 'Mediterranean trade in the sixteenth century,' *CEHE* (2nd edn), IV, 155–67.

90. Cf. R. Bautier, *The Economic Development of Medieval Europe* (London, 1971), p. 194; I. Lapidus, 'The grain economy of Mamluk Egypt,' *Journal of the Social and Economic History of the Orient*, 12 (1969), 1–15; and J. Parry, 'Transport and trade routes,' *CEHE* (2nd edn), IV, 155–222, at pp. 155–6.

91. *ibid.*, p. 156.

92. L. Güçer, the leading authority on grain movement inside the Ottoman domains, claims that he has seen no evidence at all for the introduction of foreign grain into Ottoman territory over the 104–year span (mid-sixteenth to mid-seventeenth) which his studies covered: *XVI–XVII asırlarda Osmanlı İmparatorluğunda hububat meselesi ve hububattan alınan vergiler* (Istanbul, 1964), p. 28. On pp. 8 and 9 of this study Güçer provides a table showing local grain famines in Ottoman provinces during the period 1578–1637.

93. Aymard names quite a number of Greek places supplying wheat to Western traders: *Venise, Raguse et le commerce de blé pendant la seconde moitié du XVIe siècle* (Paris, 1966), p. 47. To these B. Cvetkova would add the mouth of the Struma, where, according to Pierre Belon, Ragusan and Venetian ships might linger as long as two months selling merchandise and loading wheat, wool and skins coming down river from Seres: 'Vie économique de villes et ports Balkanique aux XV et XVI siècles,' *Revue des Études Islamiques*, 38 (1970), 322. Parry, 'Transport,' p. 158, mentions in addition Corfu, Crete (as a Venetian colony), Salonica and Prevesa. To the north, Fekete suspected he saw in the customs records of 1571 leakage of grain in the direction of Vienna via the Danube, despite interdiction: L. Fekete and Gy. Kaldy-Nagy, *Rechnungsbücher Türkischer Finanzstellen in Buda (Ofen), 1550–1580* (Budapest, 1962), p. 716.

94. Aymard, *Venise*, p. 46. T. Gökbilgin has published a series of documents dating from 1536 to 1541, all inferring the legal sale of wheat to Venetian merchants by the Ottoman authorities: *Venedik Devlet Arşivindeki Vesikalar Külliyatında Kanuni Sultan Suleyman Devri Belgeler*, I (1964), 119–220.

95. Orijentalni Institut u Sarajevu, *Monumenta Turcica Historiam Slavorum Meridionalim Illustrantia*, I, 49; R. Mantran and J. Sauvaget, *Reglements fiscaux ottomans: les provinces syriennes* (Beirut, 1951), p. 20.

96. Aymard, *Venise*, pp. 177, 178, 185.

97. Hobsbawm, 'Crisis,' p. 34; S. Woolf, 'Economic problems of the nobility in the early modern period: the example of Piedmont,' *Economic History Review*, 17 (1964–5), 267–83; Braudel, *Mediterranean*, I, 594–604.

98. A graph showing the impact of the Danzig grain is included in F. Braudel and R. Romano, *Navires et marchandises a l'entrée du port de Livourne (1547–1661)* (Paris, 1951), p. 107.

99. Cf. Helleiner, *CEHE* (2nd edn), IV, 77–85.
100. Aymard, *Venise*, p. 125.
101. L. Güçer, 'XVI Yüzyıl sonlarında Osmanlı Imparatorluğunun dahilinde hubu-bat ticaretinin tabi olduğu kayıtlar,' *Istanbul Üniversitesi Iktisat Fakültesi Mecmuası*, 12 (1951–2), 79–80.
102. M. Cook, *Population Pressure in Rural Anatolia, 1450–1600* (London, 1972), pp. 2–5.
103. Wätjen, *Niederländer*, pp. 166, 171.
104. The capitulations (*ahitnames*) were technically unilateral declarations, hence not entirely comparable to treaties, at least during this earlier period. See H. Inalcık, 'Imtiyāzāt,' *Encyclopedia of Islam*, 2nd edn.
105. *ibid.*
106. From Article 8 of the 1604 French capitulations, published in G. Noradounghian, *Recueil d'actes internationaux de l'empire ottoman*, 4 vols (Paris, 1879–1903), I, 95; also in I. de Testa, *Recueil des traités de la Porte ottomane avec les puissances étrangères* (Paris, 1864–1901), I, 144–5.
107. Cf., for instance, the English capitulations of 1675, the Dutch capitulations of 1680, the French capitulations of 1673 and 1740, and the Russian capitulations of 1783 in Noradounghian, *Recueil* and de Testa, *Recueil*.
108. Masson, *XVIIIe siècle*, p. 645.
109. H. Luke, *Cyprus under the Turks, 1571–1878* (London, 1921), pp. 138–46.
110. Masson, *XVIIIe siècle*, p. 462.
111. See R. Davis, *The Rise of the English Shipping Industry* (London, 1962), p. 247; Wätjen, *Niederländer*; Masson, *XVIIIe siècle*, p. 463; J. P. Filippini, 'Livourne et l'Afrique du Nord au 18e siècle,' *Revue d'Histoire Maghrebine*, 7–8 (1977), 125–49, esp. pp. 137–9; L. Valensi, *Fellahs Tunisien: l'économie rurale et la vie des campagnes aux 18e et 19e siècles* (Paris, 1977), pp. 330–40; L. Bergeron et al., *L'Ankylose de l'économie méditerranéene au XVIIIe et au début du XIXème siècle* (Nice, 1973), pp. 11, 16–17; R. Mantran, 'L'Évolution des relations entre la Tunisie et l'empire ottoman du XVIe au XIX siècle,' *Les Cahiers de Tunisie*, 26/27 (1959), 319–32.
112. Masson, *XVIIe siècle*, pp. 393, 428–9.
113. Cf. Masson, *XVIIIe siècle*, pp. 458–67; Braudel and Romano, *Navires*, passim; Paris, *Levant*, pp. 107, 383, 447, 478, 481–2.
114. Svoronos, *Salonique*, pp. 207, 208, 277, believes that most of the wheat exports of this zone were headed for Istanbul at the behest of the official buyers, the *mubayaajıs*. But official control was decidedly more tight at Salonica than on other Greek coasts; cf. Olivier, *Voyage*, p. 71; Leake, *Travels*, III, 254; Luke, *Cyprus*, p. 101; Braudel, *Mediterranean*, I, 584.
115. S. Papadopoulos (ed.), *The Greek Merchant Marine, 1453–1850* (Athens, 1972), pp. 30–41.
116. A. Otetea, 'Le second asservissement des paysans roumains (1746–1821),' *Nouvelles Études d'Histoire* (Bucarest, 1970), pp. 299–312, at 300; cf. V. Neamtu, *La Technique de la production céréalière en Valachie et en Moldavie jusqu'au XVIIIe siècle* (Bucharest, 1975).
117. H. Inalcık 'Adaletnâmeler,' *Belgeler* (Turkish Historical Society, Ankara), II/3–4 (1965), 126, 128; M. Akdağ, 'Genel cizgileriyle XVII yüzyıl Türkiye Tarihi' (Ankara Üniversitesi Dil, Tarih, ve Cografya Fakültesi), *Tarih Araştırmaları Dergisi*, IV/6–7 (1966), 203.

118. B. Ohlin, *Interregional and International Trade* (Cambridge, Mass., 1957), p. 209.
119. S. van Bath, *Agrarian History*, pp. 166–8.
120. J. Parry, 'Transport,' p. 160; L. Wätson, *Niederländer*, p. 334.
121. C. Wilson, 'Cloth production and international competition in the seventeenth century,' *Economic History Review*, 2nd ser., 18 (1960), 217–18; R. Davis, 'English Imports from the Middle East, 1570–1780', in Cook (ed.), *Studies*, p. 200.
122. Masson, *XVIIIe siècle*, p. 441; H. Sahillioğlu states that there were six French agents at Ankara maintained by French commercial houses in Istanbul (not Smyrna): 'XVIII yüzyıl ortalarında sanayi bölgelerimiz ve ticari imkânları,' *Belgelerle Türk Tarihi Dergisi*, II/11 (1968), 65.
123. Paris, *Levant*, p. 518. A graph appearing on p. 607 of Paris's book demonstrates the continuing predominance of the Anatolian goat and camelhair trade within the Levantine animal fiber trade as a whole throughout the eighteenth century.
124. For details, see Svoronos, *Salonique*.
125. For accounts of the decline of the cloth industry at Venice itself, see D. Sella, 'Les mouvements longs de l'industrie lainière à Venise aux XVIe et XVIIe siècles,' *Annales: économies, sociétés, civilisations*, 12 (1957), 29–45; also *idem*, 'Commerci e Industrie a Venezia nel Secolo XVII,' *Annales: économies, sociétés, civilisations*, 12 (1957), 29–45; also *idem, Commerci e Industrie e Venezia nel Secolo XVII* (Venezia, 1961); C. Cipolla, 'The decline of Italy: the case of a fully matured economy,' *Economic History Review*, 2nd ser., 5 (1952), 178–87.
126. F. Carter, citing figures offered by V. Vinaver, in 'The commerce of the Dubrovnik Republic, 1500–1700,' *Economic History Review*, 24 (1971), 382; cf. V. Vinaver, 'Dubrovačka trgovina u Srbiji i Bugarskoj krajem XVII veka, 1600–1700,' *Istorijski Časopis*, 12–13 (1961–2), 189–237; also J. Tadić, 'Le commerce en Dalmatie et à Raguse et la décadence économique de Venise au XVIIe siècle' in *Convegno Aspetti e Cause della Decadenza Economica Veneziana nel Secolo XVII* (Venice–Rome, 1961), pp. 235–72.
127. Sella, *Commerci*, p. 115; also D. Sella, 'Crisis and transformation in Venetian trade' in B. Pullan (ed.), *Crisis and Change in the Venetian Economy in the Sixteenth and Seventeenth Centuries* (London, 1968), p. 102.
128. Svoronos, *Salonique*, p. 195.
129. Tadić, 'Raguse,' p. 270; Carter, 'Dubrovnik,' passim.
130. For Ragusa's decline as the great Balkan middleman, see V. Vinaver, *Dubrovnik i Turska u XVIII Veku* (Beograd, 1960).
131. Svoronos, *Salonique*, p. 197; H. Halm and I. Sakazov, *Bulgarische Wirtschaftsgeschichte* (Berlin & Leipzig, 1929), p. 253.
132. Masson, *XVIIIe siècle*, p. 612.
133. Davis, *Aleppo*, p. 143.
134. The Dutch had already lost interest in Levantine (i.e. Persian) silk by the late seventeenth century, according to Glamann, *Trade*, p. 121. The best explanation of the Levantine silk trade is found in the works by R. Davis already cited.
135. In Lösch's words, *Location*, p. 452: 'As the price of agricultural products rises with proximity to a demand center, so also do the value of land of the same quality and the wages of labor.' The same reasoning could, of course, be applied to the United States in the nineteenth century. There were both climatological *and* economic reasons for cotton being raised *where land prices were lowest* – quite aside from the

slavery *versus* free labor controversy which has enlivened recent literature on the economic history of the American South.

136. H. Inalcık, 'Bursa and the commerce of the Levant,' *Journal of the Economic and Social History of the Orient*, 3 (1960), 136, 139.

137. S. Clough and C. Cole, *Economic History of Europe* (Boston, 1952), p. 261.

138. T. Willan, 'Some aspects of English trade with the Levant in the sixteenth century,' *English Historical Review*, 70 (1965), 403–9.

139. M. Bakhit, 'The Ottoman Province of Damascus in the sixteenth century' (unpublished Ph.D. dissertation, University of London, 1972), p. 183. Bakhit's work also indicates a record of incessant Beduin raiding in the latter half of the sixteenth century and a resultant interruption of agriculture. This harmonizes with what Barkan noticed about population trends at Aleppo and Damascus: following a general trend upward in the first half of the sixteenth century, Syrian population showed a pervasive decline in the second half of the same century. Pressure from Beduin tribes seems to have persisted as a chronic drag on agriculture throughout the Ottoman period. See H. A. R. Gibb and H. Bowen, *Islamic Society and the West*, I, pt 1, p. 233; A. Hourani, *The Ottoman Background of the Middle East* (London, 1970), p. 14; P. Holt, *Egypt and the Fertile Crescent, 1516–1922* (Ithaca, N.Y., 1966), p. 102; and A. Cohen and B. Lewis, *Population and Revenue in the Towns of Palestine in the Sixteenth Century* (Princeton, 1978), pp. 20–1.

140. Sakazov, *Wirtschaftsgeschichte*, (relying on Beaujour and Masson), p. 201.

141. Glamann, *Trade*, p. 131.

142. Davis, *Aleppo*, p. 27; *idem*, 'English imports', p. 200; A. Wood, *A History of the Levant Company* (Oxford, 1935), p. 74; Luke, *Cyprus*, pp. 87, 91.

143. Masson, *XVIIe siècle*, pp. 374, 383; Charles-Roux, *Échelles*, p. 8.

144. Levantine imports in cotton seem to form the bulk of total cotton imports at Marseilles which Masson elsewhere indicates as being 15,000,000 livres worth of raw cotton in 1789 and 2,000,000 livres worth of cotton cloth: cf. P. Masson (ed.), *Les Bouches du Rhone*, XI: *Le Mouvement économique: le commerce*, p. 238.

The Paris figures appear on p. 541 of his work, cited above many times; for the graphs offered by Paris relating to cotton, see *ibid.*, pp. 605, 606.

For Salonica, see also Svoronos, *Salonique*, pp. 247, 253.

145. Masson, *XVIIIe siècle*, p. 616.

146. Smilyanskaya, 'Razlozhenie,' p. 228, where she gives the (erroneous) impression that the Syrian cultivation of cotton is an innovation.

147. V. Paskaleva, 'Osmanlı Balkan Eyaletlerin Avrupalı devletlerle ticaretleri tarihine katkı (1700–1850),' *Iktisat Fakültesi Mecmuası*, 27 (1967–8), nos. 1–2, 37–74.

148. *ibid.*, p. 54.

149. *ibid.*, p. 56.

150. I. Erceg, 'Aussenhandel der Nordadriatischen Seestädte als Faktor im Entstehen der Kapitalistischen Beziehungen in Österreich im 18 und 19 Jahrhundert,' *Vierteljahrschrift für Sozial und Wirtschaftsgeschichte*, 55 (1968–9), 469.

151. W. Kaltenstadtler, 'Der Österreichische Seehandel über Triest im 18 Jahrhundert,' *Vierteljahrschrift für Sozial und Wirtschaftsgeschichte*, 56 (1970), 42; P. Braunstein, 'A propos de l'Adriatique entre le XVe et le XVIIIe siècle,' *Annales: économies, sociétés, civilisations*, 26 (1971), 1278; J. Hildt, 'Uebersicht des tuerkischen Handels ueber Semlin mit den österreichischen Staaten, vom 1sten Nov.

1795 bis 31sten Oktober 1796,' reproduced in N. Michoff, *Contribution à l'histoire du commerce de la Turquie et de la Bulgarie* (Sofia, 1971), pp. 65–6.

Notes to chapter 2, pp. 45–79

1. F. Braudel, *La Méditerranée et le Monde méditerranéen à l'époque de Phillipe II*, 2 vols. (Paris, 1966), ii, 67.
2. M. Weber, *Economy and Society*, 3 vols (New York, 1958), iii, 1072–9, and *idem*, *Religion of India* (New York, 1958), p. 58: 'The comparable . . . occidental parallel is not the medieval fief but the purchase of offices and prebends during the papal *seicento* or during the days of the French *Noblesse de Robe.*'
3. The *akche* is a small silver coin, identical with the *asper*.
4. N. Beldiceanu (ed.), *Code de lois coutumières de Mehmed II: Kitabi-i Qavanin-i Örfiyye-i Osmani* (Wiesbaden, 1967), pp. 9v–10r. Beldiceanu dates this code between 1477 and 1481.
5. R. Anhegger and H. Inalcık (eds.), *Kannuname-i Sultani ber Muceb-i Örf-i Osmani* (Ankara, 1956), p. 25.
6. N. Beldiceanu, *Code*, pp. 10r–10v.
7. *ibid.*, pp. 10v–11r.
8. (Ahmed Aşıki) Aşıkpaşazade, *Tevarih-i Al-i Osman* in C. Atsız (ed.), *Osmanlı Tarihleri*, i (Istanbul, 1949), chs 15 and 16 (pp. 104–5), chs 30 (p. 117), 34 and 36 (pp. 120–2), 41 (p. 125), 53 (p. 131), 55, 59 (132, 139).
9. Feridun, *Münşeat es-Selatin* (first pub. Istanbul, 1264 A.H.), i, 71 and 109 respectively. The report from Emir Süleyman is especially interesting as it mentions not only the distribution of *timars* at Qonur and Gelibolu but also the creation of a register (*defter*) and an inspection system (*yoklama*) – all elements in the fully developed control system.

    Although the authenticity of some items from Feridun Bey's collection has been doubted, the items referred to here are defended by I. Beldiceanu-Steinherr in *Recherches sur les actes des règnes des sultans Osman, Orkhan, et Murat I* (Monachii, 1967), pp. 43–9. For a discussion which brings out Feridun's general reliability, see the article '*Feridun Beg*' in *Encyclopedia of Islam*, 2nd edn, by Mordtmann and Menage.
10. H. Inalcık (ed.), *Hicri 835 Tarihli Suret-i Defter-i Sancak-i Arvanid* (Ankara, 1954).
11. The *Kavanin-i erbab-i timar-i ara'i* appearing in Haci Halfa's *Takvim et-Tevarih*, discussed by Franz Babinger, *Beiträge zur Frühgeschichte der Türkenherrschaft in Rumelien 14–15 Jahrhundert* (Munich, 1949), p. 58.
12. C. Cahen, 'Selçuki Devletleri Feodal mi idi?,' *Iktisat Fakültesi Mecmuası*, 17 (1955), 348–58, at 349; cf. H. Maine, *Ancient Law* (London, 1930), pp. 318–19.
13. See for instance, P. Charanis, 'On the social structure and economic organization of the Byzantine Empire in the thirteenth century and after,' *Byzantinoslavica*, 12 (1951), 94–153, at 132f.
14. A bibliography on the development of prebendal institutions in earlier Muslim states appears at the end of the article '*Ikta*' in *Encyclopedia of Islam*, 2nd ed.; see also C. Cahen, 'L'évolution de l'iqta du XIe au XIIIe siècle,' *Annales: économies, sociétés, civilisations*, 8 (1953), 25–46; also A. Lambton, 'Reflections on the Iqta' in G. Makdisi (ed.), *Arabic and Islamic Studies in Honor of Hamilton A. R. Gibb*

(Cambridge, Mass., 1965), pp. 358–76; F. Köprülü, 'Bizans Müesseselerinin Osmanlı Müesseselerine Tesiri,' *Türk Hukuk ve Iktisat Tarihi Mecmaması*, ɪ (1931), 219–40; cf. *idem*, 'Ortazaman Türk–Islam Feodalizmi,' *Belleten*, 5 (1941), 319–34, in which he attempted to cast doubt on the value of much previous work done on Islamic 'feudalism' (by Becker, Poliak, Deny, Wittek, and others), while suggesting Turco-Mongol rather than Islamic origins for the Ottoman system. See also Ö. L. Barkan's article '*Timar*' in the Turkish edition of the *Encyclopedia of Islam*.

15. See, for instance, N. Filipović, 'Osvrt na neka pitanja iz ranije istorije Osmanskog timara,' *Radovi Filozofskog Fakulteta Sarajeva*, ɪ (1963), 61–118, at 74.

16. H. Inalcık, 'Islam Arazi ve Vergi Sisteminin Teşekkülü ve Osmanlı Devrindeki Şekilleriyle Mukayesesi,' *Islam Ilimleri Enstitüsü Dergisi*, ɪ (1959), 1–18, at 15–16. I. Beldiceanu-Steinherr, by contrast, sees a full development of the *timar* system in the Seljuk period, 'Un Transfuge Qaramanide auprès de la Porte Ottomane,' *Journal of the Economic and Social History of the Orient*, 16/2–3 (1973), 155–67; cf. N. Beldiceanu and I. Beldiceanu-Steinherr, *Recherche sur la province de Qaraman au XVIe siècle* (Leiden, 1968).

A further area of controversy is whether to trace the Seljuk *ikta* and the Ottoman *timar* back through the Muslim *ikta* tradition, as seems to be Cahen's inclination, or whether to see it as a product primarily of Turkic and Mongol non-Islamic inspiration. This latter course is represented by O. Turan's earlier work, 'Türkiye Selçuklarında toprak hukuku: miri topraklar ve hususi mülkiyet şekilleri,' *Belleten*, 12 (1948), 549–74, at 549; by F. Köprülü, 'Ortazaman,' and by Z. Togan, *Umumi Türk Tarihine Giriş* (Istanbul, 1970), pp. 288–91.

17. Cf. N. Filipović, 'Pogled na Osmanski feudalizam,' *Godišnjak Istoriskog Društva Bosne i Hercegovine*, 4 (1952), 6–39; B. Djurdjev, 'O uticaju turske vladavine na razvitak naših naroda,' *Godišnjak Istoriskog Društva Bosne i Hercegovine*, 2 (1950), 34–81; B. Cvetkova, 'Sur certaines réformes de régime foncier au temps de Mehmet II,' *Journal of the Economic and Social History of the Orient*, 6/1 (May 1963), 104–20; V. Mutafčieva, 'De l'exploitation feodale dans les terres de population Bulgare sous la domination Turque au XV et XVI s.,' *Études Historiques* (Sofia, 1960), pp. 145–70; and F. Milkova, 'Sur la teneur et la caractère de la propriété d'état des terres miriye dans l'empire Ottoman du XVe au XIXe s.,' *Études Balkaniques*, 5 (1966), 155–68. On the 'Asian mode of production' cf. F. Tökei, *Sur la mode de production asiatique* (Budapest, 1966); S. Divitçioğlu, *Asya Üretim Tarzı ve Osmanlı Toplumu* (Istanbul, 1967); H. Islamoğlu and Ç. Keyder, 'Agenda for Ottoman history,' *Review*, 1/1 (Summer 1977), 31–55, at 37 (footnote).

18. H. Inalcık, *The Ottoman Empire: The Classical Age: 1300–1600* (New York, 1973), p. 110.

19. Both laws are published in the collection edited by Ö. L. Barkan, *XV ve XVIinci asırlarda Osmanlı imparatorluğunda zirai ekonominin hukuki ve mali esasları: ɪ: Kanunlar* (Istanbul, 1943), pp. 297–300 and 296–7 respectively. Barkan's extensive discussion of the *mirî* principle appears in his contribution to *Tanzimat* (Istanbul, 1940), pp. 329f. Inalcık's discussion of Ebusuud's Skopje/Salonica law appears in his very detailed article on the foundation of the Islamic land and tax system: 'Islam arazi ve vergi sisteminin teşekkülü ve Osmanlı devrindeki şekilleriyle mukayesesi,' *Islam Ilimleri Enstitüsü Dergisi*, ɪ (1959), 1–18.

20. This analogy appears to one of the *kanunnames* published in *Milli Tetebbu'lar*

Mecmuasi, 1–2 (1915), 52; cf. also the *fetva* collections published by M. Düzdağ, *Şeyhulislam Ebusuud Efendi Fetvaları Işığında 16 Asır Türk Hayatı* (Istanbul,1972).

21. V. Skarić, 'Postanak i razvitak kmetstva u Bosni i Hercegovini,' *Pregled* (Sarajevo), 13 (1937), 481–9, at 483–5.

22. D. Bojanić, 'O srpskoj baštini i soću u Turskim zakonima,' *Istorijski Časopis*, 20 (1973), 157–80, at 171.

23. Inalcık, 'Islam,' p. 10. Details on the fiscal categories of the original Arab conquerors also appear in F. Lökkegaard, *Islamic Taxation in the Classic Period* (Copenhagen, 1950); especially interesting is Lökkegaard's discussion of *hima*, a Beduin concept entailing a limited right to the collective use of land, p. 20.

24. 'Osmanlı Imparatorluğunda kuruluş devrinin toprak meseleleri,' *Ikinci Türk Tarih Kongresi* (Istanbul, 20–25 Sept. 1937), pp. 1002–13; other essays by Barkan touching upon the development of the Ottoman land regime: 'Aperçu sur l'histoire des problèmes agraires des pays balkaniques,' *Revue de la Faculté des Sciences Économiques de l'Université d'Istanbul*, 7 (1945–6), 120–72; 'Osmanlı Imparatorluğunda bir iskân ve kolonizasyon metodu olarak vakıflar ve temlikler,' *Vakıflar Dergisi*, 2 (1942), 279–386; 'Istilâ devrinin kolonizator Türk dervişleri,' *idem*.

25. M. F. Köprülü, 'Ortazaman,' p. 332; Köprülü is faulted for not giving sufficient attention to the matter by Filipović, 'Osvrt,' p. 62. Cf. I. Beldiceanu-Steinherr, 'Fiscalité et formes de possession de la terre arable dans l'Anatolie pre-Ottomane,' *Journal of the Economic and Social History of the Orient*, 19/3 (1976), 233–322, at 296.

26. Cf. Turan, 'Türkiye,' p. 549; and Filipović, 'Osvrt,' p. 116.

27. V. Minorsky, 'Nasir al-Din Tusi on Finance,' *Bulletin of the School of Oriental and African Studies*, 10 (1940–1), 755–89, at 774; and H. Ülken, 'Türkiye tarihinde sosyal kuruluş ve toprak rejiminin gelişmesi (Osmanlılara kadar),' *Vakıflar Dergisi*, 10 (1973), 1–62, at 47–9.

28. For the rents, taxes, services and other disabilities typical of the *paroikos*, cf. A. Laiou-Thomadakis, *Peasant Society in the Late Byzantine Empire* (Princeton, 1977); Charanis, 'Thirteenth century'; Ostrogorsky, 'Agrarian conditions in the Byzantine Empire in the Middle Ages,' *CEHE* (Cambridge, 1966), ı, 213–31. *Historija Naroda Jugoslavije* (Zagreb, 1953), ı, 418–29, 584–5, offers parallel information on the dependent cultivators of the South Slav successor states which immediately preceded Ottoman rule.

29. M. Finley, *The Ancient Economy* (Berkeley, 1973), p. 66; cf. Ö. L. Barkan, 'Le servage existait-il en Turquie?,' *Annales: économies, sociétés, civilisations*, 11 (1956), 54–60.

30. H. Inalcık, *The Ottoman Empire: The Classical Age, 1300–1600* (New York, 1973), p. 109.

31. *Monumenta Turcica*, ı (Sarajevo, 1957), 531; cf. the law of the province of Silistre (1569), Barkan, *Kanunlar*, p. 282, where a very similar clause appears with the added proviso that if and when someone else takes over the original holding and cultivates it, the man who has moved no longer need pay a double tithe. Limitations on taking the *chift bozan* tithe or tax also appear in the laws of the provinces of Musul (Murat III period), *ibid.*, p. 174; Diyarbekir (1540), *ibid.*, p. 132; and Yeni Il (1583), *ibid.*, p. 79.

32. *ibid.*, p. 332.

33. *ibid.*, p. 312. Similar clauses appear in the laws for the provinces of Niğbolu (Süleyman's reign), *ibid.*, p. 271; Silistre (Süleyman period), *ibid.*, p. 273; another Silistre law (1569), *ibid.*, p. 288. Inalcık has found evidence of a three-year *chift bozan* rule going back to Abbasid times – 'Islam arazi ve vergi sistem,' p. 13. No doubt the three-year rule is linked to fallow practices of great antiquity: one clause in one of the Silistre laws cited (Barkan, *Kanunlar*, p. 286) says that if a *reaya* comes back to his place at the end of three years there has been no offense, while the law for the province of Sofya (Sofia) (1525) stipulates that though it is permissible for some fields to be left fallow for two years, if they are not cultivated the third consecutive year, then the *sipahi* should turn them over to someone else, *ibid.*, p. 254.

34. *ibid.*, p. 24. The fifteen-year statute of limitation on fugitives (and twenty in the city) appears in the Fatih code on *reaya* affairs: Beldiceanu, *Code*, p. 51r. However a law for the province of Vize (1539), Barkan, *Kanunlar*, p. 234, specifies ten years. Perhaps this represents some local condition or perhaps there was some confusion with the rule found in the Sofya law (1525), *ibid.*, p. 253, which specifies that if a *reaya* switches holdings locally he will be registered on the new holding after ten years. The same law also suggests a continued need for labor: if a *reaya* instead of moving locally comes in from a great distance he should be registered as a *reaya* in the new place at once (even though this contradicts the rule on 'collecting' fugitive *reayas*; apparently there was ambivalence as to whether the *reaya* would be more useful in the old place or in the new).

35. *ibid.*, p. 68. Similar clauses appear in the laws for Gurcistan (Georgia) (1570), Silistre (1569) and Musul (Mosul) (Murat III period), *ibid.*, pp. 199, 285–6, 174 respectively.

36. *Monumenta Turcica*, I, 78. Similar distinctions between the *sahib-i arz* and the *sahib-i reaya* (or *kendi zabit*) appear in quite a number of provincial laws, usually stipulating a division of taxes between them with the *reaya* taxes (e.g. *ispence, salariye*) going to the latter (i.e., the *reaya*'s original *sipahi*): the laws for Karesi (1521), Kütahya (1528), Iç Il (1584), Diyarbekir (1540), Mosul (Murat III period), Küdüs (Palestine zone, n.d.), Silistre (1569), Ohri (1613), Sirem (Srem, Szerem, Murat III period), Kopan and Samanturna (Selim II period), in Barkan, *Kanunlar*, pp. 22, 26, 47, 51, 133, 174, 218, 284, 295, 308 and 321 respectively.

37. *Monumenta Turcica*, I, 78–9.

38. D. Bojanić, *Turski zakoni i zakonski propisi iz xv i xvi veka za Smederevska, Kruševacka, i Vidinska oblast* (Beograd, 1974), p. 85.

39. Barkan, *Kanunlar*, p. 299; the same understanding, virtually without changes, was written into the Morean law of 1716 which specifies that these rules still apply in neighboring Rumelia! *ibid.*, p. 362.

40. *Monumenta Turcica*, I, 82. Once again one is struck by the looseness with which the term *sahib* was used. Here it obviously refers to the peasant cultivator.

41. Barkan, *Kanunlar*, p. 326. For the original statement drafted by Ebusuud himself, cf. *ibid.*, pp. 297 and 299 (laws for Budin and Üskub/Selanik respectively). However, the earlier Cretan land law (1670) was strangely contradictory, depicting newly conquered soil as the absolute property (*mülk*) of the holder: *ibid.*, p. 352.

42. *Monumenta Turcica*, I, 52.

43. Barkan, *Kanunlar*, pp. 299, 297.
44. *ibid.*, p. 286, and Beldiceanu, *Code*, p. 44v.
45. Beldiceanu, *Code*, p. 45v.
46. *Monumenta Turcica*, ı, 82 and Barkan, *Kanunlar*, p. 362, respectively.
47. The legal requirement for registration of changes, transfers and vacancies was imperiously expressed. According to the 1519 *sipahi* law of *Rum* (Tokat), when *timars* fell vacant they should be registered on the same day, when given out they should also be registered on the same day, and copies of these records should be sent every three months both to the district judge as well as to Istanbul, Barkan, *Kanunlar*, p. 110.

    For the range in incomes possible within the Ottoman prebendal system as well as their modest size on the average, see Inalcık, *The Ottoman Empire*, pp. 115–16.
48. An interdiction of far-reaching significance!: H. Hadjibegić, 'Kanunnama Sultana Sulejmana Zakonodavca,' *Godišnjak Zemaljskog Muzeja* (Sarajevo), n.s. 4–5 (1949–50), 295–381, at pp. 318–19 (this edition of the TOEM *kanunname* has been corrected with Bosnian manuscripts); *Monumenta Turcica*, ı, 51–2; B. McGowan (ed.), *Defter-i Mufassal-i Liva-i Sirem* (Ankara, Turkish Historical Society, still in press), from the *kanunname*. The interdiction is repeated in M. Nuri, *Netayic ül-Vuku'at: Tekmileleri* (Ankara, 1961), ı, 53. On protection of common pasture: Ö. L. Barkan (ed.), *Edirne Askeri kassam'ına ait Tereke Defterleri: Belgeler*, 3 (Ankara, 1968), 48.
49. On the diminution of the prebendal demesne (*hassa çiftliği, kılıç yeri*) in the latter sixteenth century, see Inalcık, *The Ottoman Empire*, p. 110; cf. Barkan, 'Aperçu,' p. 142, who emphasizes that even while the *sipahi* had a demesne, he was not legally permitted to use corvée labor to work it. The reasons for the diminution of the demesne of the *sipahi* are unclear – possible this is a reflection of a need for his undistracted services, possibly of a trend among the *sipahis* to live away from their prebends; still other economic or administrative factors can easily be inferred. Empirical evidence on their gradual disappearance is offered by M. Cook, *Population Pressure in Rural Anatolia, 1450–1600* (London, 1972), p. 74; and by V. Mutafčieva, 'K'm v'prosa za čiflicite v Osmanskata imperiiă prez XIV–XVII v.,' *Istoričeski Pregled*, 14/1 (1958), 34–58, at 47–57.
50. It is the guarantees of status which seem impressive in the partial code of Mehmet II, dated 1477–8: 'so long as a *sipahi* answers the call and goes to battle upon the announcement of an imperial campaign and even afterwards, after he has retired, he should not be registered as a *reaya*; he is military,' Beldiceanu, *Code*, pp. 34v–38r; this passage is followed by several others refining the criteria for granting military status, i.e. who was, and who was not to be regarded as 'military' (*askeri*). However in the *sipahi* law of Rum dated 1519, it is the limitations upon status which are most striking: 'And with regard to retired *sipahis* the imperial ruling is as follows: if a *sipahi* is discharged and does not take another *timar* after seven years, then they should take (from him) the *sher'i* taxes and the other taxes, just as with the other *reaya*. And for those *sipahis'* sons whose fathers did not have a *timar* but whose forebears may have held a *timar* for a time, such as these are like the rest of the *reaya*; let there be taken the *sher'i* taxes and the other regular and occasional levies.' Quoted in Barkan, *Kanunlar*, pp. 109–10; cf. Inalcık, *Ottoman Empire*, pp. 115–16. Braudel has used the term 'noblesse' in speaking of

the Ottoman *timarlı* class. While we can surely call the *timarlıs* a status group, or (more doubtfully) a class, it seem inappropriate to use the term 'noblesse' with its strong connotation of better blood, transmitted genealogically. The Ottoman sense of status was situational, their respect for merit stronger than their respect for family origins (though this is not to say that they were not interested in such things). In terms of their numerical strength within their society the Ottoman prebendal class might reasonably be compared with the Polish *szlachta*, the Hungarian gentry, and perhaps the middle service class of Muscovy. For a discussion of the variety of attitudes surrounding 'nobilities' in various parts of Europe, see O. Forst de Battaglia, 'The nobility in the European Middle Ages,' *Comparative Studies in Society and History*, 5 (1962), 60–75.

Most persuasive is the argument that the Rum *seljuks* and the Ottomans intersected at two different points the long Byzantine career. 'The Byzantine *pronoia* was in its "infancy" in the eleventh century, but by the fourteenth the *pronoia* system had spread over the entire Byzantine domains and over those of the South Slavs': S. Vryonis, *The Decline of Medieval Hellenism in Asia Minor and the Process of Islamization from the Eleventh Through the Fifteenth Century* (Berkeley, 1971), pp. 467–8. V. Menage, reviewing Vryonis's book, adds another to the list of items which the Ottomans can be presumed to have taken over from the Byzantine state: the *dönüm*, the standard Ottoman land measure, 40 paces square, was not a standard Islamic measure but rather the equivalent of the Byzantine *stremma*: *Bulletin of the School of Oriental and African Studies*, 36 (1973), 661.

As for the *timarlı*'s hold over his peasants, the *sipahi* law of Rum (1519) provides a clause typifying the limitations (similar clauses are found scattered among all the extant provincial land codes): 'And formerly at the time when the European side was conquered, there used to be taken from the *reaya*, in addition to the taxes specified in the tax register, a *salarlık* and a *yemlik* (both taxes in kind on a household basis) and every year anyone who was registered as having a plowteam (*chift*) did one day's service for the *timar* holder. And each year a *kile* (just over a bushel) of barley apiece and a chicken apiece was taken and this was called "harvest tax". And fortress soldiers also got from each holding a load of straw and a load of wood. These were innovations (i.e., *bidats*, innovations to the Islamic system of taxation) and because they do not appear in the tax register they were abrogated and forbidden by the justice of the ruler': Barkan, *Kanunlar*, p. 110.

General statements on limitations of the *sipahi*'s powers over the peasantry are found in Inalcık, *Ottoman Empire*, pp. 107, 111; Barkan, 'Aperçu,' p. 142, H. Gibb and H. Bowen, *Islamic Society and the West*, ı, pt 1 (London, 1950), 45–70, 137–72, 235–75, and in many other places. With respect to laboring on the *sipahis*' erstwhile demesnes, Inalcık points out that in certain districts, contrary to the clause just cited, a requirement of one to three days' demesne service annually was enforced.

Elsewhere Inalcık also places great emphasis on the elimination of demesne service, 'a major social reform.' He agrees with Barkan that 'it was in principle forbidden to compel the peasants to any service' (by which he means service for the *timarlı*, not corvée labor for the state – which was another matter): 'The emergence of the Ottomans,' *Cambridge History of Islam* (Cambridge, 1970), ı, 287. B. Cvetkova points out that it was Ottoman policy to maintain the right of fiscal interference even on *mülk* and *vakıf* soil, though juridically these fall outside the eminent domain (*mirî*) category: 'Sur certaines reformes . . . de Mehmet II,' pp. 107–9.

51. J. Gould, 'The price revolution reconsidered,' *Economic History Review*, 17 (1964–5), 262.

52. The career of the *levend* irregulars and their provincial *segban* counterparts is skillfully summarized in a forthcoming article by H. Inalcık, 'Military and fiscal transformation in the Ottoman Empire, 1600–1700,' to appear in *Archivum Ottomanicum*. The same article contains an illuminating section on tax farming, which may be supplemented by his earlier article, 'Centralization and decentralization in Ottoman administration' in T. Naff and R. Owen (eds.), *Studies in Eighteenth Century Islamic History* (London, 1977), pp. 27–52. These fiscal explanations are a vast improvement over the sketchy nineteenth-century treatises: A. Vefik, *Tekâlif Kavaidi* (Istanbul, 1328H), and S. Sevdi, *Defter-i Muktesid* (Istanbul, 1306H). At the time at which the last named treatise was written (1890) tax farming was still in operation, cf. III, 111.

53. Tax farming, so subversive of society, was fatally convenient for the government, and not only at Istanbul. As one commentator on the contemporary English scene points out, attempts to do away with the farming of customs during the reigns of the first two Stuarts foundered on the argument, 'repeated *ad nauseum* by king and government officials alike, that certainty in revenue was the prerequisite of a sound financial system, and the best way of obtaining this certainty was through farming': R. Ashton, 'Revenue farming under the early Stuarts,' *Economic History Review*, 2nd ser., 8 (1955/6), 311.

54. 'The relationship between bureaucracy and taxation is a highly interdependent one. The efficiency of the bureaucracy depends upon the effectiveness of its taxation system; and the effectiveness of its taxation system depends upon the efficiency of the bureaucratic apparatus. Thus any increase in the bureaucratic load or decrease in taxation capacity may generate a vicious circle of decentralization of power': D. Lockwood, 'Social integration and system integration' in G. Zollschan and W. Hirsch (eds.), *Explorations in Social Change* (Boston, 1964), p. 254.

55. See Inalcık, 'Fiscal transformation,' forthcoming in *Archivum Ottomanicum*; also B. Cvetkova, 'Recherches sur le system d'affermage (*iltizam*) dans l'Empire Ottoman,' *Rocznik Orientalistyczny*, 27 (1964), 111–32.

56. Ayni Ali is cited in B. Cvetkova, 'L'évolution du régime féodal turc de la fin du XVIe jusqu'au milieu de XVIIIe siècle,' *Receuil d'études historiques à l'occasion du XIe congrès international des sciences historiques* (Sofia, 1960), p. 195; W. Wright (ed.), *Sarı Mehmed Pasha, the Defterdar: Ottoman Statecraft: The Book of Counsel for Vezirs and Governors (Nasaih ül vüzera vel ümera)* (Princeton, N.J., 1935), p. 73.

57. See H. Inalcık, 'Capital formation in the Ottoman Empire,' *Journal of Economic History*, 29 (1969), 97–140. Ottoman attitudes towards participation in these activities contrast sharply with those prevailing in contemporary France. See, for example, R. Grassby, 'Social status and commercial enterprise under Louis XIV,' *Economic History Review*, 2nd ser., 13 (1960), 19–38.

58. The expression *chiftlik* has at least three meanings: (1) the prebendal demesne suppressed in the latter sixteenth century, (2) the *reaya*'s holding (also called in

the Balkans *bashtina*), (3) a larger consolidated estate organized for commercial production, the usage intended here. Cf. H. Inalcık, 'Chiftlik,' *Encyclopedia of Islam*, 2nd edn.

59. H. Gandev, 'L'apparition des rapports capitalistes dans l'économie rurale de la Bulgarie du Nord-Ouest au cours du XVIIIe siècle,' *Études Historiques* (Sofia, 1960), pp. 207–20.

60. For the significance of changing patterns of commercial traffic towards the end of the eighteenth century, see above, chapter 1.

61. The importance of this move will be immediately appreciated by students of West European agrarian history. See, for instance, J. Thirsk, 'Farming techniques,' and 'Enclosing and engrossing' in H. Finberg (ed.), *The Agrarian History of England and Wales* (Cambridge, 1967–), IV, 161–99, 200–55 respectively.

62. A discussion of dispossession and the actual use of land and labor in a concrete situation follows in the Manastir study (chapter 5).

63. The long list of pretexts used by *softas, jelalis* and renegade government men to oppress the peasants of Anatolia beyond endurance is described in detail in the 'justice decrees' published with his comments by H. Inalcık, 'Adaletnâmeler,' *Belgeler*, II, nos 3–4, 126, 128 and passim.

64. A. Sućeska, 'O nastanka čifluka u našim zemljama,' *Godišnjak društva istoričara Bosne i Hercegovine*, 16 (1965), 37–57.

65. Cvetkova, 'L'évolution,' p. 182.

66. Selanikî, *Tarih-i Selanikî* (Istanbul, 1281 AH).

67. Cvetkova, 'L'évolution,' p. 182.

68. Wright, *Sarı Mehmed Pasha*, p. 73. Kochi Bey was already railing against false 'properties' and pious estates (*vakıfs*) in his time, and Ali Çauş of Sofia records the overwhelming extent to which *vakıf* had come to dominate Ottoman towns of the early seventeenth century.

69. Various nineteenth-century observers estimated the extent of *vakıf* to be between half and three-quarters of all the arable and built-upon property in the Empire, with Istanbul itself almost wholly so; see R. Davison, *Reform in the Ottoman Empire, 1856–1876* (Princeton, 1963). Inalcık also describes conversion of so-called wasteland (*mevat*), though no doubt much of what was called wasteland was either newly abandoned arable or intermittently cultivated abandoned village sites (*mezraas*, the *Wüstungen* of Kulischer, *et al.*): Inalcık 'Ottoman decline,' p. 14.

70. Cvetkova, 'L'évolution,' p. 186.

71. On the historical significance of the one-sided battle for the commons in other places, cf. Thirsk, 'Enclosing'; R. Zangheri, 'The historical relationship between agricultural and economic development in Italy' in E. Jones and S. Woolf, *Agrarian Change and Economic Development* (London, 1969), pp. 23–40, at 33; Bloch, *French Rural History*, p. 135; van Bath, *Agrarian History*, p. 183.

72. Cf. H. Inalcık, 'Chiftlik,' *Encyclopedia of Islam*, 2nd edn.

73. Also inherent in this distinction is the fact that the tax position of the usurper of the peasant's position (the *sahib-i alaka*) will be quite different from the position of the 'owner' of a property-like great *chiftlik*.

74. 'Die Privatisierung des Bodens durch die Lehensherren war für diese eine Notwendigkeit, da sie nur so dem bäuerlichen Produktionsfaktor Arbeit beikommen konnten und nur so zu vermeiden vermochten, dass sie von den Untertanen und

deren Arbeitswillen abhängig wurden': R. Busch-Zantner, *Agrarverfassung, Gesell-schaft und Siedlung in Südosteuropa* (Leipzig, 1938), p. 33.

75. Inalcık, 'Ottoman decline,' pp. 13–14.
76. The law of the province of Hatvan (Mehmed IV period, 1648–87), Barkan, *Kanunlar*, p. 317.
77. Sućeska, 'O nastanku čifluka,' p. 40 and passim.
78. R. Jennings, 'Loans and credit and early seventeenth century Ottoman judicial records,' *Journal of the Economic and Social History of the Orient*, XVI, pts 2, 3 (1973) 168–216.
79. Cvetkova, 'L'évolution,' p. 199.
80. D. Bojanik (ed.), 'Edno Ohridsko Kanunname,' *Glasnik na Institut za Nacionalna Istorija* (Skopje), 3, no. 1 (1959), 292. There are indications that the three-field system was in use in the northern Balkans at least. The sale of a fallow plot would presumably interfere with fallowing practice. See D. Warriner, 'Some controversial issues in the history of agrarian Europe,' *Slavonic and East European Review*, 32 (1953–4), 175. On the use of fallow land within the 'short fallow' system, see E. Boserup, *The Conditions of Agricultural Growth* (Chicago, 1965), pp. 15–16, 37–9. Cutting fodder for the *sipahi* is mentioned in some of the sixteenth-century provincial laws; but the fodder is cut on the *sipahi's* own land, hence little can be inferred from that about the use of *reaya* land.
81. Sućeska, 'O nastanka čifluka,' 39–40. Intensive waves of usurpation naturally created resentment and tension, and on the European side were certainly important for setting the stage for the Serbian rebellion of 1804, the Boynica rebellion (Bulgaria) in 1849, and the Bosnian–Herzegovinian rebellion of 1874–5. See H. Inalcık, *Tanzimat ve Bulgar Meselesi* (Ankara, 1943); T. Stoianovich, 'Land tenure and related sectors of the Balkan economy, 1600–1800,' *Journal of Economic History* (1953), pp. 398–411; and J. Tomasevich, *Peasants, Politics and Economic Change in Yugoslavia* (Stanford, 1955), pp. 34, 98–105, 120–4.
82. A. Sućeska, 'Malikâna,' *Prilozi za Orijentalnu Filologiju*, 8–9 (1958–9), 111–42. According to Sućeska the *Malikâne* holder had the right as well of confirming the inheritance and transfer of peasant holdings (as had the *sipahi*) and of selling, leasing or gifting his *malikâne* or entrusting it to another for management. Inalcık assigns a leading role to *malikâne* (life-lease) holdings in preparing the ground for *chiftliks*: 'Fiscal transformation' (forthcoming).
83. A petition from the villagers around Damascus (c. 1745) is reported in Inalcık's, 'Capital formation,' p. 131. The villagers complain that since 1737 the usurers of Damascus had been loaning them money at interest to enable them to pay taxes, but the accumulation of interest payments had reduced them to being unable to pay these debts; the interesting question here is: did the usurers expect to receive their capital back, or did they prefer to go on receiving interest? Clearly, much archival research needs to be done in elucidating these and other local situations. For useful remarks on the Syrian (or at least the Aleppan and Damascan) landholding situation in the eighteenth century, cf. H. Bodman, Jr, *Political Factions in Aleppo, 1760–1826* (Chapel Hill, 1963), p. 8; A. Hourani, 'The Fertile Crescent in the eighteenth century,' *Studia Islamica*, 8 (1957), 91–118. A. K. Rafeq discusses the shifting trade position of Aleppo and Damascus in *The Province of Damascus, 1723–1783 (Beirut, 1966)*, cf. A. Hourani, *The Ottoman Background of the*

Middle East (London, 1970), p. 14; P. Holt, *Egypt and the Fertile Crescent, 1516–1922* (Ithaca, N.Y., 1966), p. 102; Gibb and Bowen, *Islamic Society*, I, pt 1, 258–275. Along with Gibb's discussion of Egyptian agriculture in this period there are comments by S. Shaw, *The Financial and Administrative Organization of Ottoman Egypt* (Princeton, 1962), pp. 21–3. For a useful discussion of lower Iraq around 1800, see J. Rousseau, *Description du Pachalik de Baghdad* (Paris, 1809), pp. 117–22. In Iraq, as in parts of Ottoman Syria, communal use of land was the rule (called in Syria *mushaa*). It seems probable that this sort of communal usage has its origins in tribal life in the desert, in which case it is related logically and culturally to the already cited concepts of *hima* and *fay*. However, communal use and perennial redivision of the *mushaa* type can also be seen elsewhere, as in Russia. It would be interesting to see how the *mushaa* system affected relations with the tax farmer, or the tenant-in-chief.

84. Interestingly, 'protection' under a late Ottoman landholder would bring the *reaya* back to a position close to that of the sharecropper (*ortakchı*) who in fifteenth-century law was protected from having to pay all irregular taxes: Beldiceanu, *Code*, p. 474. Regarding the situation of the *reaya* who must pay the double tithe, cf. Sućeska, 'Die Entwicklung,' p. 104, and Inalcık, 'Ottoman decline,' p. 15.

85. V. Mutafčieva, 'K'm v'prosa za čiflicite v Osmanskata imperiiǎ prez XIV–XVII v.,' *Istoričeski Pregled*, 14/1 (1958), 34–58, esp. pp. 47–57.

86. H. Gandev, *Zaraždane na kapitalisti českiteotnošeniǎ v čiflikoto stopanstvo na severnoza-padna B'lgaria prez XVIII v.* (Sofia, 1962), pp. 31–6; S. Dimitrov, 'Za agrarnite otnošeniiǎ v B'lgariiǎ prez XVIII v.,' *Paisii Hilendarksi i negovata epoha . . .* (Sofia, 1962), pp. 129–65.

87. M. Kunt, Sancaktan Eyalete, *1550–1650 arasında Osmanlı ümerası ve il idaresi* (Istanbul, 1975), p. 90.

88. H. Inalcık, 'The Ottoman decline and its effects upon the peasantry' (paper read at the AISEE convention in Athens, April 1970).

89. A. Sućeska, 'Neke osobenosti u procesu čiflučenja u Bosni i Hercegovini u XVIII stoljeću,' *Godišnjak Pravnog Fakulteta u Sarajevu*, 21 (1973), 331–42, at 336–8.

90. *ibid.*, pp. 336–8.

91. This situation is already lamented in a law for the Ohrid district promulgated in 1613: 'Many *bashtinas* have been lost and their *jizyes* and *ispenjes* swallowed up because a *reaya* has died and his son, overtaken by destitution and out of extreme hardship has separated a field or a certain amount of land from the *bashtina* and has either sold it to another or has put it up as a pledge on a loan. Henceforth this practice must be eliminated and *bashtinas* no longer broken up. . . . The *sipahi* should recover the entire *bashtina* from the seller and the buyer, reconsolidate it, and give it to someone who wants it so that the imperial *jizye* and the *sipahi*'s *ispenje* should not be lost,' from BVA Tapu Defter 717, quoted in D. Bojanić, 'Edno Ohridsko Kanunname,' *Glasnik na Institut za Nacionalna Istorija* (Skopje), 3/1 (1959), 285–95, at 292. What the law seems not to foresee is that the *sipahi* himself may wish to break up the *reaya chiftlik* for his own purposes.

92. Gandev, *Zaraždane*, p. 18.

93. See G. Ostrogorski, *O vizantiskom feudalismu* (Beograd, 1969), pp. 362–4, or *idem*, *Quelques problèmes d'histoire de la paysannerie Byzantine* (Wetteren, 1956).

94. Cf. Y. Özkaya, 'XVIII inci yüzyılda çıkarılan adaletnamelere göre Türkiye'nin iç durumu,' *Belleten*, 38/151–2 (1974), 445–91, at 459–61.

95. A. Matkovski, *Kreposništvoto vo Makedonija vo vreme na Turskoto Vladeenje* (Skopje, 1976).

96. The shift of status to the land also had its parallel in Byzantium as well as in Western Europe in the late Middle Ages; cf. P. Charanis, 'On the social structure and economic organization of the Byzantine Empire in the thirteenth century and after,' *Byzantinoslavica*, 12 (1951), 94–153, at 138.

97. See the *ferman* published by I. K. Vasdravelli, *Arheion Veroias* (Thessaloniki, 1954), pp. 210–12.

98. Cf. N. Konstandinović, *Selo Beogradskog Pašaluka do polovine XVII veka* (Beograd, 1973), pp. 84–9; and V. Skarić, 'Postanak i razvitak kmetstva u Bosni i Hercegovini,' *Pregled*, 13/163–4 (Sarajevo, 1937), 481–9.

99. B'lgarska Akademia na Naukite, *Istoria na B'lgariā*, 2 vols (Sofia, 1954–5), I, 362.

100. Boserup's statement comes to mind: 'When population becomes so dense that the land can be controlled, it becomes unnecessary to keep the lower class in personal bondage; it is sufficient to deprive the working classes of the right to be independent cultivators: E. Boserup, *The Conditions of Agricultural Growth* (Chicago, 1965), p. 73. She forgets that land can be occupied by paper as well as by men.

101. Cf. D. Bojanovski, 'Anketa za čiflugarstvo Prilepska okolija,' *Pregled*, 2/2 (1952), 35–44, and P. Kiroski, 'Čiflugarstvoto vo Polog' in *Kiril Pejcinoviḱ i Negovoto Vreme* (Tetovo, 1973), pp. 115–20. The rather diminutive average size of demesne holdings of two or three *chiftlik* units may be compared with the five to eight 'houses' of arable soil which comprised the typical demesne holding of seventeenth-century Poland; cf. B. Baranowski *et al.*, *Histoire de l'économie rurale en Pologne jusq'au 1864* (Wroclaw, 1966), p. 78.

102. Recent and good on this issue is S. Cheung, *The Theory of Share Tenancy* (Chicago, 1969). On direct farming *versus* tenantry, see J. Hicks, *A Theory of Economic History* (Oxford, 1969), p. 110.

103. Mercantile peonage is discussed by T. Stoianovich, 'Land tenure and related sectors of the Balkan economy, 1600–1800,' *Journal of Economic History*, 13 (1953), 398–414.

104. This interview took palce on 23 August, 1975 in the company of John Thirkell, an authority on Macedonian history from the University of Kent at Canterbury, England. Tankoski had gone to America and had returned as an old man. He showed us where the old *chiftlik kule* (tower) had stood and where the families (about 18 of them since this was a larger *chiftlik*) had had their huts. Alert and friendly, Tankoski was still capable of a lively rendition of Krali Marko and several other epics. The 50–50 split with the *bey* was meant to mean after the government's collector had taken his 10 per cent, so that the rent split was really 45–45. This is quite in harmony with the account of William Leake, who wrote that a 50–50 split had been widespread all over Greece at the beginning of the nineteenth century: *Travels in Northern Greece* (London, 1835), 4 vols., passim.

105. A. Spiesz, 'Czechoslovakia's place in the agrarian development of Middle and East Europe of modern times,' *Studia Historica Slovaca*, 6 (1969), 7–62, at 41.

106. Cf. A. Oteţea, 'Le second asservissement des paysans roumains (1746–1821),'

Nouvelles Études d'Histoire (Bucharest, 1960), pp. 299–312; V. Mihordea, 'La crise du régime fiscal dans les principautés Roumaines au XVIIIe s.,' *Nouvelles Études d'Histoire* (Moscow, 1970), pp. 121–32; S. Stefanescu, D. Mioc and H. Chirca, 'L'Évolution de la rente féodale en travail en Valachie et en Moldavie aux XIVe–XVIIIe siècles,' *Revue Roumaine d'Histoire*, 1(1962), 39–60; H. Stahl, *Les Anciennes communautés villageoises roumaines: asservissement et pénétration capitaliste* (Bucharest, 1969); R. Florescu, 'The Fanariot regime in the Danubian Principalities,' *Balkan Studies*, 9 (1968), 301–18; S. Pascu, 'La question agraire dans les pays Roumains à l'époque moderne (jusq'au la réforme de 1864),' *Revue Roumaine d'Histoire*, 9 (1970), 661–76; and V. Georgescu, 'Reflexions sur le status juridique des paysans corvéables et la politique agraire de la classe dominante en Valachie dans la seconde moitié du XVIIIe siècle,' *Nouvelles Études d'Histoire* (Bucharest, 1970), pp. 139–56.

107. Cf. A. Maczak, 'Zusammenhänge zwischen Fernhandel und ungleichmässiger Entwicklung polnischer Wirtschaftsgebiete im 16 und 17 Jahrhundert,' *Jahrbuch für Wirtschaftsgeschichte*, 3 (1971), 19–227; L. Zytkowicz, 'Production et productivité de l'économie agricole en Pologne aux XVe–XVIIIe siècles,' *Third International Conference of Economic History, Munich, 1965* (Paris, 1969), 149–65; A. Kaminski, 'Neo-serfdom in Poland and Lithuania,' *Slavic Studies Review*, 34/2 (June 1975), 253–68; J. Topolski, 'Economic decline in Poland from the sixteenth to the eighteenth centuries' in P. Earle (ed.), *Essays in European Economic History, 1500–1800* (Oxford, 1974), pp. 127–42; also *idem*, 'La regression économique en Pologne,' *Acta poloniae historica*, 7 (1962), 28–49; W. Rusinski, 'Hauptprobleme der Fronwirtschaft im 16 bis 18 Jhd. in Polen und den Nachbarländern,' *First International Conference of Economic History: Communications* (Stockholm, 1960), pp. 415–23; K. von Loewe, 'Commerce and agriculture: Lithuania, 1400–1600,' *Economic History Review*, 26 (1973), 23–37; A. Klima and J. Macurek, 'La Question de la transition du feudalisme au capitalisme en Europe Centrale (16e–18e siècles),' *XIe Congrès International des Sciences Historiques: Rapports IV* (Uppsala, 1960), pp. 84–105; with respect to other parts of Europe, P. Leon, *Économies et sociétés préindustrielles*, II: *1650–1778* (Paris, 1970).

108. Prominent among earlier work on *chiftliks* in Ottoman Europe were R. Busch-Zantner, *Agrarverfassung, Gesellschaft, und Siedlung in Südosteuropa* (Leipzig, 1938), which exhibits a geographer's approach to the subject; and T. Stoianovich, 'Land tenure and related sectors of the Balkan economy, 1600–1800,' *Journal of Economic History*, 13 (1953), 398–411, much more historical in its perspective.

109. *Tevzi* lists in two Karaferye *sijils* dated 1771 and 1785 indicate as many as 800 '*chifts of chiftlik*' in this district west of Salonica.

110. See, for instance, Leake, *Travels*, an outstanding contemporary witness who reported Greek rural conditions exhaustively; and J. Petropulos, *Politics and Statecraft in the Kingdom of Greece, 1833–1843* (Princeton, 1968), p. 28; B. Hrabak, 'Albanija od Konačnog pada pod Turska vlast do sredine XVIII vek' in Društvo Istoričara Srbije, *Iz Istorije Albanaca* (Beograd, 1969), pp. 45–73; Cook, *Population Pressure*, p. 42.

111. S. Dimitrov, 'K'm istoriata na čiflikčiistvoto v Rusensko,' *Istoričeski Pregled*, 14/4 (1958), 84–98. It is striking that the number of *chiftliks* and dependent cultivators remained more or less stable at Ruse throughout the eighteenth century, a

parallel to the situation at Manastir in Macedonia where, however, about twice the scale of cultivation is apparent (i.e. 1100 cf. 700 cultivators).

112. The issue is discussed by N. Todorov in D. Kosev *et al.* (eds.), *Problemi na B'lgarskata Istoriografiià sled vtorata svetovna voina* (Sofià, 1973), pp. 265–81, at 272–3.

113. H. Kaleši, 'Kosovo pod Turskom vlaščju' in *Kosovo Nekad i Danas* (Beograd, 1973), pp. 129–76, at 149.

114. Cf. R. Tričković, 'Čitlučenje u Beogradskom pašaluku u XVIII veku,' *Zbornik Filosofskog Fakulteta*, 11/1 (Beograd, 1970), 525–49; A. Sućeska, 'O nastanku čifluka u našim zemljama,' *Godišnjak Društva Istoričara Bosne i Hercegovine*, 16 (1965), 37–57, and *idem*, 'Neke osobenosti u procesu čiflučenja u Bosni i Hercegovini u XVIII stoljeću,' *Godišnjak Pravnog Fakulteta u Sarajevu*, 21 (1973), 331–42, at 332, 335; also B. Djurdjev, 'O uticaju turske vladavine na razvitak naših naroda,' *Godišnjak Istoriskog Društva Bosne i Hercegovina*, 2 (1950), 19–82.

115. See the report of Consul Chaumette de Fossés, in M. Šamić, *Les Voyageurs Français en Bosnie* (Paris, 1960), p. 217; cf. B. Djurdjev, 'Bosna' in *Encyclopedia of Islam*, 2nd edn.

Sarajevo *sijil* no. 21, dated 1196H/1782 AD, consulted at the Oriental Institute in Sarajevo, showed 80 *chiftiks* in Visoka *nahiye*, 84 in Fojnica *nahiye*, and 42 in Saray *kaza*. Apparently some of these were larger estates because the number of *gurush* levied as *taksit* contribution ranged from 1 to 15. But the average number of *gurush* levied was 3 to 4. *Tevzi* lists in other Bosnian *sijils* of the same period show no *chiftliks*: Mostar no. 5, Travnik no. 26, Blagaj no. 25, Ljubinje no. 15.

Notes to chapter 3, pp. 80–104

1. See T. H. Hollingworth, *Historical Demography* (Ithaca, N.Y., 1969), pp. 111–18.

2. Barkan's tables appear in M. Cook (ed.), *Studies in the Economic History of the Middle East* (London, 1970), pp. 168, 169; cf. R. Jennings, 'Urban population in the sixteenth century: a study of Kayseri, Karaman, Amasya, Trabzon and Erzerum,' *International Journal of Middle East Studies*, 7/1 (1976), 21–57. Barkan's original article on population growth in the sixteenth century appeared first as 'Tarihi demografi araşırmaları ve Osmanlı tarihi' in *Türkiyat Mecmuası*, x (Istanbul, 1951–1953), 1–26; this is republished as 'Essai sur les données statistiques des registres de recensement dans l'Empire Ottoman aux XV et XVIe siècles' in *Journal of the Economic and Social History of the Orient*, I (1957–8), 9–36. Barkan offers a map, without accompanying explanation, purporting to show the distribution of the households of a large part of Ottoman Europe around the beginning of the sixteenth century as an endpiece in *Iktisat Fakültesi Mecmuası*, II (Istanbul, 1949–50). The only work known to the author pertaining to the Ottoman domains in which pre-modern household size is abstracted upon the basis of complete data is the very limited sample represented by a Sava suburb of Belgrade studied by Dušan Popović and reported by T. Stoianovich, 'Model and mirror of the pre-modern Balkan city,' *Studia Balcanica*, 3 (Sofia, 1970): *La Ville Balkanique XVe–XIXe ss.*, 83–110, at 103–4. The source here was an Austrian census made in 1733; average household size was 3.7 with a range of 2 to 8; however, so limited a statistical base can hardly be put forward as a challenge to the conventionally accepted multiplier used by Barkan.

3. Regarding the *jizye* reform: H. Inalcık, '*Djizya*' (part II) in the *Encyclopedia of Islam*, 2nd edn; for its earlier collection on a household basis: H. Hadjibegić, *Glavarina u osmanskom carstvu* (Sarajevo, 1966).
4. Examples of these are found in the BVA Kâmil Kepeci (hereafter abbr. KK) and Maliyeden Müdevver (abbr. MM) collections; e.g. MM 6251, MM 515, KK 3531, KK 3532.
5. Examples of abuses in *jizye* collection are found in the following: B. Cvetkova, 'Changements intervenus dans la condition de la population des terres bulgares (depuis la fin du XVe jusqu'au milieu du XVIIIe siècle),' *Études Historiques*, V (1970), 291–318, and E. Grozdana, 'S' biraneto na dan'ka dzizie v b'lgarskite zemi,' *Istoriceski Pregled*, 26/5 (1970), 75–90. The interest of this last scholar in the subject of the Ottoman poll tax was extended in *idem*, 'Nalog dzizye s balkanskih zemel' v sisteme dohodov gosurdarstvenno; Kazn'i osmanskoi imperii (po tureckim dokementam XVII–XVIII vv.)' in A. Tveritinova (ed.), *Vostoch'ie Istočniki po istorii Narodov Iugo-Vostočnoi i central'noi Europi*, III (Moscow, 1979), 161–234; this study includes several facsimiles of *jizye* documents. The study itself concentrates on the period before the 1691 reform.
6. The 1490 figures, taken from register OAK 214/5 housed in the Oriental Section of Sofia's Kyril and Metodi Library, appear in N. Todorov, 'Za demografskoto s'stoianie na Balkanskiiâ Poluostrov prez XV–XVI v.,' *Godišnik na Sofiiskiiâ Universitet: Filosofsko–Istoričesko Fakultet*, 53/2 (1959), 191–232. They are repeated here. Figures in parentheses represent households headed by widows.

Paşa	133,679	(11,247)	Hersek	21,141	(133)
Köstendil	42,973	(3,219)	Bosna	20,421	(1,340)
Kruševac	41,642	(1,555)	Elbasan	20,345	(—)
Vlora	34,423	(917)	Evea	19,744	(1,645)
Yanina	30,693	(—)	Sofia	19,226	(1,938)
Trikala	30,540	(5,267)	Nikopol	18,208	(1,271)
Morea	29,743	(3,093)	Smederevo	17,700	(777)
Vılcıtrin	28,542	(2,524)	Silistre	12,483	(1,412)
Ohrid	24,358	(989)	Şkodra	10,996	(739)
Prizren	23,970	(1,886)	Vidin	10,332	(—)
Preveza	23,218	(2,585)	Mitilin	5,907	(620)
			Dukakin	1,550	(—)

In making comparisons, Mitilin (Mytelene) was excluded from all totals though Evea (Euboea) was not.

7. Todorov's nineteenth-century figures are taken from his *Balkanskiat Grad XV–XIX vek* (Sofia, 1972), p. 296; the source for these is E. Z. Karal's edition of the 1831 census, *Osmanlı İmparatorluğunda ilk nüfus sayımı 1831* (Ankara, 1943); Đ. Pejanović, *Stanovništvo Bosne i Hercegovine* (Beograd, 1955); and *Državopis Srbije III* (Beograd, 1866). The Ottoman figures include males of all ages as do the Greek figures. The Serbian figures include all persons of both sexes.

Other estimates from the late eighteenth and early nineteenth centuries appear in C. Issawi, 'The Ottoman Empire in the European economy: 1600–1914' in K. Karpat (ed.), *Social Change and Politics in Turkey* (London, 1973), p. 108.

The Ottoman figures (1831)

Tuna *vilayet*	(incl. 159,249 Muslims)	477,862
Edirne *vilayet*	(incl. 158,249 Muslims)	421,721
Solun *vilayet*	(incl. 100,249 Muslims)	240,411
Manastir *vilayet*	(incl. 81,736 Muslims)	208,222
Bosna *vilayet*	(incl. 175,177 Muslims)	444,478
Total	(incl. 674,719 Muslims)	1,792,694

The Greek figures (for 1821)

	Christians	Muslims	All
Continental			
Greece	247,850	20,865	268,715
Peleponessus	458,000	42,750	500,750
Islands	169,300	—	169,300
Totals	875,150	63,615	938,765

The Greek figures (for 1828)

	Christians	Muslims	All
Continental			
Greece	172,850	11,450	184,300
Peleponessus	400,000	—	400,000
Islands	169,100	—	169,100
Totals	741,950	11,450	753,400

The Serbian figures (1833)

Both sexes (incl. 4,560 non-Christians)	678,192

8. Cf. M. Reinhard, A. Armengaud and J. Dupâquier, *Histoire générale de la population mondiale* (Paris, 1968), pp. 220ff.

9. Olga Zirojević's study of the 'royal road' from Belgrade to Sofia contains numerous examples of settlements which simply disappeared owing to their position at roadside: *Carigradski Drum od Beograda do Sofije (1459–1683)* in *Zbornik Istorijskog Muzeja Srbije*, 7 (1970).

10. The shrinking of Balkan towns in the seventeenth century and their slight recovery in the eighteenth has, however, been noticed; Edirne, Sarajevo, Skopje, Novi Bazar, Beograd and Banja Luka are named in this connection. See T. Stoianovich, 'Land tenure and related sectors of the Balkan economy,' *Journal of Economic History*, 13 (1953), 398–411.

11. For a full discussion of typhus, see H. Zinsser, *Rats, Lice and History* (Boston, 1935). More about epidemics in the Balkans can be learned from an investigator who sees cholera as the important epidemic disease of more recent Balkan history: A. Ünver, 'Les épidémies de choléra dans les terres Balkaniques aux XVIIIe et XIXe siècles', *Études Balkaniques* (1973/4), pp. 89–97; for epidemics in earlier times: B. Hrabak, 'Kuga u Balkanskim zemljama pod Turcima od 1450 do 1600 godine,' *Istoriski Glasnik* (1957), pp. 19–37, reviewed by B. Krekić, 'Pestes Balkaniques des XVe et XVIe siècles,' *Annales: économies, sociétés, civilisations*, 18/3 (May–June 1963), pp. 594–5; Stoianovich, 'Tenure,' p. 108, is of the opinion that

losses through epidemic hovered between 10 and 20 per cent but makes this generalization without specific reference to typhus.

12. About 60,000 Russian troops perished from disease at Ochakov in 1738; near Belgrade at about the same time 80 to 100 soldiers per day were dying of 'plague, malaria, and dysentery': L. Cassels, *The Struggle for the Ottoman Empire, 1717–1740* (London, 1966), pp. 152–3.

13. The contemporary debate on climatic variation seems to date from the publication of a 1914 treatise on sun–moon–earth alignments by the oceanographer Otto Peterson. For historians the controversy begins to come alive with the appearance of an article by G. Utterstrom, 'Climatic fluctuations and population problems in early modern history,' *Scandinavian Economic History Review*, 3 (1955), 3–47. Since then the literature on the subject, only a small portion of it written by historians, has burgeoned. Perhaps the most serious individual effort to settle the matter is that of E. Le Roy Ladurie, *Histoire du Climat depuis l'an Mil* (Paris, 1967), republished in English. A later return to the subject is found in the same author's *The Peasants of Languedoc* (Urbana, 1974), pp. 292–5. Important contributions to the literature which have appeared more recently include H. Lamb, *Climate: Present, Past, and Future*, vol. I: *Fundamentals and Climate Now* (London, 1972); A. Pittock *et al.* (eds.), *Climatic Change and Variability: A Southern Perspective* (London, 1978); M. Parry, *Climatic Change, Agriculture and Settlement* (Folkestone, 1978); J. Gribbin, *Climatic Change* (London, 1978); and J. Eddy, 'The case of the missing sunspots,' *Scientific American* (May 1977), pp. 80–92.

14. For the fullest accounts of Austrian military operations in the Balkans during the war of 1683–99: P. Röder von Diersburg, *Des Markgrafen Ludwig Wilhelm von Baden Wider die Türken*, 2 vols (Carlsruhe, 1839–42), and K. K. Kriegsarchive, *Feldzüge des Prinzen Eugen von Savoyen* (Vienna, 1876).

15. B. Djurdjev, 'Bosna' in *Encyclopedia of Islam*, 2nd edn; cf. H. Inalcık (ed.), 'Saray-Bosna şer'iyye sicillerine göre Viyana bozgunundan sonraki harp yıllarında Bosna,' *Tarih Vesikaları*, 2 (1942–3), 178–87, 372–84. For Yugoslav views on the growth of Serbian population during the eighteenth century, see *Historija Naroda Jugoslavije* (Zagreb, 1959), II, 1361, 1368, 1369; also B. Drubnjaković, 'Stanovništvo u Srbiji za vreme prvog ustanka' in *Geografski Lik Srbije u Doba Prvog Ustanka* (Beograd, 1954), pp. 36–54.

16. J. Cvijić, *La peninsule Balkanique: géographie humaine* (Paris, 1918), pp. 112–52, the culmination of decades of ethnographic investigation; more recently, B. Djurdjev, *et al.*, *Historija Naroda Jugoslavije*, II (Zagreb, 1959), 845–6.

17. The Bosnian figure is offered *en bloc*, as is the figure for the Belgrade bloc, which seems to include most of what became the Serbia of the early nineteenth century. One recent study suggests loss rather than gain during the eighteenth century: F. Carter, 'Urban development in the western Balkans' in F. Carter (ed.), *An Historical Geography of the Balkans* (London, 1977), pp. 147–95.

18. W. Miller, *Essays on the Latin Orient* (Cambridge, 1921), p. 418.

19. F. Pouqueville, *Histoire de la régénération de la Grèce*, I (Paris, 1824), 44–8.

20. For the Russian campaigns in the Dobrudja and northern Bulgaria during the course of Catherine's wars, see P. Longworth, *The Art of Victory: The Life and Achievements of Generalissimo Suvorov (1729–1800)* (London, 1965), pp. 73–98, 136–74; cf. H. Inalcık, 'Dobrudja' in *Encyclopedia of Islam*, 2nd edn.

21. Cf. A. Vacalopoulos, *History of Macedonia, 1354–1833* (Thessaloniki, 1973), p. 379, and Institut za Nacionalna Istorija, *Istorija na Makedonskiot Narod*, 3 vols. (Skopje, 1969), I, 294; II, 12.

Notes to chapter 4, pp. 105–14

1. The existence of the Ottoman *avarız* as early as the reign of Murat I is known from formulas for exemption from that tax appearing in some early *vakıfnames*; cf. I. Beldiceanu-Steinherr, *Recherches sur les actes des regnes des sultans Osman, Orkhan, et Murad I* (Monachii, 1967), pp. 137, 175, 195.
2. Ö. L. Barkan, 'Avarız,' *Islam Ansiklopedisi* (Istanbul, 1940), I, 15; M. Akdağ, *Celali Isyanları (1550–1603)* (Ankara, 1963), pp. 32–3; cf. B. Cvetkova, *Izvnredni danoci i državni povinosti v Blgarskite zemi pod Turska vlast* (Sofia, 1959). The two Manastir lists are found in Manastir *Sijil* no. 6, pp. 72–3 (20 December 1639) and *Sijil* no. 8, pp. 85–7 (17 February 1691), both housed in the Macedonian National Archives at Skopje. The Karaferye data are found in Kâmil Kepeci 2890 at the BVA in Istanbul.
3. BVA Mühimme Defter (MD), no. 32, item 614, p. 336 (13 Muharrem 987).
4. BVA Maliyeden Müdevver (MM), no. 118 (1542/949); MM no. 499 (1543/950); MM no. 457 (1588/996).
5. MM no. 118.
6. MD no. 60, items 557 and 558 (1585/994).
7. Ö. Barkan, *XV ve XVI asırlarda Osmanlı İmparatorluğunda zirai ekonominin hukuki ve mali esasları*, I: *Kanunlar* (Istanbul, 1943), pp. 41, 18. Barkan believes that the Karaman *Kanun* really dates back to the time of Bayezit II or even Fatih Mehmet, though his own published version was authorized in 924H. For evidence on the existence of a tax called the *avarız*, or *arıza*, in earlier Turkic states, see H. Horst, *Die Staatsverwaltung der Gross-selğuken und Horezmshahs (1030–1231)* (Wiesbaden, 1964), pp. 55, 56, 64, 80. Likewise for the *nüzül, ibid.*, p. 80.
8. Akdağ cites an example of *nüzül zahiresi* being raised from the *kaza* of Edremit in 1516.
9. The term *sürsat* seems first to have been used for sheep, then later for grain. This tax may also be characterized as compulsory sale, since, unlike the *nüzül*, the *sürsat* involved at least symbolic compensation for the seller.
10. E.g. in the *muafiyet ferman* for the *karye* of 'Girgos,' a *has karye* of Niğbolu *sanjak*, in 1547/954: BVA Fekete Tasnifi no. 321.
11. B. McGowan (ed.), *Defter-i Mufassal-i Liva-i Sirem* (Ankara, in press).
12. From the '*Kanunname-i Canbazan-i Vilayet-i Rumeli*' in Barkan, *Kanunlar*, p. 247.
13. Ö. L. Barkan, 'The price revolution of the sixteenth century: a turning point in the economic history of the Near East,' *International Journal of Middle Eastern Studies*, 6/1 (January 1975), 3–28, or *idem*, 'XVI Yüzyılın İkinci Yarısında Türkiye'de Fiat Hareketleri,' *Belleten*, XXXIV/136 (1970), 557–607.
14. H. Hadzibegić, 'Rasprava Ali-Čauša iz Sofije o timarskoj organizaciji u XVII stoljeću,' *Glasnik Zemaljskog Muzeja u Sarajevu* (1947), no. 2, 144.
15. H. Hadzibegić, *Glavarina u Osmanskoj Državi* (Sarajevo, 1966), pp. 44, 62, 70–5.
16. *ibid.*, p. 67.
17. Manastir *Sijil* no. 2 (at the Macedonian National Archives, Skopje) p. 516/II (31

August 1622/23 Şevval 1031) gives the *bedel-i avarız* rate as 360 *akçes* per '*hane*' which includes the collector's fees, or *mubashirlik*. It is of interest that the expression *bedel-i avarız* was still being used at this late date; certainly the term *bedel* does not here refer to a contemporary substitution of cash for kind, but is rather a traditional usage which still ocasionally appears. Cf. Manastir *Sijil* no. 2, p. 616/ı (1622).

18. BVA Fekefe Tasnifi no. 2620. Cf. Fekete Tasnifi nos 2607, 2606, 1895, 4434, 2254 and 3145; also Ibn ul-Emin Tasnifi / Maliye no. 2298; and MD 72, p. 100, quoted in D. Šopova (ed.), *Makedonija vo XVI i XVII vek: Dokumenti od Carigradskite Arhivi (1557–1645)* (Skopje, 1955), p. 77; also MD 73, item 955, p. 432; MD 52, item 853, p. 322; MD 73, item 312, p. 133; MD 73, item 329, p. 141; also BVA Ali Emiri Tasnifi: Ahmet I, nos. 240, 258, 264.

19. Manastir *Sijil* 3, p. 98/ı (14 June 1634/18 Muharrem 1044).

20. Manastir *Sijil* 4, p. 236/ı (22 May 1636/15 Zilhicce 1045).

21. Barkan, 'Avarız,' p. 15.

22. The Ottoman 'budget' of 1669–70, published by Barkan, shows that the contribution of the *avarız* and *nüzül* combined was at that time 122,186,163 *akches* out of total *mirî* revenues (i.e. those actually collected) amounting to 592,528,960 *akches*, or 20.6 per cent. Nine years earlier their contribution to total revenues was substantially the same. Cf. Ö. L. Barkan, 'Osmanli Imparatorluğu Bütçelerine dair Notlar'; '1079–1080 (1669–70) Mali Yılına ait bir Osmanlı Bütçesi ve bir Mukayesesi,' *Iktisat Tarihi Mecmuası*, pp. 193–224, 225–303, 304–47 respectively, esp. 212, 214, 303.

23. A single early seventeenth-century tax house register, dated 1029н, is unfortunately quite incomplete. Matkovski has cited a document from the *kaza* of Karaferye, dated 19 October 1843, which says that 69 propertyless *chiftchis*, who had been attached to one Habit Pasha, had fled, so that their registration in the *avarız–nüzül* register was prevented. This could prove to be the latest reference to the system: A. Matkovski, *Kreposništvoto vo Makedonija vo Vreme na Turskoto Vladeenje* (Skopje, in press), typescript, pp. 199–200.

24. MD no. 73, item 188, p. 80 (14 Şevval 1003). Thus when an occasional levy of grain was demanded from a border area such as Hungary, the basis of the collection was the *jizyehane*, not the *avarızhane*; see KK no. 3525 (1072н), pp. 7b–8a.

25. Matkovski, *Kreposništvoto*. Thus it is easy to understand the passage, appearing in a *hükm sureti* of 1606 dealing with *askeri* categories subject to the *kaziasker's resm-i kismet*, which runs as follows: 'Ve nasib tasarruf mülazim külliyen askeridir ve ol makule kimesneler fevt oldukta aslından *avarız taifesinden idi, reaya taifesinden idi*, sonra ehl-i berat olmuştur deyü kadilar dahledermis,' cited in I. H. Uzunçarşılı, *Osmanlı Devletinin Merkez ve Bahriye Teşkilati* (Ankara, 1948, p. 241).

26. In a *ferman* issued to several Macedonian *kadis* in 1779 in response to a complaint by numerous *sipahis* and *zaims* that *reaya* had been fleeing the depredations caused by Albanians and other brigands and were taking shelter in towns and on *chiftliks*: 'As the result of an investigation at the archives of my Sublime Porte it has been shown that those registered as the sons of *reaya* in the *defters* on *zaim* and *timar* villages, if they leave their village and settle in nearby towns and villages and are not reregistered there in *avarız defters* and where ten years has not passed since

their resettling, they must be returned forcibly to the villages where they resettled. But if they are registered in the *avarız defters* in the place where they resettled and if ten years has passed since then, this sort of *reaya* is not to be permitted to return but must pay *reaya* taxes in keeping with the law, so that an authorized person in the original village be informed that he has paid his taxes,' in L. Lape, *Odbrani Tekstovi za Istorijata na Makedonskiot Narod* (Skopje, 1959), vol. i. Instructions on drawing up a register of this kind appear as a regular feature in *fermans* authorizing *avarız* or *nüzül* collections in the seventeenth century: 've ne miktar neferden ve kaç haneden alınursa sihhatı üzere her birinin yazub defter eyleyub': *Manastir Sijil* no. 2, p. 516/ii (31 August 1622/23 Şevval 1031).

27. Ö. L. Barkan, *Edirne Askeri Kassami'na âit Tereke Defterleri (1545–1659)*, i (Ankara, 1968), 49.

28. Because the *mirî* tax mix fluctuated from year to year, the proportions of any one tax also fluctuated. Thus the proportions listed here must be accepted as merely suggestive, or illustrative, certainly no sure guide to the situation in other years or in other districts, since in each district the tax mix is bound to vary in accordance with local *mirî* requirements as well as local resources. Moreover there is no absolute guarantee that every *mirî* tax, especially if it is an occasional tax, would find its way into the *sijil* drawn up in that district. With these reservations in mind, we offer here the proportions of *mirî* taxes found in the *sijils* of Manastir on the years indicated. Note the evolution of the tax mix with the passage of time.

In 1621–2 (1031h): *jizye* 40.3%; *avarız* 14.9%; *bedel-i nüzül* 42.9%; *adet-i ağnam* 1.8%. Cf. Manastir *Sijil* no. 2, 756/i, 766/i, 51a/i, 67b/ii.

In 1633–4 (1043h): *jizye* 51.6%; *avarız* 15.8%; *nüzül* 20.0%; *adet-i ağnam* 0.3%; *bedel-i ganem (jelepkeşan?)* 5.4%; *bedel-i mekari* 5.4%; *nev yafte* 1.4%; *bargir bahasi* 0.2%. Cf. Manastir *Sijil* no. 3, pp. 1046, 98a/i, 516/i, 60b/i, 536/ii, 1056/i, 546/vii, 73a/iv, 75a/ii, 536/iii.

In 1662–3 (1073h): *jizye* 36.6%; *avarız* 23.0%; *bedel-i nüzül* 32.5%; *jelepkeşan* 6.4%; *sürsat* 1.5%. Cf. Manastir *Sijil* no. 18, pp. 84/i, 85/i, 97/iii, 104/iv, 104/iii, 106/i, 110/v, 111/iv.

In 1682 (1093h): *jizye* 36.6%; *avarız* 15.0%; *nüzül* 35.2%; *zahire baha* 2.2%; *menzilhane* 1.5%. Cf. Manastir *Sijil* no. 25, pp. 58/i, 55/i, 55/ii, 51/i, 53/ii, 54/ii.

In 1729–30 (1142h), an unusually light year since there were no entertainments: *jizye* 59.6%; *avarız* and *nüzül* combined: 19.9%; *jelepkeşan* 5.8%; *imdad-ı hazariye* 2.8%; *yag iştira* 1.9%; *salitre iştira* 7.6%; *menzil* 2.4%. Cf. Manastir *Sijil* no. 42, pp. 74/i to 75, 94/i, 88/ii, 96/iii, 97/i, 90/iii, 90/iv, 91/i, 101/v.

In 1781 (1195h), a very heavy year: *jizye* 42.2%; *avarız*: 2.0%; *nüzül*: 3.2%; *jelepkeşan* 1.7%; *imdad-ı hazariye* 0.8%; *menzil* 9.3%; an entertainment *tevzi* 1.5%; the *vilayet* expense contribution 36.8%; *segban* wages 2.4%. Cf. Manastir *Sijil* no. 63, pp. 45/iii, 45/iv, 45/v, 45/vi, 47/ii, 48/i, 54/i, 50/i, 50/ii, 50/vi, 52/ii, iii, 56/iii, 82/iii, 54/ii, 78/i, 66–68/i.

29. On the evaluation of *shakka* taxes and other taxes, such as the *imdats*, which were used at the *eyalet* level, see A. Sućeska, 'Die Entwicklung der Besteuerung durch

die avarız-i divaniye und die tekalif-i örfiye im Osmanischen Reich während des
17. und 18. Jahrhunderts,' *Südost Forschungen*, xxvii (1968), 89–130, and also a
superb study, soon to be published in *Archivum Ottomanicum*, by Halil Inalcık:
'Military and fiscal transformation in the Ottoman Empire.'

30. With regard to the graph showing the movement of tax house totals an explanation is necessary. Since the registers were not always complete, the totals from
incompleted sequences could not be included. Thus in the case of Rumeli those
provinces which were often missing were subtracted from the total for the Rumeli
bloc – these provinces were Midilli, Vidin, Mora, Kefe, Gelibolu, Ahur-ı Hayrıbolu and Ahur-ı Yanbolu. Thus Rumeli means, in this context, the *continuous core*
of the Rumelian bloc, as it appears in the registers. For Anadolu a different
method was used; when a missing entry would have upset the meaning of the
whole, the last entry before the missing one was substituted. Also some provinces
were not included in the bloc totals shown on the graph if the number of *kazas*
constituting the province is seen to have changed significantly. Ideally the
identity of an earlier province with a later province of the same name should be
proven by verifying the location of the villages comprising them, an ideal which
was, however, quite impossible of realization for this limited study. Also it should
be noted that there are frequent (but usually minor) arithmetical errors in the
registers. It was the writer's practice in these cases to accept an erroneous total on
the theory that such a total was the *official* total controlling collections.

Notes to chapter 5, pp. 121–70

1. For the construction and relative significance of the Ç/H ratio, refer to the final
pages of chapter 2.
2. D. Pop-Georgiev, *Sopstvenosta vrz Čiflicite i Čifligarskite Agrarno-Pravni Odnosi vo
Makedonija do Balkanskata Vojna 1912* (Skopje, 1956). This work relies to a great
degree upon a single legal treatise quite remote from Macedonia and its *chiftliks*:
Nedjid Chiha, *Traité de la propriété immobiliers en droit ottoman* (Cairo, 1906). A better
view of the *chiftlik* as a subject of Ottoman law is found in Ö. L. Barkan's lengthy
discussion in *Tanzimat*, i (Istanbul, 1940).
3. A. Razboinikov, *Čifligarstvoto v Makedonia i Odrinsko* (Solun, 1913) quotes a Bulgarian statistical source, *B'lgarska Sbirka*, v, 1911, offering a view of the degree of the
chiftlicization of Macedonia's villages on the eve of the Balkan Wars; according to
these statistics the district of Bitola (Manastir) was somewhat more heavily
chiftlicized than Macedonia as a whole, yet less so than the districts of Salonica
and Skopje. Cf. Pop-Georgiev, *Čiflicite*; D. Zografski, *Razvitokot na Kapitalističkite
Elementi vo Makedonija za Vreme na Turskoto Vladeenje* (Skopje, 1967), pp. 86–95. A
study offering quantitative data on the proportions of these constructual forms in
the late nineteenth-century Polog district is P. Kiroski, 'Ciflugarstvoto vo Polog'
in *Kiril Pejcinović i Negovoto Vreme* (Tetovo, 1973), pp. 115–20. A good discussion of
typical contractual relationships in English, though again with a twentieth-
century bias, is found in J. Tomasevich, *Peasants, Politics and Economic Change in
Yugoslavia* (Stanford, 1955), 122–4. Cf. also S. Vukosavljevic, *Istorija Seljačkog
Drustva*, i (Beograd, 1953), 301–9.
4. I. Ivanov, *S'verna Makedonia* (Sofia, 1906), pp. 227–32; J. Cvijić, *Balkansko Poluos-*

trvo i Južnoslovenske Zemlje, pp. 209–71ff.; R. Busch-Zantner, *Agrarverfassung, Gesellschaft und Siedlung in Südosteuropa* (Leipzig, 1938), includes a bibliography of nineteenth- and twentieth-century works dealing with land use in *chiftlik* areas, particularly those in German; Cvijic and Busch-Zantner, both writing from a geographer's point of view, influenced the work of T. Stoianovich, 'Land tenure and related sectors of the Balkan economy, 1600–1800,' *Journal of Economic History* XIII (1953), 398–411.

5. Razboinikov, *Čiftligarstvoto*, 20–6; Stoianovich, *Land;* Zografski, *Razvitokot*, 65–81; H. Hristov, *Agrarnite Otnošenitia v Makedonia prez XIV v. i načaloto na XX v.* (Sofia, 1964), pp. 38–44; N. Todorov, 'Sur quelques aspects du passage du féodalisme au capitalisme dans les territoires Balkaniques de l'empire Ottoman,' *Revue des Études Sud-Est Européennes* I (1963), 103–36, at 126ff.; I. Katardjiev, *Serskata Oblast (1780–1879)* (Skopje, 1961), pp. 39–51.

6. E.g. Todorov, 'Aspects,' pp. 121, 126–7; Zografski, *Razvitokot*, p. 69; Hristov, *Otnošenitia*, pp. 44ff.

7. The Bulgarian scholars Strašimir Dimitrov and Hristov Gandev have done some good work recently on *chiftlik* development at Ruse and at Vidin. For a bibliography of recent work on *chiftliks* in Bulgaria and elsewhere in south-eastern Europe, see the preceding chapter.

8. Busch-Zantner, *Agrarverfassung*, p. 86. Hristov, *Otnošenitia*, p. 192.

9. Zografski, *Razvitokot*, p. 31; L. Lape, 'Prilog kon izučuvanjeto na društveno-ekonomskite i politički priliki vo Makedonija vo XVIII vek,' *Glasnik na Institut za Nacionalna Istorija*, II/1 (1958), 114–48.

10. Zografski, *Razvitokot*, pp. 65–76; A. Matkovski, *Gurčin Kokalevski 1775–1836* (Skopje, 1959), pp. 13–14; Stoianovich, 'Land,' p. 402.

11. Pop-Georgiev, *Čiflicite*, p. 79; Razboinikov, *Čiftligarstvoto*, p. 26.

12. Razboinikov, *Čiftligarstvoto*, p. 32; Pop-Georgiev, *Čiflicite*, p. 91; Katardjiev, *Oblast*, pp. 33, 36.

13. U. Heyd, *Studies in Old Ottoman Criminal Law* (ed. V. L. Menage, Oxford, 1973), pp. 174, 179, 186–9. The position of the *Shar'iah* within the totality of the world's legal systems is discussed in R. David and J. Brierly, *Major Legal Systems in the World Today* (London, 1968), pp. 386, 398–9. Also worth reading in this context, despite Heyd's corrections, is the discussion of Ottoman secular law by Ö. L. Barkan in his introduction to *Kanunlar* (Istanbul, 1943).

14. For instance the (rare) *fetva* appearing in Manastir *Sijil* no. 33, p. 25/v (1709) which refers to a collection known as *Fetava-i Atayiye*. Hereafter Manastir *Sijil* will be abbreviated to MnS, followed by the archive number, the modern pagination, the order of the entry on the page, and a date: MnS 33, p. 25/v (1709).

15. Heyd's remark, *Law*, p. 227, about the frequency with which *reaya* petitions appear embedded in *fermans* which were issued in response to them is fully demonstrated in the Manastir sijils. Most *fermans* simply order an investigation. More interesting are those which order that overcollections be returned (a feature of the Köprülü years) or that the culprit be sent to Istanbul, or to the galleys, etc.

16. R. Jennings, 'Loans and credit in early 17th century Ottoman judicial records,' *Journal of the Economic and Social History of the Orient*, XVI, pts 2–3 (1973) 168–216, esp. 172. For other views on the use of *sijils* as historic sources, see J. Mandaville, 'The Jerusalem Shar'ia court records: a supplement and complement to the

central Ottoman archives' in M. Ma'oz (ed.), *Studies on Palestine During the Ottoman Period* (Jerusalem, 1975), pp. 517–24; and A. K. Rafeq, 'The law court registers of Damascus with special reference to craft corporations during the first half of the eighteenth century' in J. Berque and D. Chevallier (eds.), *Les Arabes par leurs archives, XVIe–XXe siècles* (Paris, 1976), pp. 141–59.

17. G. Elezović, 'Putopis Evlije Čelebije,' *Glasnik Istoriskog Društva*, xi/4, 273–7; xvi/6, 502–17.
18. Presumably the five were households, not individuals: MnS 18, p. 103/v (1661).
19. A *ferman* of 1694 ordering the mobilization of 624 soldiers from the district is addressed to these parties in the order given: MnS 28, p. 48/iii (1694). The meaning of *ish erleri* is not wholly clear; very probably this phrase refers to those individuals among the *ayans* who both currently and recently had (no doubt at a profit to themselves) undertaken responsibility in the district for collecting taxes, or for overseeing *mukataa*, or *vakıf* collections. Presumably Manastir also had its *muhtesib*. From numerous other entries it is clear that there also existed there a *kiracı başı* in charge of the teamsters who plied the roads from Manastir, and in the eighteenth century an officer in charge of the post house (*menzil*) service.
20. From a *buyruldu* of the *vali* ordering the transfer of the seat of his government from Sofia: MnS 90, p. 26 (1820). Later in the nineteenth century Manastir became the seat of a reorganized *vilayet*.
21. Elezović, 'Putopis.'
22. Revenues leased annually for 85,000 *akches*: MnS 28, p. 75/v (1694). From a *ferman* and accompanying *buyruldu* dated 1710 the *mukataa* of two wards (*mahalle*s) of Manastir – presumably those surrounding the market-place – being collected by a *mubashir* (one Ali, the *alaybey* of the 'left wing' of Rumeli) for a yield of 136,000 *akches*: MnS 34, pp. 18/iv and 19/i (1710). According to another *ferman*, the total of Mustafa Pasha's *has* revenues in this *kaza* was 252,000 *akches*: MnS 28, p. 65/i (1694).
23. A. Stojanovski, 'Administrativno-Teritorijalnata Podelba na Makedonija,' *Glasnik na Institut za Nacionalna Istorija* (Skopje), xvii/1 (1973), 129–45. This valuable study includes a map of the administrative subdivisions of Ottoman Macedonia in the middle Ottoman centuries.
24. MnS 8, pp. 85–7 (1641); cf. MnS 6, pp. 72–3 (1639).
25. MnS 28, p. 71 (1694) and MnS 28, p. 57/iii (1694). The number of villages listed varies slightly depending upon the fiscal purpose for which a list is drawn up. In this period lists usually include 14 to 16 villages, called '*tuğralı*' villages, which enjoyed certain privileges which distinguish them from the majority.
26. MnS 32, on the basis of many *tevzi* lists appearing in this *sijil*.
27. MnS 43, p. 83 (1809).
28. *Carte de la Macédoine*, 1:3,000,000, L'Institut Scientifique Macédonien à Sofia.
29. Some of the names on Jaranov's map show slight morphological changes away from the original form. Six names from the 1641 list which survive on Jaranov's map do not appear on the map included here: Demir Hisar to the north-east, and south of the present Greek border five villages which now officially bear Greek names, the original names being Negočani, Obšireno, Klabučišta, Rakovo, and Bituše. The latinicized morphology of the list of 1641 names offered here uses several letters from the Croatian (i.e. latinicized) alphabet: c, č, ć, š, ž, and j (instead of y).

30. Several names have twin forms – 'upper,' 'lower,' 'big,' 'small,' etc. – and in these cases it is difficult to know which of the twins survived to appear on modern maps; twinning cases include Eflahci, Bukri, Pogodin, Divjaci, Crska, Srpci, Suhodol, Kočište, Lopatica, Novoselo and Egri.

31. Hearth coefficients at various Byzantine localities are said to have varied between 3.2 and 5.2 during the centuries before the Ottoman conquest: D. Jacoby, 'Phénomènes de démographie rurale à Byzance aux XIIIe, XIVe, et XVe siècles,' *Études Rurales*, 5–6 (Apr.–Sept. 1962), 161–86, esp. p. 133. During the century following the reconquest of Srem by the Austrian house, hearth coefficients rose astonishingly; cf. the Introduction to the writer's forthcoming *Defter-i Mufassal-i Liva-i Sirem* (Turkish Historical Society, Ankara).

32. An examination of the *jizye berats* for 1683 shows that *three* different sets of *jizye* totals are involved: (1) the archaic totals from a peak period long past, (2) currently authorized *official* totals, and (3) the totals which actually arise from a local survey conducted for the purpose of apportioning the official levy among the actual surviving inhabitants of a district. Cf. MnS 25, p. 42/II (1683) and MnS 25, p. 43/III (1683).

33. BVA Kamîl Kepeci, no. 6251.

34. MnS 3, p. 105b/I (1634).

35. An explicit prohibition on such exemptions is included, for instance, in a *ferman* dealing with the methods to be used in collecting *jizye* which appears in MnS 34, p. 20/I (1710). Other *fermans* can be found which show that those who dwelled on *vakıf* estates were also liable for payment of other *mirî* taxes, such as the *imdad-i hazariye* and *seferiye* and the *bedel-i sürsat*: MnS 43, p. 88/II (1731); MnS 43, p. 114/I (1731). In the eighteenth century three large *vakıf* estates (Srpci Pasha, Egri Pasha and Bukri Pasha) show up regularly on *tevzi* lists apportioning various *mirî* taxes and levies. A *berat* specifically authorizing collection of *jizye* on several *vakıf* estates is found in MnS 25, p. 40/III (1683).

36. MnS 6, p. 7/VIII (1638).

37. MnS 8, pp. 87, 88 (1641).

38. MnS 18, p. 103/v (1661). Many series of treasury records now housed at the BVA in Istanbul commence with the Köprülü years, suggesting that fiscal reforms introduced by the family may have been fully as important as their other policies.

39. BVA Kamîl Kepeci no. 515.

40. MnS 25, p. 42/II (1683) and MnS 25, p. 43/III (1683).

41. MnS 34, p. 41/II to p. 43 (1711). This is not a *berat* but a list, showing distribution of expenses in connection with the maintenance of a contingent of '*martolos*' upon all the district's *jizye*-liable villagers. By now only 1927 of the *jizye* liable are recorded as dwelling on *chiftliks*. But this count is not quite accurate, apparently. A separate survey of '*nefer*'s (who are presumably defined in the same way for *jizye*, as for other purposes), drawn up for tax purposes, shows a total of 3362 *nefers* – 2097 living in villages, 1265 living on *chiftliks*.

42. MnS 47, p. 17/III (1740).

43. BVA Kâmil Kepeci, nos. 3531, 3580 and 3662.

44. A. Matkovski, *Kreposništvoto vo Makedonija vo Vreme na Turskoto Vladeenje* (Skopje, 1976), pp. 256–63.

45. F. Pouqueville, *Reise durch Morea und Albanien nach Konstantinopel und in mehrere andere*

Theile des Ottomanischen Reichs in den Jahren 1798, 1799, 1800, und 1801 (Leipzig, 1805), III, 126; and F. Beaujour, *Table du commerce de la Grèce* (Paris, 1800), I, 127–32, republished in L. Lape, *Odbrani Tekstovi za Istorijata na Makedonskiot Narod* (Skopje, 1959), pp. 241–2; Tatarcik Abdullah Efendi, 'Selim-i Salis devrinde nizam-i devlet hakkında mütaleat,' *TOEM* (1332H), cited in A. F. Miller, *Mustafa Pasa Bayraktar* (Moscow, 1947), p. 87.

46. Zografski, *Razvitokot*, p. 75; Lape, 'Prilog,' pp. 114–18, 121.
47. In 1748 five Macedonian merchants were present at the Leipzig fair; in 1752 twelve; in 1767 thirty-four; in 1774 sixty-nine. These figures appear in E. Hasse, *Geschichte der Leipziger* (Messen, 1885) and are quoted by A. Matkovski, *Gurčin Kokalevski, 1775–1863* (Skopje, 1959), p. 45. Among the 134 Ottoman subjects who functioned as resident merchants at Vienna, according to an official list drawn up in 1766, 30 were from Macedonia (though only one was from Manastir/Bitola): D. Zografski, 'Za Trgovskite vrski na Makedonija sa Avstrija vo sredinata na XVIII vek, '*Pregled* (Skopje), 1955/6, 45–59, at pp. 48–9; on Salonica trade: Lape, 'Prilog,' p. 124; on trade northward through Belgrade and Zemun: R. Veselinovic, 'Prodirange austrijske trgovine u Beograd u drugoj polovini XVII veka,' in Srpska Akademija Nauka i Umjetnosti, *Oslobodjenje gradova u Srbiji od Turaka, 1862–1867* (Beograd, 1970), pp. 163–79; V. Čubrilović (ed.), *Istorija Beograda*, 3 vols (Beograd, 1974), I, 686–90.
48. Regarding the proportions of the Macedonian export trade in the 1780s: F. Beaujour, quoted in Zografski, *Razvitokot*, p. 58. Regarding the predominance of cotton among Macedonia's eighteenth-century exports, cf. F. Beaujour, *Schilderung des Handels von Griechenland* . . . (Weimar, 1801), p. 139, quoted in N. Michoff, *Contribution a l'histoire du commerce de la Turquie et de la Bulgarie* (Sofia, 1971), pp. 59–60; J. Hildt, 'Übersicht des türkischen Handels über Semlin mit den österreichischen Staaten, vom 1sten Nov. 1795 bis 31sten Oktober 1796,' pp. 65–6, *Handlungszeitung oder wochentliche Nachrichten von Handel, Manufakturwesen, Künsten und neuen Erfindungen* (Gotha, 1797), quoted in N. Michoff, *Contribution*, p. 65; *Kurzgefasste Beschreibung der Handlung der vornehmten europaischen Staaten* (Liegnitz and Leipzig, 1778–9), II, 212, quoted in N. Michoff, *Contribution*, p. 31.
49. H. Gandev, 'T'rgovskata obmie'na na Europa s' B'lgarskitie zemi prez XVIII i načalato na XIX Vek,' *Godišnik na Universiteta Sv. Kliment Ohridski* (Sofia), *Istoriko-Filologičeski Fakultet*, 40 (1943/4), 1–36, at 18–19.
50. N. Michoff, *Beitrage zur Handelsgeschichte Bulgariens* (Sofia, 1943), pp. 21–6, based on official French statistics published in *Das Ausland*, VIII (Stuttgart and Tübingen, 1835), no. 63, pp. 249–50.
51. Matkovski, *Gurčin*, and Katardjiev, *Oblast*, pp. 49, 51, 68; Zografski, *Razvitokot*, p. 75.
52. Katardjiev, *Oblast*; Zografski, *Razvitokot*, p. 35.
53. In 1705, for instance, a *ferman* to the *vali* of Rumeli and the *kadis* of Manastir, Prilep, Prespa and Ohrid districts states that because of the death of Zeynal Abedin Pasha, his treasury debt would have to be repaid by selling off at the currently authorized prices the grain (*mahlut*) he had stored at Prilep and the grain (*tereke*) on his various *chiftliks* in other *kazas*. MnS 32, p. 21/II (1705).
54. MnS 78, p. 31 (1800), from a *ferman* revoking the ban ostensibly because the *reaya* had a need to sell their surpluses in other places. Another *ferman*, dated 1801, is an

attempt to suppress speculation on wheat and barley at Manastir: MnS 78, p. 65 (1801).

55. For instance, the *chiftlik* of Bayram Bey at Tušadinci, in Sirem, registered during the reign of Selim II; this estate employed seventeen field hands, six of them shepherds: B. McGowan (ed.), *Defter-i Mufassal-i Liva-i Sirem* (Ankara, Turkish Historical Society, forthcoming).

56. A 'justice paper' (*adaletname*) dated 1609 names the flight of the villagers as the precondition for the rise of the *jelali* era *chiftliks*; also noteworthy is the mention of the use of the land for pastoral purposes, *Mühimme Defter* no. 78, p. 899, published in transcription in Ö. L. Barkan, *Edirne Askerî Kassamına âit Tereke Defterleri (1545–1659), I, Belgeler,* III (Ankara, 1968), 49.

57. MnS 4, p. 126/VI (1636); MnS 8, p. 27/VIII (1641); MnS 18, p. 34/XI (1662).

58. For a good discussion of the whole question: V. Mutafčieva, 'K'm v'prosa za čiflicite v Osmanskata imperiā prez XIV–XVII v., '*Istoričeski Pregled,* XIV/1 (1958), 34–58.

59. D. Bojanik, 'Edno Ohridsko Kanunname,' *Glasnik na Institutut za Nacionalna Istorija* (Skopje), III/1 (1959), 285–95, from p. 295. This law is dated 1613 and appears in *Tapu Defter* 717, BVA, Istanbul.

60. MnS 32, p. 10/I (1707). Following an investigation of *kadi* found in favor of the *chiftlik* holders. Perhaps it is significant that the villagers harassing them for taxes were Muslims (the village being Presil).

61. MnS 62, p. 23/III (1778). This *ferman* is accompanied by a list of delinquent *zaims* and *timarlıs*.

By this period the only *timar* patents appearing in the Manastir *sijils* were those awarding *timars* to lesser officials, such as scribes. Still officially valued at a by now insignificant 6000–7000 *akches* annual income, such *timars* were probably scarcely worth having – unless perchance they should contain a well developed *chiftlik*, the income of which did not enter into the official valuation.

62. Some earlier examples: MnS 3, p. 23/II (1634); MnS 4, p. 6b/IV (1636); MnS 18, p. 23/XII (1662); MnS 24, p. 43/II (1679); MnS 32, p. 21/I (1705). Later examples: MnS 72, p. 20/III (1794); MnS 80, p. 62/I (1803).

63. The report of a commission headed by Konstantin Jirehek into the origins of *chiftliks* in Bulgaria emphasized seizure upon pretext as the means by which they were created. But this report, dated 1880, referred to the recent past and was aimed at Bulgaria: K. Jirechek and M. Sarafov, *Raport na Komisijata, Ispratena v Kiustendilskia okr'g da izuči položenieto na bezzemlenite seliani* (Sofia, 1880). Certainly spates of force and terrorism were known in parts of Macedonia, such as at Seres in the latter half of the eighteenth century; cf. Katardjiev, *Oblast,* pp. 33–9.

64. MnS 8, p. 36/IV (1641); also MnS 30, p. 7/II (1704) cited by L. Lape, *Odbrani Tekstovi,* I, 221 and the instances found in A. Matkovski (ed.), *Turski Izvori za Ajdutstvoto i Aramistvoto vo Makedonija (1620–1650),* I (Skopje, 1961), nos. 2, 3, 16, 19, 30, 71, 72 and 89; vol. II (*1650–1700*) (Skopje, 1961), no. 23; and vol. III (*1700–1725*) (Skopje, 1973), nos. 64, 119 and 124.

65. The concern of the Porte here was less with the *reaya* than with the revenues lost, and the solution demanded was that the burden be shifted to the new *chiftlik* holders: 'Whoever has at his disposal land on which *reaya* have previously destroyed their *avarız* houses and have turned it into *chiftlik,* you shall on the basis

of the old law register and inscribe it in the register for *avarız* houses according to what it can bring in,' MnS 8, p. 100/ı (1640). In a *ferman* of 1606, addressed to the inspector at Ohrid, the Porte had already admitted the pernicious effects which moneylending was having in the countryside: 'It has been reported that some people in your district have been giving money to *reaya* by way of loan and that later when the time for settling accounts arrives have taken excessive amounts of money and have oppressed them causing many a *reaya* to flee his land . . .': *Mühimme Defter* 77, p. 613 (1606), quoted in D. Šopova, *Makedonija vo XVI i XVII vek, Dokumenti od Carigradskite Arhivi (1557–1645)* (Skopje, 1955), p. 87.

66. MnS 7, p. 15/ı (1640); MnS 7, p. 15/ıı (1640); MnS 7, p. 3 (1641); MnS 7, p. 2b/ıı (1641); MnS 8, p. 116 (1640); MnS 8, pp. 85–6 (1641); cf. also MnS 8, p. 17b/vıı (1640); MnS 8, p. 52/vıı (1641); MnS 8, p. 23b/ııı (1641); MnS 8, p. 16/ııı (1640); MnS 8, p. 16/x (1640); MnS 8, p. 17/xıı (1640).

67. MnS 8, p. 12b/ıv (1640); MnS 8, p. 32/ııı (1640); two more villages are recorded as having fled under similar conditions in 1662: Dragos and Bituše. MnS 18, p. 45/ıv (1662); MnS 18, p. 48/v (1662).

68. MnS 8, p. 13/vıı (1640).

69. This *ferman*, appearing in MnS 51, p. 55/ıı (1748), touches on a number of fundamental problems.

70. Rare but not unheard of. Two cases in 1662 demonstrate that – possibly through the laxity of an individual judge – some breaches of the long-held norms did take place earlier. In one, Hüseyin Subashı of Manastir stated that Stoyko Rogle of Trnovci (in all probability *reaya*) had sold him land (a *bashtina*) for 3000 *akches* which he, Stoyko, had abandoned thirty years earlier. The *subashi* complained that the villagers of Trnovci were denying him the use of it: MnS 18, p. 50/ı (1662). In the other case the *reaya* Jovan of Lahci was trying to recover a vineyard which he had put up as a pawn to one Mustafa against a loan of 1350 *akches* which he claimed to have repaid (this case would have been more clearly a breach of principle, it is true, if the pawned land had been an arable field or pasture instead of a vineyard): MnS 18, p. 23/ıx (1662).

71. 'Osmanlı Kanunnameleri,' *Milli Tetebbu'lar Mecmuası*, 1–2 (1915), 49–112, 305–48, esp. pp. 52–3; M. Düzdağ, *Şeyhülislam Ebusuûd Efendi Fetvaları Işığında 16 Asir Türk Hayatı* (Istanbul, 1972), p. 167; S. Albayrak, *Budin Kanunnamesi ve Osmanlı Toprak Meselesi* (Istanbul, 1974), p. 108; Ö. L. Barkan, 'Türk Toprak Hukuku Tarihinde Tanzimat ve 1274 (1858) Tarihli Arazi Kanunnamesi,' *Tanzimat*, ı (Istanbul, 1940), 349, 383. The 'knowledge' or 'consent' of the *timarlı* is in fact, frequently referred to in entries in the Manastir *sijils* which deal with transfers of fields and pastures.

72. Albayrak, *Budin Kanunnamesi*, p. 129. Direct descent was known as *intikal*, the right of more distant relatives as the *hakk-ı tapu*: Pop-Georgiev, *Čiflicite*.

73. MnS 8, p. 33/v (1641).

74. Ö. L. Barkan, *Edirne Askerî Kassamına âit Tereke Defterleri (1545–1659)*, ı (Ankara, 1968), 47.

75. Barkan, *Tanzimat*, ı, 347–8; taken from *Kanunname* no. 4798, p. 26, at the Bayezid Library, published in 1033 H and still in force in 1181 H.

76. Barkan, *Tereke Defterleri*, p. 48. This excerpt is taken from a *kanunname* located in the library of the General Directorate of the Archives; no date is offered.

77. Matkovski, *Kreposništvoto.*
78. MnS 4, p. 24/II (1636). Aleksandar Matkovski refers to a similar *ferman* in 1634: 'La Résistance des Paysans Macédoniens contre l'attachement à la glebe pendant la domination Ottomane,' Rapport de l'Association Internationale d'Études du Sud-est Européen, III (Sofia, 1969), 705.
79. MnS 5, p. 366/II (1638).
80. MnS 8, 100/II (1641).
81. Matkovski, *Kreposništvoto.*
82. As for instance, in three *fermans* dating from 1777, 1778 and 1779: MnS 61, p.69/I (1777); MnS 62, p. 13/II 1778); and I. K. Vasdravelli, *Arheion Veroias* (Thessaloniki, 1954), pp. 210–12.
83. MnS 43, p. 110/IV (1731); MnS 43, p. 84/I (1732); MnS 61, p. 10/II (1776).
84. Over 85 per cent of the military men of the Manastir district were living in the town itself, as revealed by a list of campaign-liable personnel: MnS 3, pp. 94 and 95 (1635).
85. MnS 2, p. 15b/XI (1622); MnS 2, p. 22/IV (1623); MnS 3, p. 120/III (1634); MnS 3, p. 77/I (1635); MnS 3, p. 77/III (1635); MnS 4, p. 5b/III (1636).
86. MnS 32, p. 39/I (19 March 1707).
87. MnS 43, pp. 81–3 (January 1732).
88. MnS 61, pp. 43–4 (13–22 September 1777).
89. MnS 72, p. 20/I (26 November 1795).
90. This is hard to prove from lists of *chiftlik* holders, however, since they are invariably identified, not as *sipahis*, *timarlıs* or janissaries, etc., but as *ağas*, *beys*, *efendis* and *chelebis.*
91. On the *timar* system in the late eighteenth century, see S. Dimitrov, 'Politikata na upravliavstvata v'rhuska v Turtsia spriamo spahiistovoto prez vtorata polovina na XVII v.,' *Istoričeski Pregled*, XVII (1962), no. 5, 32–60; cf. also B. Cvetkova, 'L'évolution du régime féodal turc de la fin de XVIe jusqu'au milieu du XVIIIe siècle,' *Recueil d'études historiques à l'occasion du XIe congrès international des sciences historiques* (Sofia, 1960), pp. 171–206.
92. Bojaniḱ, 'Ohridsko Kanunname,' p. 295.
93. MnS 8, p. 15 (1800).
94. MnS 24, p. 41/III (1679); MnS 24, p. 43/VI (1679); MnS 28, p. 76/II (1693).
95. MnS 29, p. 31/I (16 June, 1695).
96. MnS 3, p. 1056/II (1634); cf. MnS 8, pp. 87–8 (1641); MnS 18, p. 104/I (1662).
97. MnS 28, p. 75/II (1694); MnS 28, p. 63/I (1699).
98. MnS 29, p. 35/II (1695).
99. MnS 25, p. 57/II (1682).
100. MnS 28, p. 62/III and p. 63/II (October 1694). The *deruhdeji* relationship proved to be a particularly persistent form of protection. In 1830 we find that virtually the entire Manastir district had been divided among *deruhdejis*. However, the connotation of the term may have shifted. In 1830 *deruhdejis* were responsible not for individual villages but for a specified number of *chiftliks*, which might be scattered among several villages. See the discussion which follows in connection with the *tevzi* data.
101. Entries dealing with banditry appear in every *sijil*. The 1661 raid is spoken of by Evliya Chelebi. Two raids on Manastir in 1711 are the subject of a *ferman* of the

same year; in the first raid money, livestock, food and other goods were extorted not only from the town but from surrounding villages; in the second the bandits took hostages and demanded that they be recognized as the militia (*armatolis*) of the town: Vasdravelli, *Veroias*, pp. 117–18.

102. Lape, 'Prilog,' pp. 114–48, gives a quite detailed account of these times; cf. Katardjiev, *Oblast*, p. 51. *Sijil* no. 61, covering 1776–7, holds many entries reflecting the new and more ambitious scale of the brigandage. Bands were often led by *pashas*, who frequently attacked other *pashas*. No clear line could be drawn between outright brigandage and brigandage incidental to the feuding between powerful families.

103. These prices are cited in Matkovski, *Gurčin Kokalevski*, p. 23.

104. R. Walpole, *Travels in Various Countries of the East . . .* (London, 1820), pp. 176–7.

105. Wheat values cited here appear in MnS 63, p. 34/II (1782); MnS 63, p. 36/III (1781); MnS 63, p. 43/I (1782); MnS 80, p. 10/I (1804); and MnS 80, p. 12/III (1802). The 1782 *akche/gurush* exchange rate was inferred from a *ferman* authorizing *nüzül* collections, MnS 61, 29/IV (1777).

106. H. Gandev, *Zaraždane na kapitalističeski otnošenia v čifliskoto stopanstvo na severno-zapadna B'lgaria prez XVIII vek* (Sofia, 1962), p. 29.

107. Vasdravelli, *Veroias*, p. 237.

108. MnS 80, p. 62/II (1804).

109. MnS 63, p. 86/I (1780).

110. Except for the *mirî* system (as expressed in the term *mal-i mirî*) these categories are imposed by the historian for the purpose of analysis: they are not categories conceived by Ottoman fiscal authorities and do not appear as such in the sources.

111. To 221 *akches* per household by 1621: MnS 2, p. 75b/II (1621); to 310 *akches* per household by 1662: MnS 18, p. 106/I (1662); to 1445 *akches* per household by 1682 (reflecting fugitives?): MnS 25, p. 53/II (1682); and to 5 *gurush* per man (in the largest of three classes): MnS 42, p. 74/I (1729).

112. MnS 24, p. 34/VII (1679); MnS 34, p. 32/II (c. 1710); MnS 43, p. 93/II (1730).

113. Cf. B. Cvetkova, 'Les Celeps et leur rôle dans la vie économique des Balkans á l'époque ottomane XVe – XVIIIe s,' in M. Cook, *Studies in the Economic History of the Middle East* (London, 1970).

The *jelepkeshan*, a tax to cover the imperial household's outlays for the sheep it consumed, froze at about 48 *akches* per head of sheep; moreover, the number of sheep recorded for the Manastir district also froze at a purely fictitious level of 3595 sheep: it was this number on which the *jelepkeshan* was supposedly based.

114. Irregular taxation at the provincial level is thoroughly discussed in H. Inalcık, 'Military and fiscal transformation in the Ottoman Empire, 1600–1700' in *Archivum Ottomanicum* (forthcoming).

115. MnS 61, p. 9/II (1776) and MnS 61, p. 62/I (1777). Cf. MnS 28, p. 35/II (1695); MnS 25, p. 47/I (1683); MnS 24, p. 38/VI (1679); MnS 24, p. 39/I (1679). However a high valuation might be placed on grain if it was the *bedel* which was being raised: MnS 28, p. 61/III (1694).

116. MnS 65, p. 34/I (1788).

117. A list of these provincial *tekâlif* with brief descriptions, is offered by A. Sućeska, 'Vlijaneto na odanočuvanjeto na rajata so nametite avâriz-i dîvânîye, tekâlif-i örfîye i tekâlif-i šaqqa vrz razvojot na procesot na čifličenjeto vo Makedonija vo

XVII vek, '*Glasnik na Institut za Nacionalna Istorija* (Skopje), XIV/1 (1970), 71–86 – also published as 'Ekonomske i društveno-političke posljedice pojačanog oporezivanja u osmanskom carstvu u XVII i XVIII stoljeću,' *Godišnjak Pravnog Fakulteta u Sarajevu*, XIII (1965), 223–39. The most common of the provincial *tekâlif* at Manastir were the *zahire baha* and the *kaftan baha*, which seem to have been raised on an annual basis. Cf. Inalcık, 'Transformation.'

118. As, for instance, to defray the expenses of a fourteen-day visit at Manastir by the *müfettish* Shahin Ağa and his retinue in 1683: MnS 25, p. 46/II.

119. MnS 25, p. 45/I (1679).

120. See the discussion of A. Sućeska, 'Taksit: prilog izučavanju dažbinskog sistema u našim zemljama pod turskom vlašću,' *Godišnjak Pravnog Fakulteta u Sarajevu*, VIII (1960), 339–62, at p. 341. Suceska finds a precedent for the *imdad-i seferiye* in the *seferiye* tax collected in wartime by the central government as early as the reign of Bayezid II; however as a tax in support of the provincial governor the *imdad-i seferiye* appears only at the end of the seventeenth century. Cf. Inalcık, 'Transformation,' for the resort to the *imdat* by the central government during the seventeenth century.

121. MnS 43, p. 111/I (1730).

122. MnS 62, p. 36/I (1779).

123. MnS 62, p. 27/V (1779).

124. MnS 28, p. 30/II (1695).

125. MnS 42, p. 76/II (1729); MnS 47, p. 10/V (c.1740); MnS 62, p. 37/V (1779); MnS 63, p. 77/VI (1781).

126. MnS 63, p. 54/II (1781). These provincial expense accounts became increasingly elaborate and detailed in the early nineteenth century.

127. Cf. MnS 25, p. 58/I (1682); MnS 43, p. 105/I (1731); MnS 43, p. 75/IV and p. 76/I (1732).

128. E.g. MnS 63, p. 48/I (1781).

129. For the *piyade* levy in 1694, MnS 28, p. 48/III (1694).

130. MnS 2, pp. 75b/I, 51a/I, 76b/II (1621–2).

131. MnS 3, pp. 104, 98/I, 51b/I, 53b/I, 105b/I, 54b/VII, 53b/III (1633–4).

132. MnS 18, pp. 84/I, 100/III, 85/I, 97/III , 104/IV, 104/III, 106/I, 110/V, 111/IV (1662–3).

133. MnS 25, pp. 58/I, 55/I, 55/II, 51/I, 53/II, 54/II (1682).

134. MnS 42, pp. 74/I, 94/I, 88/II, 89/I, 90/III, 90/IV, 91/I, 101/V (1729–30).

135. MnS 63, pp. 45/III, IV, V, VI, 47/II, 48/I, 54/I, 50/I, II, 52/II, III, 56/III, 82/III, 54/II, 78/I (1780–1).

136. F. Babinger (ed.), *Das Qânûn-nâme-i sultânî ber mûdscheb-i 'örf-i osmânî* (Munich, 1956), p. 271. Similar arrangements were resorted to by the Byzantines in attempts to shore up their fiscal integrity: G. Ostrogorsky, 'Agrarian conditions in the Byzantine Empire in the Middle Ages,' *Cambridge Economic History of Europe*, I: *The Agrarian Life of the Middle Ages* (Cambridge, 1966), 213 (regarding the *allelengyon* system); K. Setton, 'On the importance of land tenure and agrarian taxation in the Byzantine Empire, from the fourth century to the Fourth Crusade,' *American Journal of Philology*, 74/3 (1953), 257; and N. Svoronos, 'Sur quelques formes de la vie rurale à Byzance: petite et grande exploitation,' *Annales: économies, sociétés, civilisations*, 11/3 (1956), 335.

137. MnS 3, p. 75a/II (1635) and MnS 6, p. 7a/VIII (1638).
138. MnS 6, p. 11b/VI (1640).
139. MnS 18, p. 95/I (1661); MnS 18, p. 96/I (1661).
140. MnS 28, p. 57/IV (1694).
141. MnS 28, p. 61/III and p. 58/I (1694).
142. MnS 25, p. 58/I (1682).
143. MnS 34, pp. 30/II, 32/I (1710).
144. The Prota apparently thought the Belgrad *vezir* imagined that each of the *avarız hanes* was an actual household headed by an adult male; but the *vezir* unquestionably understood the system better than the Prota. The English translation of these passages is borrowed with gratitude from L. Edwards (tr.), *The Memoirs of Prota Matija Nenadović* (Oxford, 1969), p. 28.
145. MnS 28, pp. 62/III and 63/II (1694).
146. From a *jizye tevzi* of 1683: MnS 25, p. 41/III (1683).
147. A *tevzi* list including *chiftliks* had appeared in the Ruse (Ruschuk) district on the Danube as early as 1657: S. Dimitrov, 'K'm istoriata na čiflikčiistvoto v Rusensko,' *Istoričeski Pregled*, XIV/4 (1958), 84–98. Inalcık's 'Transformation' emphasizes the role of the life-lease (*malikâne*) system in the genesis of the *chiftliks* of this period.
148. MnS 29, p. 31/I (1695). A similar situation still existed a hundred years later, as we can see in a *ferman* of 1795 in response to a complaint by the villagers of Mogila who repeat the long familiar story, namely, that *chiftlik* holders (*sahibs*) and other influential individuals were not paying their share of the *avarız* and other such taxes: MnS 72, p. 38/I (1795).
149. MnS 33, pp. 31–4 (1709). Occasionally a name is doubtful – for instance, Albanian names. It may be that the inclusion of the *chiftlik* holders on a *tevzi* introduced a long needed easement; a few months later a *tevzi* list drawn up to meet the payment of the annual *avarız–nüzül* shows that twenty villages will be passed over because of flight and material weakness – a concession all too rare: MnS 33, p. 36/IV (1709).
150. Examples of applications of these principles, in order of citation: MnS 33, pp. 31–4 (1709); MnS 34, pp. 30/II, 31/I, II, 32/I (1710); MnS 34, pp. 11/III to 12 (1710); MnS 43, pp. 91, 92 (1731).
151. Apparently there was more than one way of counting *chiftliks*, at least in the early eighteenth century; although in 1709, there are 419 *chiftliks* indicated; in the *tevzi* of 1710 there were 362 listed; and in the *tevzi* of 1711 there were 333: MnS 33, pp. 31–4 (1709); MnS 34, pp. 11–12 (1710); MnS 34, pp. 41–3 (1711). And while in 1729 there were shown 476 *chiftliks*, in 1731 only 380 are indicated: MnS 42, p. 92/III (1729); MnS 43, pp. 91–2 (1731). In each case the higher number was chosen for the graph, the assumption being that these differences in enumeration reflected differences in power and status so that whereas *all* the *chiftliks* might appear on one *tevzi*, only *most* of them appear on another *tevzi*. A similar explanation is offered for the two series of *chifts*, see below.
152. MnS 34, pp. 11/III to 12 (1710). A 1711 *tevzi*, showing 1274 *reaya* living on 333 *chiftliks*, yields an average number of 3.8 *nefers* per *chiftlik*: MnS 34, pp. 41–3 (1711). The distribution of *chifts* on a 1788 *tevzi* is very similar, the highest reading in this case being 75: MnS 65, pp. 4–5 (1788).
153. MnS 42, p. 92/III (1729).

154. MnS 43, pp. 19–92 (1731).
155. P. Kiroski, 'Čifligarstvoto vo Polog,' in *Kiril Pejčinovik i Negovoto Vreme* (Tetovo, 1973), pp. 115–20.
156. MnS 34, pp. 30–2 (1710); MnS 51, p. 52/ɪ (1748); MnS 61, p. 15/ɪ (1776); MnS 65, pp. 4–5 (1788); MnS 78, p. 73 (1813); MnS 91, pp. 37–8 (1824).
157. MnS 42, p. 92/ɪɪɪ (1729); MnS 65, pp. 4–5 (1788); MnS 80, pp. 69, 75, 76, 79 (1803–4); MnS 43, p. 23/ɪ (1809); MnS 91, pp. 6, 11, 12, 14, 20, 23, 27, 29 (1820–1).
158. MnS 87, p. 4 (1816).
159. MnS 34, pp. 41–3 (1711); there is a discrepancy here, of course, from the number used on the graph, which was the *'nefers'* cited in MnS 34, pp. 30–2 (1710).
160. The *tevzi* of 1788 is unique. Each village is entered, then the identity of the holder of each *chiftlik*, then the identities of each of the cultivators working on each *chiftlik*, followed by the number of *chifts* of land which each cultivator has in his charge. As one would expect from the numbers offered on the graph, most *chiftliks* have more than one *chifchi* (cultivator) on them, and some *chifchis* have charge of more than one *chift* (25 acre unit). MnS 65, pp. 4–5 (1788).
161. MnS 80, pp. 69, 75, 76, 79 (1803–4); MnS 43, pp. 33/ɪ (1809); MnS 85, pp. 7, 15, 17, 19, 24–30 (1814).
162. MnS 85, pp. 3b, 4, 5, 7, 15, 17, 19, 24–30 (1814); MnS 92, pp. 9/ɪ, 16/ɪ, 24/ɪɪɪ, 30/ɪɪ (1822); MnS 91, pp. 6, 11, 12, 14, 20, 23, 27, 29 (1820–1).
163. MnS 93, p. 13/ɪᴠ (1823).
164. MnS 94, pp. 16/ɪ, 16/ɪɪɪ, 18/ɪ, 18/ɪɪɪ, 19/ɪ, 24/ɪɪɪ and 27/ɪɪɪ (1824).
165. MnS 87, p. 19 (1816).
166. MnS 93, p. 1 (1824).
167. MnS 91, pp. 37–8 (1824).
168. MnS 98, pp. 31/ɪɪɪ to 32 (1830).
169. Matkovski, *Kreposništvoto*, p. 99.
170. MnS 99, pp. 20/ᴠɪɪɪ (19 November 1830). For examples of the *chift tevzis* of 1830, cf. MnS 99, p. 20/ɪᴠ, 12/ɪᴠ, 12/ᴠ, 12/ᴠɪ, 15/ɪ, 39/ɪɪ, 13 (1830).
171. In MnS 101, pp. 39–40 (1834) *chifts* of the district (*kaza*) were shown as numbering 2648. The relation of this number to numbers cited earlier is obscure. Cf. also MnS 101, pp. 41–2 (1835–6).

Notes to Conclusion, pp. 171–2

1. G. Veinstein, '"Âyân" de la region d'Izmir et commerce du Levant (deuxième moitié du XVIIIe siècle,' *Études Balkaniques*, 12/3 (1976), 71–83.
2. H. Inalcık, 'Centralization and decentralization in Ottoman administration' in T. Naff and R. Owen (eds.), *Studies in Eighteenth Century Islamic History* (London, 1977), pp. 27–52.
3. An interesting beginning limited to one locality has been made by A. Cohen, *Palestine in the Eighteenth Century: Patterns of Government and administration* (Jerusalem, 1973).
4. Y. Nagata, *Some Documents on the Big Farms (Çiftliks) of the Notables in Western Anatolia* (Studia Culturae Islamicae no. 4, Tokyo, 1976).
5. This point is also emphasized by R. Mantran, 'The transformation of trade in the Ottoman Empire in the eighteenth century' in Naff and Owen, *Eighteenth Century*, pp. 217–35.

Glossary

(F) French   (G) German   (S) Serbian

akche	small silver coin, the asper
Anadolu	western Anatolia
arpalık	interim prebend, held between offices or as income security
avarız	tax collected by the central government, originally to meet emergencies
ayan	class of provincial notables, influential in fiscal affairs
bashtina (S)	typical *reaya* holding, usually about one *chift* in size
berat	patent empowering bearer to perform some service
bey	prominent Muslim landholder
beylerbey	governor of a major province (e.g., Rumeli, Anadolu)
buyruldu	patent issued by the provincial governor
caravanaire (F)	coastal intra-Ottoman trader, trading ship
chift	standard unit of land, about 25 acres; also occasionally the draft team which would ordinarily work a holding of that size
chift bozan	penalty upon *reaya* who abandoned their holdings
chiftlik	landholding of indeterminate size, in the seventeenth and eighteenth centuries usually the holding of the superior tenant
deruhdeji	agent of a collective of tax payers
Djurdjevdan (S)	6 May (St George's Day)
échelle (F)	French trading colony
eyalet	major province (e.g., Rumeli, Anadolu)
ferman	decree, sometimes also an enabling patent
Grundherrschaft (G)	feudal economy based on rents
gurush	larger silver coin, Ottoman or non-Ottoman (*grossus, groschen*)
gürihte	fled, fugitive
Gutsherrschaft (G)	feudal economy based on direct exploitation of labor on a consolidated estate
hane	house, household, often (fiscally) a group of households
has	prebend of large size
hassa	portion of land under direct control of the prebend-holder
hatt-ı humayun	imperial rescript
haymana	unregistered cultivator, often a fugitive
hüjjet	notarial certificate issued by the *kadi*
iltizam	rent leasing, tax leasing, often by auction

219

imdat	tax collected in the seventeenth century by the central government, in the eighteenth century by the provincial government, originally to meet emergencies; hence the *imdad-i seferiye* of wartime became the *imdad-i hazariye* in peacetime
ishtira	compulsory sale of commodities at fixed price
jabi	collector, usually for a *sipahi*
jizye	hearth tax or (after 1691) head tax on adult males of the non-Muslim communities
kadi	judge–administrator at district level
kanunname	provincial or general law code
kapanlı	government buyer
kaza	judicial–administrative district, subdivision of *liva*
kirjalı	bandit
kmet (S)	Serbian or Bosnian peasant
knez (S)	Serbian headman, village chief
liva	province, subdivision of an *eyalet*
malikâne	holding leased for life, life-leasing
mevat	wasteland, unclaimed land
mevkufat	division of the Ottoman treasury which collected *avarız–nüzül*
mirî	belonging to the state, or to the imperial treasury (as opposed to the *has*, or sultanic treasury)
Mitrovdan (S)	8 November (St Dimitri's Day)
mubayaa	compulsory commodity sale at fixed price
mukataa	rent lease unit, rent lease system (cf. *iltizam*)
nahiye	subdivision of a *kaza*
naib	substitute *kadi*
nefer	adult male individual
nüzül	tax collected by the central government, originally an occasional tax
pasha	title used by generals, governors
reaya	registered peasant cultivator, the peasantry (a collective noun often used as a singular, or as an adjective)
Rumeli	Rumelia, south-eastern Europe south of the Danube, excluding Bosnia
sahib	holder (sometimes tantamount to 'owner')
sahib-i alaka	non-*reaya* individual who holds a *reaya*'s right to a holding, inferior tenant
sahib-i arz	holder of land, superior tenant
Shar'iah	Muslim holy law (used as an adjective – *sher'i*, or *shar'i*)
sijil	record book of the *kadi*'s court and of his district (*kaza*)
sipahi	cavalryman, often the holder of a *timar*
subashı	bailiff, collector for a provincial governor, or other important person
tahrir	survey register of the sixteenth-century type
tapu, tapuname	deed-like land transfer document issued by *timar* holder
tekâlif	irregular, or unauthorized taxes
tekâlif-i shakka	province level taxes, often of dubious legality
temessük	notarial document issued by the *kadi*(cf. *hüjjet*)
temlik	property-like landholding
tevzi	tax apportionment at district level
timar	smaller prebend
timarlı	holder of a smaller prebend

vakıf	pious estate under Muslim holy law, technically ownerless, ostensibly dedicated to some charitable or religious purpose
vali	governor of an *eyalet*
zaim	holder of a *ziamet*
ziamet	middle-sized prebend, usually held by a military officer
zimmi	non-Muslim *reaya*

Author index

223

Subject index

For EU product safety concerns, contact us at Calle de José Abascal, 56–1°,
28003 Madrid, Spain or eugpsr@cambridge.org.

www.ingramcontent.com/pod-product-compliance
Ingram Content Group UK Ltd.
Pitfield, Milton Keynes, MK11 3LW, UK
UKHW010042140625
459647UK00012BA/1552